Library of
Davidson College

A Boundless Field

POETS ON POETRY

David Lehman, General Editor
Donald Hall, Founding Editor

New titles

Thomas M. Disch, *The Castle of Perseverance*
Mark Jarman, *Body and Soul*
Stephen Yenser, *A Boundless Field*
Philip Levine, *So Ask*

Recently published

Tess Gallagher, *Soul Barnacles*
Linda Gregerson, *Negative Capability*
Philip Levine, *The Bread of Time*
Larry Levis, *The Gazer Within*
William Matthews, *The Poetry Blues*
Charles Simic, *A Fly in the Soup*

Also available are collections by

A. R. Ammons, Robert Bly, Philip Booth, Marianne Boruch,
Hayden Carruth, Fred Chappell, Amy Clampitt, Tom Clark,
Douglas Crase, Robert Creeley, Donald Davie, Peter Davison,
Tess Gallagher, Suzanne Gardinier, Allen Grossman, Thom Gunn,
Rachel Hadas, John Haines, Donald Hall, Joy Harjo, Robert Hayden
Edward Hirsch, Daniel Hoffman, Jonathan Holden, John Hollander
Andrew Hudgins, Josephine Jacobsen, Weldon Kees, Galway Kinnell
Mary Kinzie, Kenneth Koch, John Koethe, Yusef Komunyakaa,
Richard Kostelanetz, Maxine Kumin, Martin Lammon (editor),
Philip Larkin, David Lehman, Philip Levine, John Logan,
William Logan, William Matthews, William Meredith, Jane Miller,
Carol Muske, Geoffrey O'Brien, Gregory Orr, Alicia Suskin Ostriker
Ron Padgett, Marge Piercy, Anne Sexton, Charles Simic,
Louis Simpson, William Stafford, Anne Stevenson, May Swenson,
James Tate, Richard Tillinghast, Diane Wakoski, C. K. Williams,
Alan Williamson, Charles Wright, and James Wright

Stephen Yenser

A Boundless Field

AMERICAN POETRY
AT LARGE

Ann Arbor

THE UNIVERSITY OF MICHIGAN PRESS

Copyright © by Stephen Yenser 2002
All rights reserved
Published in the United States of America by
The University of Michigan Press
Manufactured in the United States of America
♾ Printed on acid-free paper

2005   2004   2003   2002   4 3 2 1

No part of this publication may be reproduced, stored in a retrieval system, or transmitted in any form or by any means, electronic, mechanical, or otherwise, without the written permission of the publisher.

A CIP catalog record for this book is available from the British Library.

Library of Congress Cataloging-in-Publication Data applied for

ISBN 0-472-11278-3 (cloth)

Approaching thus the momentous spaces, and considering with reference to a new and greater personalism, the needs and possibilities of American imaginative literature, through the medium-light of what we have already broach'd, it will at once be appreciated that a vast gulf of difference separates the present accepted conditions of these spaces, inclusive of what is floating in them, from any condition adjusted to, or fit for, the world, the America, there sought to be indicated, and the copious races of complete men and women, along these Vistas crudely outlined. It is, in some sort, no less a difference than lies between that long-continued nebular state and vagueness of the astronomical worlds, compared with the subsequent state, the definitely-formed worlds themselves, duly compacted, clustering in systems, hung up there, chandeliers of the universe, beholding and mutually lit by each other's lights, serving for ground of all substantial foothold, all vulgar uses—yet serving still more as an undying chain and echelon of spiritual proofs and shows. A boundless field to fill! A new creation, with needed orbic works launched forth, to revolve in free and lawful circuits—to move, self-poised, through the ether and shine like heaven's own suns!

—Walt Whitman, *Democratic Vistas* (1868)

Contents

Elizabeth Bishop's Stove	1
Some Poets' Criticism and the Age *Dana Gioia, Mary Kinzie,* *Allen Grossman with Mark Halliday,* *Stephen Dunn, Mary Karr*	9
A Range of Affirmation *Philip Levine, Robert Hass,* *Robert Pinsky, Galway Kinnell*	34
Fables of Purity *Louise Glück, Linda Gregg,* *David St. John, John Ashbery*	59
Bright Sources *John Hollander, Donald Justice,* *Alice Fulton, Sharon Olds*	84
Versions of Maximalism *Susan Mitchell, Judith Hall,* *Susan Prospere, Gjertrud Schnackenberg*	119
Wild Plots *Harryette Mullen, Ann Lauterbach,* *Louise Glück, Michael Palmer*	145
Sensuous and Particular *Sherod Santos, Rosanna Warren,* *Richard Kenney*	160
A Boundless Field *Frank Bidart and C. K. Williams*	176

The Poetics of Plash and Speed 193
Susan Wheeler and Frederick Seidel

Breaking and Making 216
*Heather McHugh, Lynne McMahon,
Jorie Graham*

Elizabeth Bishop's Stove

Wondering how best to prepare this *étoufée* of essays and reviews, I find myself gazing—as I have so often gazed over the last several years—at a miniature wood-burning kitchen stove, made of tin, about 6″ × 4″ × 2″, hand-painted to represent a stove made of bricks. Is *it* the means for cooking up this concoction? My miniature stove, surely sun-bleached, is now chiefly shades of orange, but it must once have been red. It stands shiftingly on legs painted metallic turquoise, and its bottom pan rises what would be (if the stove were translated into the scale of my everyday world) some two feet above the ground. Thanks to a clever, simple hinge, the oven door, the door of the stove's combustion chamber, opens and closes, opens and closes—and on each of the stove's two burners there sits a tin pot, one with real (therefore "oversize") black beans in it, the other with grains of real white rice. (Both the beans and the rice are old—the first now a dull brown, the second dun.) Above and behind the burners, on braces that run up from the stove's sides to meet in an inverted U behind the stovepipe (itself painted forest green, like the braces), hang two miniature kitchen implements, on the left a sieve and on the right a grater. Inscribed in a circle on the oven door is the brand name—presumably also the name of the first cook—"EVA."

This miniature stove, or one very like it, evidently made by a Brazilian folk artist, belonged to Elizabeth Bishop. She reproduced it as a miniature, along with what would be (if *it* were to scale) a giant cannikin of enormous flowers, in a painting (watercolor and gouache), done in a quasi-primitive style, known as *Red Stove and Flowers*. ("Home-made, home-made! But aren't we all?" her Crusoe exults—who lived so long in a world in which a "weird scale" obtained.) In the painting, in white cursive script across the top of a black backdrop behind the stove, there runs an inscription: "May the Future's Happy Hours Bring you Beans and Rice and Flowers—April 27th, 1955—Elizabeth." The antithetical rhyme of *Hours* with *Flowers* is, characteristically, discreetly suppressed. The current whereabouts of the painting is unknown, its dedicatee uncertain. Like seven other paintings by Bishop, it is now viewable, alas, only in a color photograph. (It is reproduced on the cover of and again within *Exchanging Hats: Paintings,* by Elizabeth Bishop, ed. William Benton.) The miniature stove itself was passed along to her friend James Merrill, after whose death it came by way of a gift into my hands.

Having hoped that this set of circumstances would be heuristic, and suddenly at the risk of particularizing precociously, I now look for further help to Bishop's "Poem" (included in her last collection, *Geography III*), which is itself, title notwithstanding, "about" a *painting*. In "Poem" a great-uncle's landscape painting has been passed along collaterally to the speaker, who, meditating on it, has a revelation:

> Heavens, I recognize the place, I know it!
> It's behind—I can almost remember the farmer's name.
> His farm backed on that meadow. There it is,
> titanium white, one dab.

Later, the poet muses on her distant relative and his work:

> I never knew him. We both knew this place,
> apparently, this literal small backwater,
> looked at it long enough to memorize it,
> our years apart. How strange. And it's still loved,
> or its memory is (it must have changed a lot).
> Our visions coincided—"visions" is
> too serious a word—our looks, two looks:
> art "copying from life" and life itself,
> life and the memory of it so compressed
> they've turned into each other. Which is which?
> Life and the memory of it cramped,
> dim, on a piece of Bristol board,

> dim, but how live, how touching in detail
> —the little that we get for free,
> the little of our earthly trust. Not much.

The issue raised, which is virtually Platonic, is the nature of "recognition"—and of "knowledge" in the first place. The more deeply the observer-poet has felt herself into the painting, so to speak, the more it has become her own, or the more she belongs to it, and therefore the more she "recognizes" herself and her own past in it. Mightn't the same be said of many works of art that frame our feelings and memories for us? There might be a sense, that is, in which any evocative scene, however initially "strange" to the observer, would come to seem, by virtue of its evocations, familiar. In this instance, the "literal small backwater" represented on smooth cardboard might not be in fact that of Bishop's youth but instead simply engagingly painted. In other words, the scene is not even "literal" at all until the poet makes it so, or renders it in words—which is to say, makes the painted scene, along with that scene as reported and remembered by her, all indistinguishable, from her point of view in the first instance and the reader's in the second. "Life and the memory of it so compressed / they've turned into each other. Which is which?"

If Bishop's lines work as I think they work, any reader with any autobiographical detail whatever in common with the scene as rendered might discover the seeds of his or her past therein. It figures, then, that in the poem's last lines the scene Bishop describes is in effect that of Eden, the origin we *all* have in common, on which she ironically superimposes the eternally alluring prospect of Milton's "fresh Woods, and pastures new." All in all, from past to future, what our lives add up to is

>   Not much.
> About the size of our abidance
> along with theirs: the munching cows,
> the iris, crisp and shivering, the water
> still standing from spring freshets,
> the yet-to-be-dismantled elms, the geese.

Bishop's last line, like the first line of her poem, and like many others in it, is in sturdy, homely iambic pentameter, her normative meter in this case, which itself might be called a means of compressing "life and the memory of it."

Let me sum up what I understand about "Poem." Any reading interprets, at her implicit invitation, Bishop's poem, which interprets her great-uncle's landscape, which interprets an "original" scene, a scene that in the poet's report of its painted version—with her paradoxical fusion of time passing and time frozen—is all but explicitly tantamount to the frieze on Keats's dreamed-up Grecian urn as he spells it out.

Now let me further suggest that as her "Poem" is to her great-uncle's painting, so her own *Red Stove and Flowers* is to the folk artist's stove. In each case, one art interprets another, and the interpreted object itself represents a "common" or mundane subject. In each case, that subject (the rural scene, the miniature stove) is unprepossessing, though carefully crafted in the representation of it, and each representation invites someone's further participation, tinkering, speculation. For instance, the actual miniature stove's brand name as advertised on the stove door is "EVA," whereas the name that appears on Bishop's painting of the stove is "Magú." In the gloss on the painting as it is reproduced in *Exchanging Hats: Paintings*, the editor implies that *Magú* suggests *magic* (which definition might indirectly connect the miniature with "the Little Marvel Stove" in Bishop's "Sestina," published in *Questions of Travel*). For better or worse, however, *magic* in Portuguese is *magíca*, whereas Magú is the common nickname for Mariaugusta, which (as Bishop's younger friend Ricardo Sternberg has informed me) happened to be the given name of Bishop's acquaintance, by way of the poet's longtime intimate friend Lota de Macedo Soares, Mariaugusta de Léon Costa Ribero. In all probability, then, Bishop, having wittily exchanged the brand name of the stove for the nickname of Lota's friend, gave the now missing painting to Mariaugusta in April 1955. To say so, of course, is to begin to appropriate the painting.

The preceding paragraphs will have adumbrated some approaches and biases to come. To begin with, the spirits whom

I want to hover over my readings of thirty-six living poets are those of Elizabeth Bishop and James Merrill, who seem to me the crucial poets of the first and second postmodern generations. (She was born in 1911, he in 1926.) In the second place, the readings in this book, most of them concerned with the three generations of postmodern poets beginning with Merrill's and especially the two succeeding his, value local color (in both senses of the phrase) and are responsive to subtly calculated effects, which is to say that they are detail oriented and word specific. Third, these readings reflect my convictions that there is no such thing as "poetic subject matter" (indeed, as soon as a subject matter is perceived as "poetic," whether it be courtly love or child abuse, it needs challenging) and that poetry qua poetry is never interesting for its "ideas" (of which there are probably only a *basic* two or three in the world, after all, and those discoverable in Plato). For another thing, these essays esteem poems that are conversant with aesthetic traditions and precursors, whether in the so-called Western world or elsewhere. Their art comes from art. For yet another, however, they emphasize a poetry that at once embodies, provokes, and resists tampering thought; a poetry that is resistant to both received notions and its own premises, hence innovative, hence complex; a poetry that bears witness to a processive questioning of things (phrases, propositions, categories, first thoughts). Perhaps in sum I believe with Wallace Stevens that poetry should resist the intelligence almost successfully.

But I also believe, though again with Stevens, that "poetry is the scholar's art." I have a couple of parabolic foils. I know one poet who prides herself on the accessibility of her poems. In the course of things, she wrote a poem that, while certainly not obscure, drew upon the works of Nietzsche and other philosophers. Another reader of her poem, who liked it very much, registered both his admiration and his surprise at the unexpected range of learned reference and its attendant intellectual thickness. "Oh yeah," the poet replied, "I paid a research assistant to look up the 'truth' stuff." I have another friend who was engaged in writing a sequence based on Homer's epics. When I heard of the project, I said to him, "So:

you've been rereading the *Iliad* and the *Odyssey*." "Oh no," he said, scandalized, "that's the *last* thing I would do." It will be clear that these are the last responses that I would expect my favorite poets in their sober moments to give.

Finally, the preceding credos notwithstanding, the essays included here reflect a commitment to poems that are affectively charged—poems, that is, that implicitly value dramatic inflections. Tones of voice rather than apparently pellucid propositions or "denatured" or "deconstructed" language, undisguisedly subjective points of view rather than implicitly impersonal vantages, psychological processes and rhetorical deftness rather than philosophical or political positions, works that are essentially dramatic rather than expressive or effusive, ironic rather than ingenuous, maximalist rather than post-Imagist or minimalist: these are my prejudices, as far as I can tell them. At the same time, there are certain terms, often elsewhere used as pejoratives or honorifics, that for me are simply descriptive. They include *lyric* and *narrative* and *confessional, formal prosody* and *free verse*.

One might infer from the foregoing sentences that this collection has all too little to say about one current movement known as "neoformalism" and another known as "Language Poetry," though I have included pieces about writers associated with both. I hope that the reader will also divine a certain mute indifference to what is sometimes called—unfairly, since a majority of our best young and younger poets have roots in M.F.A. programs—"workshop poetry." In my mind, the latter term simply designates the poetry that is currently "conventional": that is written in quotidian English, or "English that cats and dogs can speak," in Marianne Moore's deathless verdict (and thus allergic to extravagant syntax and "inkhorn" terms, as they used to say); that presumes an audience of contemporaneous readers (rather than readers among the formidable shades and forthcoming generations); that depends for effect chiefly on unusual or seemingly spectacular experiences (trichotillomania, incest, dirt eating, jail time, firefights) rather than ordinary situations (kitchen stoves, cows in a field—subjects that have themselves of course been the occasions of reams of bad verse); that prizes mystery at the expense of lucidity (where *mystery* is not to be confused with *complexity* or *ineffability*); and that, to get to a bottom line at last, cares little for the concept of precisely *the line*, which I take to be the defining element of poetry. (Such carelessness in regard to lineation, by the way, is frequently manifest in fetishistic concern for regular prosody.)

So, the prose that I have included here is in search of a poetry that in its exemplary forms will be vivid and demanding but accessible, though never transparent, delicately constructed yet historically rich, emotionally loaded yet analytically undergirded, and prosodically alert withal. If (all told) I seem to forecast a predilection for certain kinds of difficulty, I have done part of my job. If, however, I seem to admire obfuscation, I have misstated my view of myself, since I hold with Frost that, while "dark sayings" are to be savored, "obscurity" is to be eschewed. Robert Lowell, reflecting some thirty years ago on "The Armadillo" and other poems by Bishop, suggested that her lines seemed to him lines composed in the next century and somehow smuggled back through time to us. That's the kind of poetry I've tried to keep in mind—poetry that seems to envision its future without losing touch with its origins and that, I think, most of the poets I've written about have tried to make.

As that last sentence suggests, most of these pieces are not adversarial. (Somewhat different is "Some Poets' Criticism and the Age," in which criticism rather than poetry is the chief subject.) Vitriol and acerbity can be fun to indulge and to witness, but those modes seek to close doors rather than to open them, and I cannot see much point these days, at the outset of a new millennium, in the closing of doors. It seems to me, as my title must have suggested, that we are in no danger of being overrun by mediocrity. While I am sharply aware of the frequent contention that much criticism of living poets is appreciative because self-serving or "politically" motivated, I am still more sensitive to W. H. Auden's admonition that even very good books are routinely ignored and that bad books need no ushering on their way to oblivion. Some of Randall

Jarrell's wittier and nastier reviews, and some of Howard Nemerov's, to conjure two masters of the modern acerb, will always be perversely delightful to read, but it's hard to think that such sharply pointed but brittle palisades themselves have kept the sacred realm of poesy from being infiltrated by infidels. Poetry with integrity constitutes its own defense.

Some Poets' Criticism and the Age

American poetry is in bad shape. Our poets not only take in one another's laundry; they also do it in public. By *poets* I mean a coterie of enervated academics who praise and in turn practice mediocrity, shun political issues, and ignore the public at large, with the result that the public returns the favor in spades. In the old days, poets either had to work for a living or to resign themselves to an honest bohemian existence; today they have got fat and lazy, thanks to sinecures at universities, honoraria for poetry readings, and grants. The pampered, short-winded American poet rarely writes a long poem these days, or at least a really good long poem, although it is important that really good long poems be written, because—well, because they keep alive venerable structures (the narrative, the didactic exposition), and so on; and in any case, the paucity of good long poems reflects and contributes to the vexatious absence of a coherent sense of things as a whole. Even worse, our lassitudinous, laconic poets have lost touch with the true formalist impulse and have turned *faute de mieux* to a paradoxically prolix, "confessional," "lyric" mode notable for its homogeneity.

I am radically paraphrasing (but not, I think, caricaturing) the first three chapters of a collection of essays by the poet Dana Gioia, *Can Poetry Matter? Essays on Poetry and American*

Review of *Can Poetry Matter? Essays on Poetry and American Culture* by Dana Gioia, *The Cure of Poetry in an Age of Prose: Moral Essays on the Poet's Calling* by Mary Kinzie, *The Sighted Singer: Two Works on Poetry for Readers and Writers* by Allen Grossman with Mark Halliday, and *Walking Light: Essays and Memoirs* by Stephen Dunn. From *Southern Review*, Winter, 1994.

Culture. (But wait . . . the mail has just come. In it I find a letter from the prominent magazine *Parnassus*, which advertises "a mammoth issue on the long poem . . . [a] nearly 500 page issue." This issue includes a number of new long poems and several essays on "old [modern] masters of the long poem." I also find the new *American Poetry Review*, which features an essay by Louise Glück, who notes that "in my generation [she is about Gioia's age], most of the poets that I admire are interested in length," and who feels compelled to *defend* "ellipsis," "suggestion," and "economy" against the creeping hegemony of "elaboration," "amplification," and "the expansive poem." What a difference a day makes, hmm?) But to resume: I could be drawing from a number of recent publications, including Joseph Epstein's notorious essay "Who Killed Poetry?" (*Commentary*, 1988), the special issue of *Crosscurrents* (1989) on "Expansionist Poetry: The New Formalism and the New Narrative," and Frederick Feirstein's anthology entitled *Expansive Poetry: Essays on the New Narrative and the New Formalism* (1989). They are all contributors to the foreseeable if belated backlash to the postmodern, the so-called but ill-defined confessional, and the free verse aesthetics predominant in this country from the 1960s through the 1980s and epitomized, for example, in Donald Allen and Warren Tallman's collection entitled *The Poetics of the New American Poetry* and—to move from the left to the center—in the popular anthologies edited by Stephen Berg and Robert Mezey entitled *Naked Poetry*.

One problem with Gioia's approach, especially in his opening chapters, mirrors the alleged problem with many of the texts he contemns, in that it is narrow-minded and argues from intuition and by fiat and ad hominem. Gioia is a classic conservative in certain respects: he is nostalgic for less "complex" apprehensions of the world; he thinks that American literary history has been all downhill for the last century or so; and he prefers the viewpoint of the (purportedly) independent businessman or entrepreneur to that of the (supposedly) beholden academician. He has a violent *parti pris,* and his book, contrary to what one might have hoped, in view of his acumen and his knowledge of his craft, is anything but a carefully thought-out undertaking.

If Gioia's book were as coldly analytical as its blurbs and its pronouncements pretend it is, it could have avoided the contradictions that beset it. I have in mind, for example, its claim on the one hand that "American poetry now belongs to a subculture" that has little if any influence on our lives and its claim, on the other, that "since there are too many poetry collections appearing each year to evaluate, the reader must rely on the candor and discernment of reviewers to recommend the best books." I have in mind, in other words, Gioia's evidently naive paradox that "the poetry boom has been a distressingly confined phenomenon." (And why "distressingly"? If our poetry is as noxious as he thinks, it's best that the boom take place in a confined space—the nearest WC will do.) I think too of Gioia's simultaneous notions that poetry has become an arcane, underappreciated art and that it has become "a modestly upwardly mobile, middle-class profession." Were it steadfastly analytical, his book would also examine, would *try* certain of its crucial claims, but it is as though Gioia has never heard of the advantages of anticipating counterarguments. Thus he can begin a notice of Tom Disch's work with the comment that "there has been a good deal of talk lately about a rebirth of formal poetry" (as there has been) and then come puzzlingly around to the opinion that, since Disch writes often in "traditional forms and genres," he is "every bit at one with his age as John Dryden would be in a surrealist café"—while I suppose Gioia himself would have been perfectly at home at Mr. Dryden's feet in Will's.

One of Gioia's "modest proposals" for the improvement of the culture is that "*Poets need to write prose about poetry more often, more candidly, and more effectively.*" It is not so much that one notes in passing how little was written by poets in prose about poetry before Dryden, who on Gioia's time line lived yesterday (nothing from Chaucer and little from Dante and the other *stilnovisti,* for instance, treatises by Philip Sidney and Samuel Daniel, yes, and Ben Jonson's *Timber*—but nothing by Edmund Spenser, William Shakespeare, John Donne, Andrew Marvell, or George Herbert). It is rather that as I contemplate this injunction, I sit at a desk surrounded by the books mentioned in the following paragraphs along with

John Hollander's two books on Renaissance poetry and his book on the figure of *Echo,* Richard Howard's exemplary *Alone with America,* James McCorkle's *The Still Performance,* J. D. McClatchy's *White Paper,* Anthony Hecht's *Obligatti* and *The Hidden Law* (on Auden), James Merrill's *Recitative,* Howard Nemerov's three volumes of criticism, in addition to books by Adrienne Rich, Donald Justice, Alfred Corn, George Garrett, David Lehman, Robert Morgan, John Matthias, Wayne Dodd, and others. Marvin Bell has collected many of his frequently published essays, and Sandra Gilbert is better known as a critic than as a poet. Alicia Ostriker's and Robert Pinsky's and Robert Hass's full-length critical works are well-known, as (in their different circles) are Charles Bernstein's poetics and Timothy Steele's weighty study of prosody. William Logan has a book of essays in press, and so does Louise Glück.... Since the catalog is virtually endless, what can Gioia mean? (A strikingly divergent and truer thing that he says is that poets interminably review one another's poetry—a circumstance he also manages to deplore.)

Other incongruities are equally breathtaking. According to Gioia, Edmund Wilson was on target when he wrote in 1934 about the moribund state of the art of verse—and so what if, as Gioia admits, Robert Frost, Wallace Stevens, T. S. Eliot, Ezra Pound, Marianne Moore, E. E. Cummings, Robinson Jeffers, H. D., Robert Graves, W. H. Auden, and others "were writing some of their best poems" even as Wilson spoke? And what if, as Gioia points out, a new generation including Robert Lowell, Elizabeth Bishop, Philip Larkin, Randall Jarrell, Dylan Thomas, and A. D. Hope (not to mention John Berryman, Theodore Roethke, Richard Wilbur) was "just breaking into print"? And what if, as Gioia fails to note, the extraordinary generation of A. R. Ammons, John Ashbery, Edgar Bowers, Allen Ginsberg, Anthony Hecht, John Hollander, Richard Howard, Donald Justice, James Merrill, W. S. Merwin, Sylvia Plath, W. D. Snodgrass, May Swenson, Mona Van Duyn, Derek Walcott, and others was on the horizon? Among Gioia's own contemporaries (to come forward a generation or so), perhaps especially his female contemporaries, there is such talent as has rarely been seen at once in American poetry: Glück, Alice Fulton, Sandra McPherson, Susan Mitchell, Gjertrud Schnackenberg, Ellen Bryant Voigt, Rosanna Warren.... Well, "Wilson's prophecies were sometimes inaccurate," Gioia concedes—as one might concede that Bishop Ussher's dating of the beginning of the world now seems to have been a bit off the mark or that Pound's predictions for fascism were not wholly borne out. Again, if on the one hand Adrienne Rich is judged to be "a major poet," "*in spite of* her overbearing polemics" (my emphasis), on the other hand "it is a difficult task to marry the Muse happily to politics" and "American poetry has not often excelled in public forms like political or satirical verse." It's not that these two points of view are incompatible but rather that their awkward fit might have provided an open-minded critic with a heuristic opportunity: the chance to try and if necessary to mitigate and to complicate the point.

But Gioia resents complications. They would get in the way of the sweep of the rhetorical sickle, and they don't sell books. He is content to say in one breath that we do not write long poems and that the obvious thriving in recent years of the sequence does not count "because it is a new-fangled form" (nothing need be said, evidently, of Dante or Petrarch or the many sonnet sequences of the later Renaissance or Jonson's "Celebration of Charis" and even *The Forrest,* Herbert's *The Temple,* James Thomson's *Seasons,* D. G. Rossetti's *House of Life,* Elizabeth Barrett Browning's *Sonnets from the Portuguese,* George Meredith's *Modern Love*...) and then to say in the next that "since 1960 there has been relatively little formal innovation done by the mainstream either in metrical or free verse." It is not only that this is an egregious contradiction—which might be resolved if he weren't so precipitate, since he probably means *form* in different senses—but also that each of the contravening elements is itself wrong. Apart from the many sequences that he peremptorily excuses from consideration, Gioia ignores the dozens of recent long poems, as diverse as Ammons's *Tape for the Turn of the Year* and *Sphere,* Ashbery's *Litany* and *Flow Chart,* Ronald Johnson's *Ark,* Merrill's *Changing Light at Sandover,* Pinsky's *An Explanation of America,* Frederick Turner's *The New World,* Vikram Seth's

Golden Gate, Derek Walcott's *Omeros.* . . . On the other end, he overlooks such diverse evidence of innovation as the resurrection of the canzone (by Merrill, followed by Hecht, Hollander, Marilyn Hacker, and others), the resuscitation and then the redefinition (by Hollander in *Kinneret*) of the pantoum, the novel use of many of the fanciest Provençal and other forms in W. D. Snodgrass's *Führer Bunker* (Is this last a sequence? A book? A long narrative poem?), and the creation of forms that prove their uniqueness by not having names (see Elizabeth Bishop's "Cirque d'Hiver," Snodgrass's "At the Park Dance," Ashbery's "Finnish Rhapsody," and so on and on). My own guess is that there has never been so much formal diversity in American poetry as in the last fifteen years.

A similar narrowness of mind and reading lies behind Gioia's patronizing of Rich's politics and his utter neglect of the politics of Philip Levine, Galway Kinnell, W. S. Merwin, Robert Bly, James Wright, Judith Grahn—not to mention Amiri Baraka, Audre Lorde, Michael Harper, and such younger African American writers as Rita Dove, Elizabeth Alexander, Thylias Moss, and Harryette Mullen. For someone who accuses his peers of "a conspicuous lack of diversity," Gioia has astonishingly little to say of women—he includes an essay on Bishop and very short reviews of books by Margaret Atwood and Maxine Kumin—and even less to say of ethnic minorities.

Indeed, a Martian—or Gioia's own representative alien, an "eighteenth-century . . . gentleman"—might well gather from this book that our most neglected minority is the businessperson-poet. To the extent that they were and are businesspeople as well as poets, Gioia idolizes Eliot, Stevens, Ted Kooser—and Tom Disch, evidently one of the all too few "self-supporting writers." (As all current and aspiring academics reading this paragraph will be delighted to learn, professors who write poems can therefore be supported by their institutions.) Is it—I am sure that it must not be, because otherwise he would surely have acknowledged the circumstance—that at least until recently (when he has tested the crowded, tepid academic waters first at Johns Hopkins and then at Sarah Lawrence) Dana Gioia was himself a businessman-poet?

What impresses me most about Gioia's book is that, although it appeals, persistently and even obsessively, to empirical and rationalistic criteria, it cannot itself begin to measure up according to such standards. Based on prejudices, blinkered to alternative modes of expression, fearful of difference, it is of significance chiefly to those who already feel as Gioia does: that metrical orthodoxy combined with prose virtues, and reasonableness, and quotidian speech, and in short the ultimate plain style, are of unsurpassable value. So much for Berryman, Thomas, Hart Crane, Hopkins, surely Walt Whitman, Emily Dickinson, et al.

When Gioia is not scolding or lecturing, he can be an interesting commentator on specifics—especially when the specifics are products of poets not much written about by others. His essays on Weldon Kees and Robinson Jeffers, though not ground-breaking, revive two poets continually in need of revival, and his essay on Ted Kooser is a welcome introduction. He is a generous, perceptive reader of Kees's work, which he praises in terms that Donald Justice found useful before him: "a conversational tone," "'natural words in a natural order,'" "deceptive informality," "a believable speaking voice and a clear dramatic situation." What has happened to the peevish tone of Gioia's earlier chapters? It's here, just somewhat muted: "the sheer flexibility of his talent, the clarity and precision of his language, made him untrustworthy to critics trained to explain the obscure and celebrate the idiosyncratic. . . . His poetry . . . did not reek of the university." "The university": Is there after all but one? Can a poet be at once idiosyncratic and like all the other poets? Are all people in "the university" alike? Are they more alike than people who are in business?

Gioia does not mention Mary Kinzie, nor does Kinzie mention Gioia in her collection of essays, and in each case I'm surprised, since I think of them as kindred spirits. In a note to a poem in her strong first book of poems, Kinzie eulogized her teacher Earl Wasserman: "I have never seen anyone who kept the text in front of him so constantly, who returned to it so loyally. His thought was not original, but practically unique in another way: he was not trying to devise interpretations for the poetry, but rather to school himself to think like his subjects." An admirable project, touchingly related. But the title of her recent collection of prose, *The Cure of Poetry in an Age of Prose: Moral Essays on the Poet's Calling*, knowingly tips a hand of a different kind, suggesting as it does the didactic, even the censorious; and in the essays themselves her dissatisfaction settles like a thin dust over most of her subjects.

But I have got off on the wrong foot. Kinzie is rebarbative, bracingly thoughtful, as well as well educated, admirably responsible and persistent, delightfully knowledgeable about other arts, and self-examining. At the same time, she has her ax to grind, and it looks a lot like Gioia's: the "plain style" or more narrowly the "classical plain style," especially as it has been interpreted in the twentieth century. This style is above all else reasonable, flexible within definite limits, controlled, straightforward, and highly allergic to extravagance. As far as I can tell from Kinzie's remarks, it is also likely to be ironic, austere, learned, and politically as well as prosodically conservative ("The only poem acceptable to the Left may eventually be the completely ill-written and inchoate one," she jeers in an unguarded moment). Kinzie disdains the "confessional" mode and a related mode that she has characterized and named the "rhapsodic," which overlaps with the "increasingly popular metaphysical-diaphanous mode indebted to the late romantics" and which verges on what she calls "the romance of the perceptual."

Her essay on Seamus Heaney's work is representative. Beginning with praise that she hastens to hedge, she goes on to detail the shortcomings in the poetry ("casuistry," "evasion," "cutting of corners," "flawed prosaism," "aversion to the mellifluous," "descriptive excess," "unclarity," "barbarous peculiarity of diction and rhythm"), and in the course of things turns to *Sweeney Astray*, which she judges "not an original work: It diverges very little from the interpretation of the narrated events by the work's only other modern translator, J. G. O'Keeffe, in 1913." Well, that's news, one thinks—and thanks Kinzie for doing the homework. But within two pages she allows that "Heaney's book does something the O'Keeffe does not," then spends another 150 words saying what that something is, and finally summarizes thus: "The difference between the earlier [O'Keeffe's] version and *Sweeney Astray* is like that between a dull encrusted gemstone and its beveled and polished resplendence." The bemused reader might feel on firmer acidic ground by essay's end, where Kinzie argues that certain "truths of technique have long been known and eloquently expounded by Seamus Heaney in his prose [*Preoccupations* is 'one of the most splendid examples of poetic criticism by any writer since Eliot'], but have seldom been so perfectly, and precariously, embodied in his own verse."

Or there is her take on John Ashbery. This essay, suggestively entitled "'Irreference,'" which foregrounds "Houseboat Days," opens with an illuminating comparison of the poet with Henry James, an exploration of the one's nebulous antecedents and the other's shrewdly contextualized dilatoriness. As the argument picks up momentum, however, the more or less appreciative glow (which in retrospect seems to have been lent by the presence of the revered master) begins to dissipate, to give way to a manner that is affectless, doggedly if not obsessively analytical, schematic. This manner in turn is infiltrated by pejoratives. About fifteen pages into the essay, for example, though Kinzie has not overtly criticized Ashbery, we learn that "Dylan Thomas is often *guilty* of [Ashbery's] sort of *forced* over-application of metaphoric keys"; then that Ashbery "*cannot* work with naturalism and accident in and for themselves, *only* with his own angle of refraction of their details"; and then that it is "as if, while moving toward the *prosaic* in his manners, he were also moving toward prose in his rhythms" (my emphasis).

Kinzie programmatically uses *prose* in a derogatory fashion, since to her *poetry* means "*true* poetry" or "superb literature." When writing about one poem she dislikes, she refers in contradistinction to "the magical sense of that world of true poetry in which the expression is always the *right* one." By the same token, she occasionally refers to work ordinarily called prose as poetry, as long as it meets an impressionistic standard evidently as hard (or easy) to define as A. E. Housman's famous criterion ("when I am shaving of a morning . . . if a line of poetry strays into my memory, my skin bristles so that the razor ceases to act"). Kinzie repeatedly calls J. M. Coetzee's novel *Age of Iron* a "poem." "It is never very far from poetry to a consciousness of a spiritual realm," she opines, as she tightens the connection between the poetic and the mystical, whereas the remove of "prose" from soul is great indeed.

Once or twice in the book she seems on the verge of realizing that the distinctions that must be made are (1) between prose and poetry (where *poetry* indicates words framed in lines and thus not to be justified by the printer) and (2) between good work and bad, whether prose or poetry—yet she never does so. But surely there is nothing—*nothing*—that poetry can do that prose cannot do, *except* to the extent that its effect has to do with measure. The distinction between *poetry* and *verse* is a facile distinction, and *prose poem* is a contradiction in terms. Poetry is in verse—free or not—and prose is not. (Or *usually* not—John Lyly and James Joyce and William Gass, for instance, on occasion write in discernible "lines"; but even then the ostensible absence of the margin, that negative white space into which the lines eat like acid in an etching, is significant.) To presume otherwise is to dissolve a useful difference into an evaluation that can only be subjective and also necessarily and mean-spiritedly to denigrate that which is—by one means or another—in prose, and at last, and perhaps most important, to muddy intellectual waters at their source. (When Homer nods, does he slip into prose? Kinzie finds Ashbery prosaic and Coetzee poetic according to standards that might determine that Djuna Barnes's *Nightwood* is poetic and Marianne Moore's poems are often prosaic.) It is ironic and reassuring that, elsewhere, Kinzie is a taxonomist, who tirelessly distinguishes hypotaxis from parataxis, low diction from high diction, and so on.

On the way to her finely shaded and increasingly predictable conclusion about Ashbery, Kinzie—as rhetorician and grammarian—sheds much light on his means. It is a light that is tinged, however, by the smug smog of disapproval. Wait—since it's mine, I'll twist that metaphor. One might say of a sunset in Santa Monica, "How much more beautiful if the atmosphere were pristine!"; or one might say, "How wonderful that smaze contributes to beauty in the world." Kinzie sees not what is there to be seen but rather what might be there to be seen if it weren't for—Imagism? The Industrial Revolution? The Fall? Being a deep-dyed antimeliorist, she is sure that things were better in the Golden Age (though, since she never specifies when that might have been, one has to imagine that it is an abstraction, a kind of Gold Standard). Her final assessment of Ashbery is that "he is . . . one of the great poets of cliché, consenting to appear tainted by the banalities over which he broods." That is a nicely turned, superficially laudatory, cunningly qualified judgment, gainsaying itself at every juncture, which in the end condemns its subject. If I were Mary Kinzie, I'd call it poetry.

One poet who earns Kinzie's ungrudging approbation is Louise Bogan, who is commended for weaving a "dense web of heartbroken implication" in a "verse as serene and perfected and memorable as any American poet has produced: pure feeling of loss, transmuted into pure achievement of verse." Well, purity—especially redoubled—can hardly be disputed. Moreover, as other essays here make clear, Kinzie is sufficiently familiar with Dickinson and Whitman, with Frost and Eliot and Stevens and Bishop, to believe that her phrase "any American poet" is truly justified. It does Louise Bogan no disservice to note that Kinzie thus follows Yvor Winters in his appreciation of the allegedly underread—Jones Very et al.—and in his correlative attempt to deflate the reputations of "major" poets. Kinzie has serious reservations about Seamus Heaney's accomplishment. She impugns most of the work of Robert Lowell. She has little but contempt for Theodore Roethke. Anne Sexton is an embarrassment. She treats Wallace Stevens chiefly as the purported progenitor of an alleged line of poets that somehow includes A. R. Ammons as well as Mark Strand, Ted Hughes as well as Robert Pinsky, Ben Belitt as well as Louise Glück—though at one point Kinzie also refers mysteriously to Glück as one of "Bishop's imitators." Go figure. Connections and influences there have to be, if we believe that poets read other poets. But such an assortment might seem to represent a tradition less than it does a congeries of grievances.

Kinzie also writes warmly and with deserved acuteness about Howard Nemerov, Eleanor Wilner, and John Koethe. But regardless of Wasserman's example, empathy is not her strong suit. She is usually in the first place judging (so much in the first place that it can look like *pre*judice) and therefore condescending. She cannot suspend disbelief when it comes to poets with dissimilar aesthetics who are her contemporaries. High-church, so to speak, she distrusts most enthusiasms and the inner light altogether—so Crane, Lowell, Berryman, Plath et al. are either dismissed or hardly mentioned—and she cherishes ardent asceticism. If she approves of Nemerov's approval of Goethe's maxim that "The attitude of belief is fertile, while the attitude of skepticism is sterile, even if one is compelled to skepticism by the age in which one lives," her own emphasis has to be on that last clause. What she means is that there has been a "'pure' poetry: it used the line without clunky inversion or crowding; it used trope commensurate with an illustrative or expressive end; its syntax ranged across the whole keyboard of the instrument . . . ; and [it] articulated a view of life based on insight, dignity, and depth of feeling." Her argument favors commonsense pithiness, moderation, and decorum. There is strong precedent. Poets, Plato thought, are likely to voice extremes of expression, which is one reason that most were banished from his Republic.

His spirited blurb tells us that Allen Grossman is an admirer of Kinzie's criticism. But his own criticism is of an altogether different sort. Consider the following excerpts:

> In the lyric "space of appearance" all being is celebratory. (This is true in the same sense that all representation has about it the quality of celebration.) . . . The speaker in lyric has not lost heart. To go on speaking, not to lose heart, is an occasion of celebration and an attribute of majesty.

> The poem is an occasion, across vast reaches of space and time, for the performance of the ceremony of hospitality in which the stranger is greeted and the contracts of sociability are recovenanted. This is because the poem as a common place is like a festive table where persons renew their relation to the substance of being in colloquy. The poem has no other life than the relationships it facilitates, and these relationships reproduce the proudest human covenant, which is the covenant of language through which they give and obtain the world simultaneously, and only obtain the world when they give.

> Interpretation is a crisis in the community because it makes apparent the diversity of economically divergent interests in the community, a diversity which is concealed when the canonical text is merely sung. . . . But the community can be healed when the members turn away from the text and toward one another. . . . This is the beginning of *hermeneutic friendship.* . . .
>
> The meaning of speaking is always absent, and requires to be constructed. . . . In speaking we are in one another's hands. Speaking is an ontological puzzle . . . or maze, which is only solved or completed when the absent person is confirmed as *discovered.* It is a maze colored with hope . . . but it is a maze which cannot be solved in theory. Reading requires an act, the completion of inference, acknowledgment.

It is hard to stop quoting from *Summa Lyrica,* which is the second part of *The Sighted Singer: Two Works on Poetry for Readers and Writers,* by Grossman with Mark Halliday. I mean to call attention both to the quality of abstraction of the discourse, which implicitly assures us what his allusions indicate, that Grossman knows the Western philosophical tradition from Plato on, and to the tone of ebullience or enthusiasm that can be fueled only by acquaintance with the Western literary tradition from Homer on. (Homer's *eidos*—not Plato's and not Aristotle's—is the pivotal term in this difficult, illuminating, and addictive text.) Especially the latter feature (which is thrown into relief by the former) distinguishes this book from the two glanced at earlier. Whereas Gioia and Kinzie are concerned chiefly to erect standards and to censure individual poets and kinds of poetry, Grossman emphasizes the hymnal element in poetry. There are no castigations or jeremiads in *The Sighted Singer.* Rather than fearful of the pestiferous, Grossman is tipsy with possibility. Notwithstanding his dark early observation that poetry "is an art which has been driven into a corner, which requires justification; it is an art which has more practitioners than readers; an art the function of which is hard to discern"; and notwithstanding his contention that "my poetry is throughout a skeptical poetry . . . a poetry that assigns a structure to hope but no structure to the universe"—

notwithstanding such disclaimers, his is an expansive, sanguine work.

The two parts of this book are quite different. The *Summa Lyrica* is solely by Grossman. Its numbered sections recall more rigorous procedures—Wittgenstein's in *Philosophical Investigations*, say—and its aphoristic, sometimes oracular paragraphs remind one now of Schlegel's *Athenaeum* fragments and now of Stevens's *Adagia*, while its frequent quotations make it a kind of commonplace book, complete with glosses, scholia, and marginalia. The first testament, on the other hand, which is called *Against Our Vanishing: Conversations on the Theory and Practice of Poetry*, and which has been made in conjunction with Halliday (a younger poet and critic), is dialogic in its form and often concerns itself with craft at a personal level. To the extent that *Against Our Vanishing* is an interview with Grossman on subjects of general interest, it is as compelling as the *Summa Lyrica;* but to the extent that it is a kind of Socratic dialogue that utilizes autobiographical particulars, it bursts the bounds of its genre. If Plato's dialogues are not altogether dramatically plausible to us, they are implausible in a familiar way—a way we know how to allow for—and in any case for most of us the speakers, apart from Socrates, have the thinnest of historical existences. Grossman and Halliday, unhallowed by death and tradition, strike us not unreasonably as living people with vested interests, so that the evident inequality between them can be disconcerting, as can their evident ambitions. Grossman does not mean to condescend to an ephebe, but that effect is inescapable. To put that the other way around, Halliday often seems to be playing the straight man—whereas one increasingly yearns for Lear's fool. Late in the second half of *Against Our Vanishing*, recorded some nine years after the first half, Grossman asks Halliday why it is that "we haven't had many jokes . . . this time we talked." Halliday responds that "It's because of my attempt this week to impersonate a grownup." One feels a painful truth in that response, though at the same time one might feel that the earlier hierarchy has not really been challenged in this second section, as the following exchange suggests:

H I think "H" wins this one.
G I don't think so.
H Fortunately for you, there's no ultimate judge.
G That's what you think. Look. . . .

One's unease can only be aggravated by the recurrent quotations and discussions of poems by each of our authors. If we admire the candor involved in such self-exposure, we might also wonder at the self-promotion implied, and if so the candor takes on the tincture of audacity. Wouldn't the pursuit of truth be better served by exclusive reference to poets who have no obvious reason to defend themselves? The situation is exacerbated by a tiresome convention that apparently demands that each speaker ask permission of the other to "read" aloud a poem of his own—or a poem by someone else.

When someone else's poem is the subject, the resulting comeditation is usually deeply engaging; anyone can learn from the glosses on Stevens's "World without Peculiarity" and Dickinson's "Again—his voice is at the door" and Thomas Hardy's "At the Railway Station, Upway." And when Grossman is developing his central notions of poetry as the composer of the "countenance" or the preserver of "the images of persons" (by which he means not images of the poet or of the self but rather of the beloved as "mediated by the principle of representation toward an audience which would constitute a future for the beloved")—notions that I believe are indebted to Whitman's exposition of "personalism" in *Democratic Vistas*—he writes (or "speaks") a prose of passionately circumspect eloquence. No accident that he, in contrast to Kinzie and to Gioia, locates in the mislabeled "confessional" watershed a source of renewal in American poetry. Although no meliorist, Grossman wants to recognize recent innovations for what they are and to look to future improvisations, rather than to recommend reversions of the past.

Grossman's tome is an ambitious, intense, massively informed, magisterial enterprise; Stephen Dunn's *Walking Light: Essays and Memoirs,* as its deft title intimates, is a comparatively cavalier undertaking. Dunn is good-natured, chatty, relaxed, rambling and gambling. He is not much interested in the subjects that drive Grossman, Kinzie, and Gioia:

> I have never been a systematic thinker, nor am I inclined to promulgate theory or theories. I'm more inclined to occupy certain territory for a while, sometimes as a settler or surveyor, other times as a raider, the kind who makes forays and with luck shoots accurately as he tries to identify where the gold is, hoping to escape with a few nuggets.

As that last sentence demonstrates, with its combination of mixed metaphors and happy-go-lucky and oddly sinister overtones, he often declines to weigh his words. More fun to loot than to assay, it seems. Casual in method to the point of serendipity, right down to his proofreading, and romantic in temperament (Ingmar Bergman's films, Pablo Picasso's "Guernica," Galway Kinnell's *Book of Nightmares,* and Dylan Thomas's "Fern Hill" constitute one characteristic constellation of exemplary artists), Dunn is an unpretentious, rarely rigorous, never captious writer.

The easygoing, catch-as-catch-can style of *Walking Light* accommodates inconsistencies that will seem hobgoblins to little minds. Thus Dunn sensibly warns that "for a personal poem written in the first person to be good the poet must work against the dangerous tendencies of the 'I'—self-congratulation, solipsism, untransformed confession." But then his own essays have room for anecdotes like the following:

> I lived in a poor part of town in an old house with thin walls. The gun-toter lived in the other apartment on the ground floor.... I could have been shot. But if I had backed away after he had seen me, I think he would have made my life miserable from then on.... Something about living on my own terms impelled me forward.

(I'm not sure how self-gratulatory this passage will seem to another reader; but when one realizes that in fact the "gun-toter" was not angry at Dunn, one looks again at a passage elsewhere in the book where he quotes Barry Lopez approvingly: "the person who feels compelled to dramatize the risks . . . is either smugly complacent or eager to demonstrate his survival skills.") At one interesting juncture, Dunn avers as follows: "If you approach poetry writing without reading great poetry, you will reach, at best, the level of your ignorance." Well put. How is it, then, that his range of allusion in this book is limited, with scattered exceptions, to twentieth-century poets?

Still, Dunn's tone is convivial, engaging. Reading *Walking Light* is rather like listening to a friend in a bar—yes, *Oh No,* yes, *maybe* so—without being able to break into the monologue. At the same time, this is a book in process, revising itself from moment to moment. Although Dunn must be one of the poets with whom Gioia (and Kinzie) would have little patience, he agrees with Gioia that "most people" don't believe they have any reason to read poetry and that there is even "a gulf . . . between the poet and the willing, intelligent reader." He remonstrates with readers who are "satisfied with poem as content" and asks for "a more discriminating sense of what content involves" and for attention to "the arrangement of detail." The reader who applauds these desiderata, however, might come with some surprise on Dunn's quotation of William Carlos Williams's well-known irony: "William Carlos Williams said, 'It's difficult to get the news from poems, but men die miserably every day for lack of what is found there.'" The thing is that Williams "said" this in verse ("Asphodel, That Greeny Flower," bk. 1). The claim about the fatal effect of not reading poems is *in* a poem—and it is there in a special prosody. In fact, in another essay, Dunn quotes Williams (almost) accurately:

> It is difficult
> to get the news from poems
> yet men die miserably every day
> for lack
> of what is found there.

Why, then, when he is explicitly concerned with detail, does he omit lineation in the first of these versions?

Nor is it clear to me how, in this same context of sensitivity to minutiae, he would justify quoting and glossing Goethe's "Selige Sehnsucht" in Robert Bly's translation. My point is not so much Dana Gioia's, that Bly is an unreliable translator who has "usually provided prose translations, often curiously awkward ones, lineated as verse," as that Dunn never refers to the original German, even in the title. When he explicates the poem, it's Bly's version that he deals with. I'm reminded of Charles Kinbote's commentary on his uncle Conmal's version of Shakespeare's *Timon*. In the same essay, Dunn discusses a poem by Carlos Drummond de Andrade in a translation by Mark Strand without reference to the Portuguese. Perhaps most painfully, in another essay, Dunn offers the Twenty-third Psalm as an instance of "great poetry" and proceeds to laud "the distinctiveness of the psalm's phrasing and rhythm" and the singular sensibility of its "author." "Even though many of the psalms feel as though they were composed by committee, this one has on it the distinctive imprint of a single maker." The ironies provoked by the last sentence give one pause. The "single maker"—if indeed there was one—was writing in Hebrew, and in verse, whereas the King James Version (1604) from which Dunn quotes is in English, and in prose, and composed as far as we know precisely by a "committee" of fifty-four clergymen and scholars who were revising the Bishop's Bible (1568), which revised the Great Bible (1539).

I think that the fundamental problem here is that whereas Dunn reiterates the importance of "craft" in poetry, he really has in mind aspects of what many of us consider "content." So it doesn't make much difference whether Goethe means "massman" (Bly) or "mob" (*The Penguin Book of German Verse*) when he writes "die Menge" or whether his "Stirb und werde!" means "die and so to grow" or "die and be transformed." Paraphrasable gist is what's crucial. It is perhaps telling that (apart from the Emerson tag about "a metre-making argument") I cannot think of a single reference in Dunn's book to "meter" or to any particular foot. Patterns of accent and other sonic patterns are loosely and consistently referred to as instances of "rhythm." The reliance upon the latter term, with all of its approximateness, rather than on the vocabulary of versification, keeps Dunn from examining prosodic details.

I don't know exactly what has happened to the Symbolist and post-Symbolist insistence on "le mot juste" and "rien que la nuance," but my suspicion is that it has gone the way of "difficulty." "That [certain parabolic poems] might be more difficult, demand more of us, is of course understandable and fine," maintains Dunn—whose own parabolic poems are often vivid. "But the poet must not love difficulty. That's the solipsism of the prig, the person who believes he/she has something so precious it's worth concealing." One recalls, on the one hand, all those contrary insights (W. B. Yeats's "fascination of what's difficult," John Keats's advice to Percy Shelley that he "load every rift with ore," Stevens's injunction that the poem "resist the intelligence almost successfully"). And, on the other hand, one thinks of the many literary treasures that are precisely "difficult" (literally, "not facile"). A third hand would allow us to call up the venerable hermeneutic tradition according to which poets embed sacred truths in other structures in order that they not be understood by "most people" but only by qualified initiates. To allow that the poem can be *difficult* but must not be *too difficult* is not to mediate but to temporize.

But I've begun to take things too seriously by now. To be in sync, I need to lighten up. Dunn's striking title, *Walking Light,* comes from a fine poem by William Meredith, called "Crossing Over," on which Dunn's commentary shines its own good *and* marvelously flattering light. Dunn concludes his observations with sentences that have rich implications for a study of his own poems and that also wisely qualify his assessment of "difficulty":

> We have to learn how to walk light. Or, if we must have a graver tone, we must remember what walking light means: knowing enough about the conditions of our subject that we don't let its weight sink us, that in a poem we keep alive with our discoveries, our successful movements from one precarious moment to the next. Finally, we don't stop loving because of the difficulties.

Indeed, here's to the difficulties.

Of course not all of our recent poet-critics feel even this warmly toward difficulty—or "complexity," as a feature in a recent issue of the Poetry Society of America's journal *Crossroads* terms it, and among them would be Mary Karr, well-known originally for her memoir *The Liars' Club*. Allen Grossman has also contributed a laudatory blurb to Karr's *Viper Rum*, a volume of poems that includes as its coda an essay at least momentarily notorious, "Against Decoration," originally published for some reason in *Parnassus*. That Grossman has done so is again something of a surprise, since Karr's treatise is not only more dyspeptic and less sound than the work of Kinzie and Gioia but also much briefer. Karr's bugbears, in any case, are chiefly the products of poets she regards as "decorative," though she has plenty of bile left over for "Ashbery and his heirs, the Language poets," as well as for the authors of the stereotypical free verse poem produced by "the burgeoning number of M.F.A. programs" (in several of which she seems nonetheless to have taught). Indeed, almost no one 'scapes whipping here, with the result that Karr's notion of the commendable in contemporary poetry—except perhaps for the work of Seamus Heaney, who can only be humbled by the exemption ("Like Shakespeare . . . Heaney")—is anyone's guess. But the brunt of her attack is borne by poets whom she takes to be formalist and neoformalist, including most notably James Merrill ("who may well have been the first emperor of the new formalism," though his contemporaries John Hollander, Anthony Hecht, and Amy Clampitt get tarred with the same brush and ridden out of town on the same railing) and Rosanna Warren (whose reprehensible cohort includes Brad Leithauser and Gjertrud Schnackenberg).

The condition everywhere undermining Karr's argument is that she does not know how to make an argument. Undefined terms, circular reasoning, selective quotation, gross generalization, and distorting use of authority all plague what can only be called her diatribe. Let's take Aristotle, who, she informs us, "called metaphors of all kinds the mere 'seasoning of the meat,' and believed that clarity [certainly a desideratum for Karr] resided instead in everyday words." OK. Having puzzled momentarily over the paradox that "seasoning of the meat" is itself a metaphor, we might observe that, while in part 22 of the *Poetics* Aristotle does indeed prize clarity, he is careful to qualify his view of the use of what Karr calls "everyday words":

> The perfection of style is to be clear without being mean. The clearest style is that which uses only current or proper words; at the same time, it is mean—witness the poetry of Cleophon and of Sthenelus. That diction, on the other hand, is lofty and raised above the commonplace which employs unusual words. By unusual, I mean strange (or rare) words, metaphorical, lengthened—anything in short that differs from the normal idiom. (1458a; Jowett's trans.)

In point of fact, Aristotle goes so far as to assert that "the greatest thing by far is [for the poet] to have a command of metaphor. This alone cannot be imparted by another; it is the mark of genius, for to make good metaphors implies an eye for resemblances." And here he is again in the *Rhetoric:* "now strange words simply puzzle us; ordinary words convey only what we know already; it is from metaphor that we can best get hold of something fresh" (1410b; Roberts and Bywater's trans.). "Seasoning of the meat" indeed!

"*Lack of clarity*" is one of the two principal "sins" Karr uncovers in contemporary poetry, and the other is "*absence of emotion.*" This *soi-disant* stickler for clarity elaborates as follows:

> What should I as a reader feel? This grows from but is not equivalent to what the speaker/author feels. Questioning a poem's central emotion steers me beyond the poem's ostensible subject and surface loveliness to its ultimate effect. Purely decorative poetry leaves me cold.

What can *should* mean in that first sentence? Does it imply moral obligation? Or appropriateness? And is the implication that the poet "should" make the reader feel X and yet might not? Or is it that the reader "should" feel X in response to the poem but might not? If not, whose fault is the absence of that feeling? Moreover, what can it mean that what the reader should feel "grows from but is not equivalent to what the speaker/author feels"? "Not equivalent" in the way that the feeling experienced by the observer of ardor is not equivalent to the feeling of the ardent one? That the oak is not equivalent to its acorn? That a reflection in glass is not equivalent to the object it reflects? In any event, do we not want to allow for a distinction between "speaker" and "author" and the attendant complications? (Who ever thought that Prufrock was Eliot? Or indeed the speaker of "Filling Station" Elizabeth Bishop? Who really says the last lines of "Ode on a Grecian Urn?" What about the last lines of "The Road Not Taken?") Further, is the reader's "questioning [of] a poem's central emotion" an aim the poet has—or an unwanted result? Is it somehow the same as the reader's *having* a "central emotion," as the phrase *ultimate effect* perhaps intimates? Or does *questioning* suggest an obstacle to having a "central emotion"? And what does *central* mean in this context? Does it exclude, for instance, the concept of an emotional complex or "chord"? Could a poem attest to or evoke two (or—imagine!—more) emotions equally? Does Karr's last sentence imply that "purely decorative poetry" (*purely?*) leaves *her* cold but might move others? If it moves others, what happens to her thesis that "poetry's primary purpose [is] to stir emotion"? (Why, by the way, on the one hand, do we need poetry, if the stirring of emotion is its raison d'être? Can't we make do with drugs and demagoguery, roller coasters and melodramas, polemical essays and appendices? And what, by the way, on the other hand, does Karr think of Plato's argument that one *problem* with poetry is that it so effectively stirs the emotions?) It is of course possible that Karr's last sentence is tautological and means simply that poetry that leaves Karr cold is therefore purely decorative. But then who is this "I" and "me" who represents the "reader" *I* am?

No one responsible for such a tangle of simplisms can be expected to give a poem its due, and, sure enough, Karr utterly misunderstands a poem that she thinks "commits every decorative crime" imaginable. The poem, which she calls "bad" and even refers to as "drivel," is Rosanna Warren's "History as Decoration," which I quote entire:

> Float over us, Florence, your banners
> of assassination, your most expensive
> reds: Brazil, Majorca lichen, cochineal.
> Let the Neoplatonic Arno flow
> crocus yellow. Let palazzo walls
> flaunt quattrocento dyes: "little
> monk" and "lion skin." We pay for beauty; beautiful
> and gorgeous crimes we cannot feel—
>
> they shone so long ago. And those philosophies
> too pretty in spirit ever to be real.
> City of fashion. Leonardo chose
> the hanged Pazzi conspirator for a theme:
> "Tawny cap; black satin vest," he wrote,
> "black sleeveless coat, lined; turquoise
> jacket lined with fox; Bernardo di
> Bandino Baroncigli; black hose."
>
> So dangled the elegant corpse, *bella figura*
> though its tongue stuck out. The keen, gossipy
> faces still peer from Ghirlandaio's walls
> and from the streets we elbow through today.
> History flashes in banknotes. Gold, jade, corals
> twinkle from hand to hand, while the spectral glare
> of Savonarola's sunset bonfire licks the square
> and his cries ascend and blend with Vespers bells.

After quoting exactly the first half of the poem, Karr breaks off (after the reference to the Pazzi conspiracy) and complains that she "cannot even say what this [*sic*] seeks to describe. Nor can [she] imagine the origin of the quotes, what this has to do with Leonardo, or how any river—even the Arno—can be Neoplatonic." The poem is in short one of the "worst examples" of its genre.

Such a verdict is not to be regarded lightly—or so delivered in the first place. But little enough reflection will determine that there is nothing in Warren's poem mysterious to anyone with a modicum of patience, a capacity for inference, and an education in the liberal arts—or, failing that last, an intellectual curiosity, a willingness to make inroads on ignorance. In the poem's first half, in which she emphasizes precisely surfaces that are finally (as she says straight out) "too pretty,"

Warren specifies some of the rich, carefully concocted, wittily named colors used by great Florentine painters and, by way of their own common names, a couple of the dyes used in Florentine tapestries. The Arno is obviously "Neoplatonic" because Marsilio Ficino lived on it (in Careggi, just out of Florence) in a villa that the munificent patron of the arts Cosimo de'Medici bought for him, and it was there that he dreamed up much of his "pretty" philosophy.

So much for obfuscation. Who would not be chagrined not to be able to discover (I don't say not to *know*, since reading strong poetry is by my lights always a heuristic enterprise) these facts? Beyond them, the thing is that this city, an artistic and philosophic center, was also a political crux and the source of horror as well as of beauty. Warren's apprehension of the Gordian knot that history repeatedly ties with these two qualities produces her phrase *gorgeous crimes*—a phrase that must call up Yeats's immortal oxymoron, *terrible beauty*, generated in the context of a relevant but much later conflict—and the passage about Leonardo, which Karr truncates because she despairs of anyone's ever understanding it. Well, we're here to help. Leonardo, ever intellectually curious, evidently took notes on the hanging of one of the men involved in the plot to overthrow the rule of the Medici family in 1478. (The pope's nephew was involved in the insurrection, and thereafter the papacy waged war against Florence.) Leonardo, ever the artist and philosopher, was intrigued by the fashionable garb of the executed conspirator, by the "*bella figura*" that he cut, even as his "tongue stuck out." Warren is interested, as Leonardo was, in "the elegant corpse." The topos—the relationship between superficial beauty and essential mortality—is as old as art and as vital now as ever (the pertinent line in Shakespeare's *Troilus and Cressida* is an apostrophe to a dead soldier: "O putrefied cor[p]se, so fair without"), which is why Warren, in a wonderful transition, lets the faces in Ghirlandaio's paintings (at the Church of Ognissanti?) mix with those on the streets of Florence "today." Beauty and terror, greatness and horror, aesthetic achievement and inveterate barbarism: when has this intersection not been the locus of profound art? Warren gives us an indelible image of it in her last lines, where she conjures the hanging and the burning, by the Medici, those exemplary supporters of the arts, in the Piazza Signoria in Florence, of Girolamo Savonarola (a principled Dominican friar—or, indeed, a "'little monk'" with a "'lion skin,'" proleptic phrases obscure to Karr that now have a double application). I quote Warren's admirable last lines, inspired by the martyred friar (and perhaps the conclusion of Robert Lowell's "For George Santayana"), once more:

> History flashes in banknotes. Gold, jade, corals
> twinkle from hand to hand, while the spectral glare
> of Savonarola's sunset bonfire licks the square
> and his cries ascend and blend with Vespers bells.

"Money is a kind of poetry," observes Wallace Stevens—one of the few recent poets Karr can bring herself to praise—and I cannot think of a better testimony to his pronouncement, so eminently reversible, than these verses, in which beauty and horror, flesh and currency, go together up in flames. I have to think that somewhere Horace and Yeats, Marvell and Robert Lowell, at a break in their card game, cash and chips and notes littering the green felt forever in front of them, nod in approval.

A Range of Affirmation

The black-and-white photo on the cover shows an empty vase and a couple of bunches of flowers, weighed down by rocks, resting on a stone slab covered with graffiti. We cannot know whose grave it is. No formal inscription appears, and the graffiti include at least two names, one clumsily spray-painted and barely legible, the other done with a marker and partly cropped from the photo. But then perhaps the ambiguity makes its own point, since the one name is Durruti and the other is Ferrer Guardia, and they both died fighting for the same cause. As a circled *A* scrawled over Durruti's name suggests, it could be the grave of the Spanish Anarchist movement.

Philip Levine has frequently paid tribute to the Anarquistas. He dedicated his preceding book, *The Names of the Lost*, to Durruti, the leader of the radical wing of the Iberian Anarchist Federation (FAI), and several of those poems elegized Durruti and his comrades. "Francisco, I'll Bring You Red Carnations," one of the finest poems in *7 Years from Somewhere* (published simultaneously with *Ashes,* a collection of new and older poems), honors Francisco Ascaso, another powerful figure in the FAI who died in combat. Set in a cemetery in Barcelona, it surveys "the three stones / all in a row: Ferrer Guardia, / B. Durruti, F. Ascaso" and then focuses on the latter. The swift, clean development represents Levine at his best:

Review of *7 Years from Somewhere* by Philip Levine, *Praise* by Robert Hass, *An Explanation of America* by Robert Pinsky, and *Mortal Acts, Mortal Words* by Galway Kinnell. From *The Yale Review*, Autumn, 1980.

> For two there are floral
> displays, but Ascaso faces
> eternity with only a stone.
> Maybe as it should be. He was
> a stone, a stone and a blade,
> the first grinding and sharpening
> the other.

Although this is the only poem here that deals explicitly with the Spanish Civil War, one feels that it marks a center, that this gravestone and whetstone is the omphalos of Levine's world. As his earlier work testifies, from his point of view, that war no more ended in 1939 than it began in 1931. It was instead a crucial part of a continuing political struggle. We always find "The poor packed in tenements / a dozen high; the rich / in splendid homes or temples."

Those lines refer ironically to the graves and mausoleums, but the metaphor instantly reverses itself. Levine wants us to see that Barcelona also qualifies as a "city of the dead." Suffocating in "industrial filth and / the burning mists of gasoline," it could be hell—and at the same time any city in which, as he put it in an interview several years ago, "people's lives are frustrated, they're lied to, they're cheated, there is no equitable handing out of goods." His native Detroit appears in the same infernal light. "The Gift" summons up its Stygian

> river black at night
> with darkness or with oil
> or both, gleaming with the lights
> of all the fires that burned
> beside it.

In "The Life Ahead" he remembers even more pointedly Detroit's "dark streets awash / with oil" and one in particular "that led to hell." In this far-flung urban Hades, the workers serve interminable sentences at hard labor and even undergo a certain torture: the people in the steel factories work on "with sudden gasps / of breath crying out even over the roar / of the huge descending presses." Not that they inspire pity alone. The Barcelona laborers in "Hear Me" have the fierce, contemptuous strength of folk heroes:

> If God
> cared he would send an old crone
> to waken each of them and whisper
> that in work is salvation, and
> there would be great laughter,
> for they have become work.
> That one who is still only a boy
> is first the ringing of a hammer
> on steel. If you put your ear
> to his chest you will hear the music
> of salvation breaking his heart.

Strong as they are, however, and because they are so strong, their lives travesty Ascaso's

> dream of the city
> of God, where every man
> and every woman gives
> and receives the gifts of work
> and care.

Much as he admires the Anarchists, Levine finds it hard to share their meliorism, because his disillusionment goes so deep. Capitalism simply epitomizes an indifferent universe, purposeless unless its purpose is to frustrate change. "The farmer / and his horse slowly / plowing the field they / plowed the day before" could serve as an emblem for his life and the other monotonous, pointless lives he sees all about him. "And there I was, going / nowhere and seeing nothing," he recalls in "Left on the Shore," a poem about entering middle age. In "The Face" he is still "going nowhere," and in "Let Me Begin Again" he longs to "go back to land after a lifetime / of going nowhere." In "The Last Step" he realizes that while we all have certain "companions / for a time," "nothing goes / the whole way." Perhaps we should hear that last clause in two senses. Rather like Teufelsdröckh, he steadily confronts *das ewige Nein* of existence.

But the negative, as Carlyle's figure discovered, cuts both ways. Or it is the stone on which Levine hones the knife of his own spirit. "Dawn, 1952," which concerns his refusal to join the army during the Korean War, records that early instance of his negation of negation: "But I said, No, no, I will not go, and / they let me go, knowing I was nothing." The anticlimactic repetition of *go* stresses his fecklessness, but the refusal still transforms the nugatory into something. "You Can Have It" passionately commemorates a more profound rejection on a night over thirty years ago:

> My brother comes home from work
> and climbs the stairs to our room.
> I can hear the bed groan and his shoes drop
> one by one. You can have it, he says.

Levine recalls with sardonic hyperbole that both of them worked so hard that they never lived that year of their lives: "In 1948 in the city of Detroit . . . no one walked the streets or stoked a furnace, / for there was no such year." But that's all right with him. He would gladly trade in that year and much more besides, he tells us in touching paradoxes:

> I give you back 1948.
> I give you all the years from then
> to the coming one. Give me back the moon
> with its frail light falling across a face.
>
> Give me back my young brother, hard
> and furious, with wide shoulders and a curse
> for God and burning eyes that look upon
> all creation and say, you can have it.

It would be easy to make too much of the affinity with Carlyle, but such passages rhyme in spirit with the famous repudiation: "The Everlasting No had said: 'Behold, thou art fatherless, outcast, and the Universe is mine (the Devil's)'; to which my whole Me now made answer: '*I* am not thine, but Free, and forever hate thee!'" Levine's vehement denials also affirm the human by rejecting the inhuman. This renunciation of creation is the dream of the city of God in negative.

In these poems affirmation always springs out the stoniest ground. "Words" begins almost predictably with the poet,

> alone, searching
> again for words
> that will make
> some difference
> and finding none.

A poem about the need to overcome alienation, it ends with the grim reality of a typical evening at home and the inexorable negatives. Like his father before him, Levine's son will come home from work exhausted, "slump before his dinner," and "say / nothing of how much / it costs to be 18." His wife "will say nothing / of the helplessness / she feels seeing her / men rocking on / their separate seas." As the three of them bow their heads not in prayer but "to bread and wine and meat," the windows go dark, "but the room is / quiet in yellow light. / Nothing needs to be said." It is a vibrantly equivocal last line. Like the words never discovered at the beginning, the prayer would make no difference if uttered. But these three know one another's suffering, and their silence itself constitutes a mutual blessing. When he yearns earlier in the poem to have "to rise above / nothing," he is pleading for the communication withheld at dinner. Yet it is precisely the nothing said that he does rise above in the end.

His carefully devised details call little attention to themselves in Levine's poems, most of them outfitted in the same homely prosodic uniform: short free verse lines often recklessly enjambed and rarely divided into stanzas. Because the verse is so insistently serviceable, one expects little subtlety elsewhere, but some of these poems owe their strength to it. "Andorra" sets a scene in the mountains, in the past tense and then shifts into the future. When Levine repeats and complicates the process, his purpose begins to clarify itself:

> The man I was
> smiles into the light, young
> and full of hope. He will leave
> the bridge and lean down to splash

> the freezing water on his face
> and shake his head as though he
> were saying No! No! to everything.
> He is awakening to a day as pure
> as new snow, a day like no
> other, cold and black at the edges
> and elusive as light at the center,
> a day on which he will climb
> high above the village and sing
> in his cracked voice to everyone
> and no one.

He finishes in the present tense, as the figure in his memory climbs on "out of sight." The poem bids farewell to that former self, "full of hope," but the carefully chosen tenses make it a fuller statement. As the young man "is awakening," something like his feeling returns to the older man; and as the one moves out of sight, the day on which he "will climb / high above the village and sing" has just arrived again. This "cracked" song, with its "No! No! to everything," rejects cynicism as much as it does ingenuousness. Levine lives in this penumbra between disillusionment and faith. In the homage to Ascaso, the dream of the new life "goes on in spite of slums, . . . in spite of all / that mocks it." But at least as often he believes that the dream cannot go on, and poem after poem has to prove all over again the will to continue.

Sometimes I wish he were less like that farmer who must keep on plowing the same field. Yet our very familiarity with his spiritual struggle enables his details to say more than they do. The parabolic title poem recounts a touring incident in north Africa, when Levine and his wife came to a place where "the bridge / had washed out." When he remembers wondering, "can we go back / and to what?" we sense parallels with both the rift between the bitter older poet and the sanguine young man and the discrepancy between the actual world and the city of God. Back then, some "dirty, green / eyed Berbers" appeared miraculously out of nowhere. One mysteriously took Levine's hand, and then the Berbers told them to "double / back" and they would find a bridge. But today is another story, the same old story:

> the smell of bourbon
> and sweat and another day
> with no bridge, no old city
> cupped carefully in
> a bowl of mountains,
> no one to take this hand,
> the five perfect fingers
> of the soul, and hold it
> as one holds a blue egg
> found in tall grasses
> and smile and say something
> that means nothing, that
> means you are, you
> are, and you are home.

So the volume ends with negations: "no bridge, no old city," "no one," "nothing." Or nearly ends that way. For no one can read this poem without feeling that it supplies the missing bridge— the bridge from the nowhere of the present to the dreamlike "somewhere" in the past, from the "bombed-out American / city" to the "old city" that (like Jerusalem) presages a new one. It is not for "nothing" that Levine coaxes us into recombining his metaphors so that the mountains cup the old city as carefully "as one holds a blue egg." Over the course of this last sentence, the lost experience increasingly, wondrously asserts itself until, with the importunate tenses in the last lines, the past is present. Because the dream persists in spite of all that mocks it, "the world we made / and will never call / ours" can be "home" by the poem's end. In such unexpected ways, Levine's terse, flinty, bitterly eloquent poems keep convincing him (and for this we must be grateful) that they are worth the writing.

As the title of his new book suggests, Robert Hass affirms more readily than Levine. *Praise:* one thinks perhaps of Blake's "Prayer is the Study of Art. Praise is the Practice of Art." Or of the poet's invariable answer to his questioner in Rilke's little poem: "Ich rühme." If Levine recalls the severe author of "The Snow Man" in his insistence on seeing "Nothing that is not there and the nothing that is," Hass could be replying to Stevens's poem in "To a Reader," where he conjures up his own January scene and then urges us to "look seaward," beyond the bleak appearances:

> what is not there
> is there, isn't it, the huge
> bird of the first light
> arched above first waters
> beyond our touching or intention
> or the reasonable shore.

But those lines have a Stevensian ring, and if one had to pick a single writer with whom Hass shares most—and that would not be easy, since he reads widely and assimilates easily—my choice would be Stevens, who figures importantly in "Songs to Survive the Summer," this exhilarating volume's major achievement. Like Stevens, Hass is a remarkably sensuous poet—and a remarkably gustatory one. Moreover, although you could hardly confuse Stevens's "boys" and their "maidens" who "stray impassioned in the littering leaves" with Hass's "man and the pale woman / he fucks in the ass underneath the stars," both like to include the sensual in the meditative. Indeed both in general seek to include, in Stevens's terms, "the things / That in each other are included."

Among these things for Hass are prose and verse, which he combines delightfully in "The Yellow Bicycle" and "The Beginning of September," and heroes from Kurosawa and Homer, whom he brings together to wonderful effect in "Heroic Simile." "Monticello," a lyrical meditation on the relationship between political machinery and personal feelings, takes a characteristic stance. It wittily resurrects "the age of reason" in the persons of Jane Austen and Thomas Jefferson. The latter, "if he isn't dead, / has gone down to K-Mart / to browse among the gadgets: / pulleys, levers, the separation of powers." That fine transition foreshadows the real subject:

> I don't want the powers separated,
> one wing for Governor Randolph when he comes,
> the other wing for love,
> private places
> in the public weal
> that ache against the teeth like ice.

As we might guess from his visual pun, the simultaneous isolation and exposure of *private places,* he does not want to separate forms and ideas either. They work together perfectly in "Emblems of a Prior Order," where he considers the painstaking work involved in developing both a species of "climbing rose" and the Doberman pinscher in a neighbor's yard. Because of the way in which he draws one sentence out over six tercets, the poem itself climbs and twines, and the rose and the dog—the one white and the other black, the one "bred / to fall" and the other "bred to stand"—come to seem inextricable, along with human devotion to beauty on the one hand and to means of death on the other. A succinct, affecting statement of the way things are as a whole, the poem ends by reminding us that both rose and dog "were born . . . under the lindens / that bear the morning / toward us on a silver tray." We have to hear the irony (and the echo of the German song popular during World War II), but we hear the wondering gratitude at least as clearly.

Because he wants to see things as a whole, Hass resists the sort of thinking that would separate concepts from raw experience or even words from objects. True, in "Picking Blackberries with a Friend Who Has Been Reading Jacques Lacan," he and his friend happily give up analyzing "subject and object / and the mediation of desire" for the immediate pleasures of berrying. By the poem's end, their ears "are stoppered / in the bee-hum," and his friend, "laughing wonderfully, / beard stained purple / by the word *juice,* / goes to get a bigger pot." But Hass does not really believe that the Sirens of thought can be dealt with so summarily. Even here, his ears are not wholly stopped, since that penultimate line, however much it mocks idle philosophizing, is also a bravura gesture in the direction of mediation between language and experience. He works the subject over seriously in the lovely, intriguing "Meditation at Lagunitas," which wryly undercuts one distinction and proceeds to mull over others:

> All the new thinking is about loss.
> In this it resembles all the old thinking.
> The idea, for example, that each particular erases

> the luminous clarity of a general idea. That the clown-
> faced woodpecker probing the dead sculpted trunk
> of that black birch is, by his presence,
> some tragic falling off from a first world
> of undivided light. Or the other notion that,
> because there is in this world no one thing
> to which the bramble of *blackberry* corresponds,
> a word is elegy to what it signifies.

Because "talking this way, everything dissolves," he lets the philosophical dilemmas themselves dissolve into a memory of a love affair that incorporates a digression into yet another time:

> I felt a violent wonder at her presence
> like a thirst for salt, for my childhood river
> with its island willows, silly music from the pleasure boat,
> muddy places where we caught the little orange-silver fish
> called *pumpkinseed*. It hardly had to do with her.
> Longing, we say, because desire is full
> of endless distances. I must have been the same to her.

But he has not forgotten those earlier issues, which also involve "endless distances," and he returns obliquely to them in the last lines: "There are moments when the body is as numinous / as words, days that are the good flesh continuing. / Such tenderness, those afternoons and evenings, / saying *blackberry, blackberry, blackberry.*" If his conclusion bemuses somewhat, that is because he means to encompass so much, because he wants to acknowledge dichotomies and yet to disclose connections. "*Blackberry*" is perhaps "elegy to what it signifies," but it evokes more than the fruit and has the power to call up experiences so special that they make the body itself "numinous." Particulars might obscure Platonic universals, but our concrete experiences of the numinous surely inspire our vision of "a first world / of undivided light." Desire springs from emptiness, but it is *full* of endless distances, and it leaps gaps between worlds.

Given his impatience with easy distinctions, it is no surprise to find him, in a recent interview, calling "a real idea . . . an event, and radiant." He sometimes seems to be trying to invent a language to embody such ideas—a language like that which Stevens defined in his exemplary line as "An abstraction blooded, as a man by thought." The title of "Like Three Fair Branches from One Root Deriv'd" comes from *The Faerie Queene,* but Hass is more interested in the paradoxes at the root of language than in the three sons of Agape. "I am outside a door and inside / the words do not fumble / as I fumble saying this," he begins—but the first line break gets him inside as well. He warns us of a "thinning out / of particulars," but the caveat turns out to be in part ironic, for the door becomes a gate through which we enter this magical world:

>   The gate
> with the three snakes is burning,
> symbolically, which doesn't mean
> the flames can't hurt you.
> Now it is the pubic arch instead
> and smells of oils and driftwood,
> of our bodies working very hard
> at pleasure.

As it goes through a third transformation, turning this time into marble, we gather that it is all three forms at once and that we ourselves "go / as fire, as flesh, as marble." Elusive particulars, symbols that burn, flesh that is fire and marble: we are in a world in which "the body is as numinous / as words," in which all is translation and metamorphosis. If it is impossible to designate that world "myth" or "life" or "art" alone, that seems to be the point.

While this poem, a palpable, burnished abstraction, laughs at obscurity, others here perhaps take the risk and lose. Hass's beguiling tone—intensely curious, casual, self-confident, tongue-in-cheek by turns—keeps one going and even coming back to some poems that finally mystify. Stevens thought that a poem should resist the intelligence almost successfully. Different intelligences will draw the line at different points, but I suspect that many readers will have problems with "Against Botticelli," "Santa Lucia," and "Sunrise." If so, the difficulties will involve extreme parataxis, ambiguous referents, and fragmented syntax. These poems are essentially discursive, and I am not sure that he can give up so much in the way of muscle and tendon and still get the body of thought to articulate itself. Versions of these devices are virtues, on the other hand, in "The Beginning of September," a chain of images and notes in which the counterpoise of disjunction and ligature recalls both "Thirteen Ways of Looking at a Blackbird" and Basho's *renku*.

Hass puts the Japanese influence to work beautifully in "Songs to Survive the Summer," a sequence of 369 lines divided into seventeen unequal sections made up of haiku-like stanzas. Occasioned by the death of a neighbor whose child plays with his daughter, it tries to come to terms, partly for the sake of his daughter, with mortality. Its implicit questions are the simple, unavoidable ones: What consolations can we muster? By what means or in what sense can we save ourselves? His far-ranging reflections make him a kind of explorer, like Georg Wilhelm Steller, whose experiences on the voyage with Bering Hass narrates (and rearranges). Stevens's dictum "Death is the mother of beauty"; Steller's attempts to save the crew from scurvy and to immortalize himself by putting his name to the species he discovered; recollections of people being reborn at Pentecostal meetings; his grandfather's advice not to take any wooden nickels (accompanied by a wooden nickel): he studies all these things and others, as though he were looking for "the golden key" that always turns up in the stories he reads to his daughter.

While no such key exists, Hass does forge, bit by bit, a moving response to his basic questions—a response that is as much the method of the poem as an idea in it. By method, I mean simply the recurrence, ramification, and intersection of all its chief elements: an echo of one of Ariel's songs, music in many forms, including the old village bell that tolled in threes, the three lines of a haiku about plum blossoms, the plum tree in which a Steller's jay appears ("A hard, indifferent bird, / he'd snatch your life"), death as the mother of beauty, the child's mother dead on a Sunday morning. One way to suggest the sequence's intricate exposition might be to take a closer look at that wooden nickel that his grandfather, laughing "as if it were a cosmic / secret that we shared," once gave to him. Because it has an Indian carved on one side and a buffalo on the other, and because both belong to a lost world, that shared secret is death. But the nickel has two sides in another sense, as Hass implies when he tells us that it is made of "live oak." Having been passed on to him, just as he passes this poem on to his daughter (for the title must be read in two ways), it represents continuity. Read the lines in a different light, and they mean that the secret is that we share. Because the nickel connects generations, it also connects with the art of weaving, which the dead woman taught to Hass's daughter. He continues the lessons by weaving together stories of wooden nickels, fairy tales about orphan girls, and weaving itself. Death is the very warp of it all, the thing included in everything else.

While *Field Guide* (1973) led us to expect some good poems from Hass, it could not have prepared us for "Songs to Survive the Summer." Robert Pinsky's *An Explanation of America* also follows an outstanding first volume of poems, *Sadness and Happiness* (1975). He and Hass are about the same age (both in their thirties); both have written sensitive criticism (Hass in several as-yet-uncollected essays, Pinsky in two books); and Pinsky's volume also contains a long meditative poem for his daughter. The two poets differ along lines that make one consider dusting off the terms *romantic* and *classical*. Pinsky's work is cooler, less sensuous, more consistently discursive, less mysterious, more circumspect. He has surely learned from the Auden of such poems as "In Praise of Limestone" and the Eliot of *Four Quartets*. He organizes rigorously: a brief prefatory lyric and a concluding dedicatory elegy frame the title poem, fifty-five pages long, which divides into three parts ("Its Many Fragments," "Its Great Emptiness," "Its Everlasting Possibility"), each of which has four titled sections. The twelve sections give him an "epic" arrangement and might make us think of Milton, although Pinsky, unfashionably and polemically, sees America not as a paradise lost but as the old New World.

He means his title's audacity to give way to exactness. As he admits early on, "Countries and people . . . Cannot be known or told in final terms . . . But can be, in the comic, halting way / Of parents, explained." Moreover, explanations can be "True or false." He never quite points out that *explanation* means "to open out, to spread out flat," but he might have. To put it one way, Pinsky levels with us. His vocabulary is large and varied but never arcane. His figures illustrate or carry forth arguments rather than lay claim to a unique sensibility. His carefully composed sentences never stray very far from the syntax of good conversation, and they need to be reread not for comprehension but for admiration of their lucidity. This heightened plain style seems as "Garrulous, prosy" in its way as his daughter's style in her essays, which he proudly characterizes in his first section, and it recalls Horace in the *Epistles,* one of which (1:16) he translates here. In a clause that he does not really translate, Horace writes to Quinctius, "scribetur tibi forma loquaciter et situs agri": "I will describe for you in rambling style the nature and lie of the land" (Loeb trans.). Properly glossed, that statement could sum up Pinsky's intention too. To put all this another way consonant with the word *explanation,* he unfolds and spreads out his own clearly delineated map of the country's diverse, contradictory qualities. He does so leisurely and efficiently, smoothing away wrinkles here and there even as he introduces some new wrinkle, itself to be ironed out later.

His opening will show his engaging way of getting along:

> As though explaining the idea of dancing
> Or the idea of some other thing
> Which everyone has known a little about
> Since they were children, which children learn themselves
> With no explaining, but which children like
> Sometimes to hear the explanations of,
> I want to tell you something about our country,
> Or my idea of it: explaining it
> If not to you, to my idea of you.

This modest version of epic simile nicely accommodates Pinsky's easygoing expansiveness, which in turn comports with his subject, or his idea of it. He gives one the impression that he has any amount of territory in which to expatiate, amplify, and invent. As he makes clear later, however, he also welcomes boundaries, and his carefully measured blank verse in the lines given here tells us that as well. He has something in common with the carefree Brownie Leader in the subsequent verse paragraph's lively description of his daughter's square dance lesson: she smiles and skips through the dance, and he varies his pentameter, especially by means of that terminal anapest, until it lilts. But he must also recognize himself in another Leader, "her face exalted / By something like a passion after order."

This square dance introduces a pervasive, unobtrusive analogy. The two Leaders embody conflicting impulses within the country as well as within the verse; and if, with its "home-stitched formations," the dance resembles the United States, it also resembles the poem, the unity of which depends partly on "Varying repetitions" like those in the music—as the reticulation of *idea, children,* and *explaining* in the opening lines suggests. On the whole, Pinsky weaves more loosely than Hass, but then he has undertaken a considerably longer work. His manner often reminds me of those phrases in Chopin, as described by Proust, so free and flexible, that wander far from their points of departure and indulge apparently whimsical digressions only to come back to their appointed places with all the more precision. This sort of development occurs often within individual sections. In "Serpent Knowledge," for instance, he begins by quarrelling with the assertion in his daughter's textbook that snakes innately know all they will need to know, since it seems to him that "Even a snake's horizon must expand, / Inwardly, when an instinct is confirmed." Leaving the snake behind, he muses on how the things that people of different ages know "All differ, like different overlapping stretches / Of the same highway," but then he suddenly transforms "The actual highway" into a "snake's-back" where "any strange thing may be happening, now, / Somewhere along its endless length," and this section forthwith becomes a survey of the places the highway runs through and of the instances of "random evil" that occur beside it. He details one of these "things unspeakable," which the victims survived, modulates into speculation on the feelings of the survivors of historical catastrophes, and returns implicitly to his beginning:

> Perhaps they came to see
> The state or empire as a kind of Whale
> Or Serpent, in whose body they must live—
> Not that mere suffering could make us wiser,
> Or nobler, but only older, and more ourselves.

Starting with one detail in a zoology lesson, he has moved across the country and back, and back and forth through centuries, and by the time he reprises the original idea, the snake with the inwardly expanding horizon has become both Leviathan and any individual citizen. Even while worrying that he cannot use certain words, including *Vietnam,* because they threaten to "swallow and enclose the poem," he has made the poem a kind of serpent that can swallow anything.

In a sense it even swallows itself. "Serpent Knowledge" has its tail in its mouth. And in "Braveries," at the same time that he wonders how to evoke "the boundaries of this place ... where Possibility spreads / And multiplies and exhausts itself in growing, / And opens yawning to swallow itself again," he embodies that paradox in his structure. He tells the story of the child being born during the siege of Saguntum who looked out at the horror awaiting him and retreated to the womb to die. This legend provokes reflections on the Zero Population Growth movement, whose aim contravenes the typical American "Denial of limit" and yet expands the country's potential precisely by embracing limitation. Trying to explain his sense of this country's bounded limitlessness, he resorts to the image of a girl learning to ride, whose circular progress around the ring makes "The goods of all the world seem possible" to her adoring father. These passages lead into this section's climax, with its characteristically casual puns on *born* and *goods*—and its characteristically optimistic attitude.

> The country, boasting that it cannot see
> The past, waits dreaming ever of the past,
> Or all the plural pasts: the way a fetus

> Dreams vaguely of heaven—waiting, and in its courage
> Willing, not only to be born out into
> The Actual (with its ambiguous goods),
> But to retreat again and be born backward
> Into the gallant walls of its potential,
> Its sheltered circle . . . willing to leave behind,
> It might be, carnage.

It is as though he were suggesting that countries die (as Alcemon said of people) because they cannot join their ends and their beginnings and that it need not be so here. As at other points in the poem, one begins to wonder whether his explanation has not surrendered to his rhetoric. It is one thing for "Braveries" to "be born backward" and another thing for America. Echoing *Gatsby*'s conclusion in order to correct it, these lines must nonetheless remind us of the relevance of Fitzgerald's skepticism.

But Pinsky has been there before us, and his optimism rarely narrows into naive patriotism. For one thing, just as its parts compel us to examine it as a whole—for the poem coheres in much the way that each section does, so that to pull out one strand of associations is eventually to unravel this entire "cloth / Cut shimmering from conventions of the dead"—so this explanation of America keeps turning into an explanation of the world at large. If America is a sort of "prison," as well as a "nest" and a "shelter," "the world and all its parts / Are also prisons (Chile, the Hunnewell School, / One's own deficient being . . .)." It is "Another country like others with their myths / Of their uniqueness." Moreover, Pinsky's version of the American dream is shrewdly self-conscious, especially in his conclusion, where he takes the risk of letting his view of the country's future fade into the outcome of *The Winter's Tale*, in a college production of which his daughter played Mammilius:

> The ending is happy; though the Bear eats the man;
> Though the pastoral is broken, and the King alone
> Upon the wind-scarred peak of his regret,
> It all comes right: the statue comes to life,
> And frozen Possibility moves and breathes,
> Refreshed again, although the King is older.

> Though happy endings rarely satisfy,
> That one's a model of successful failure,
> Holding Truth up against the rules of Romance.

As the last lines imply, he adopts this happy ending in the face of the realization that it "affronts belief." He even sketches the alternative conclusion, one prompted by fear rather than hope and presided over by the mountains, with their "cold and motionless remove." The more he ponders that grimmer possibility, however, the more he must acknowledge the instinct that romance formulates, the instinct that will reproduce "New Hope," if need be, even "on some stage / As bare and rarefied as the coldest mountain." It might seem revealing at first that his drama metaphor recalls Bishop Berkeley's in "On the Prospects of Planting Arts and Learning in America":

> Westward the course of empire takes its way;
> The first four acts already past,
> The fifth shall close the drama with the day:
> Time's noblest offspring is the last.

But Pinsky knows that much has happened since 1730 to call into question that phrase, "Time's noblest offspring," and in the end he pays homage not just to this country but to the human spirit, the ineradicable "passion to make new beginnings." It is this admirable poem's final paradox that its eminently lucid "explanation" leads to an affirmation of "an authority transcending power / Or even belief."

Galway Kinnell has had to face a problem that Hass and Pinsky, to the extent that their long poems seemed comprehensive and were preoccupying, must also be familiar with. In an interview in 1971, he had this to say about *The Book of Nightmares*, the superb long poem published earlier that year:

> I thought of that poem as one in which I could say everything that I knew or felt. . . . I didn't want to let that poem go. I felt I could spend the rest of my life writing it—revising and perfecting it. . . . Eventually I had to force myself to get rid of it, though I knew I would feel an unsettling

emptiness for a long time afterward. I hope I feel as totally consumed again.

"Wait," in *Mortal Acts, Mortal Words,* seems written out of that very complex of feelings. One might even hear overtones of Rilke, who meant so much to Kinnell when he was writing the *Nightmares,* in its closing lines:

> Only wait a little and listen:
> music of hair,
> music of pain,
> music of looms weaving all our loves again.
> Be there to hear it, it will be the only time,
> most of all to hear
> the flute of your whole existence,
> rehearsed by the sorrows, play itself into total exhaustion.

The connection made in the last lines characterizes this new book even as it did the preceding volume. While suffering and song are tied up for any poet, Kinnell more than most has made that relationship an explicit subject. At times, song remedies suffering, as in "The Still Time," where all of his "old voices" return to tell him that

> there is time, still time
> for those who can groan
> to sing
> for those who can sing to heal themselves.

At other, more distinctive moments, sorrow and music seem one, as they do also in the fifth section of the last of the *Nightmares,* where so many of the elements in the poem come together: when

> the violinist
> puts the irreversible sorrow of his face
> into the opened palm
> of the wood, the music begins.

That music is

> the sexual wail
> of the back-alleys and blood strings we have lived
> still crying,
> still singing, from the sliced intestine
> of cat.

It is as though crying *were* singing. As he puts it in "Brother of My Heart," "the bravery / of the crying turns it into the true song."

What then saves Kinnell's poetry—as something assuredly does—from being melodramatic and maudlin? For one thing, for all his talk about sorrow, he never makes it appear that his sorrow differs from anyone else's. Responding to an interviewer's question about Sylvia Plath, he once noted that "she thinks her own woes are the only ones and ceases to understand that other people suffer. . . . Also, it often seems she doesn't want to understand her misery so much as to intensify and perfect it. . . . But you see, I respond very much to her poems, and it is these elements in myself, as much as in Plath, that I'm trying to be clear about. All criticism is self-criticism." The last remarks suggest more strongly than the comments on Plath ever could the importance to Kinnell of recognizing his bonds with others. That recognition encourages a poetry that, however personal in its references, continually expands into larger statements. "You're tired," he tells himself in "Wait," but his next thoughts are, "But everyone's tired. / But no one is tired enough." His need to see his own feelings in a larger context can lead him into inflation and platitude, as I think it does in "Flying Home," in a long passage about his wife:

> Very likely she has always understood
> what I have slowly learned
> and which only now . . . can I try to express:
>
> that love is hard,
> that while many good things are easy, true love is not,
> because love is first of all a power,
> its own power.

But usually his generalizations rise out of striking images and crystallize in aphorisms, as in "Wait":

> Second-hand gloves will become lovely again;
> their memories are what give them
> the need for other hands. And the desolation
> of lovers is the same: that enormous emptiness
> carved out of such tiny beings as we are
> asks to be filled; the need
> for the new love *is* faithfulness to the old.

Then, too, rather than trying "to intensify and perfect" his sorrow, Kinnell tries to understand its relationship to joy. For him as for Yeats the two seem interdependent: "It is written in our hearts, the emptiness is all. / That is how we have learned, the embrace is all." If true song involves crying, it also entails laughing, as it did even for Amos, the old hobo in "Memory of Wilmington," who, happy to have eaten a stolen chicken he cooked just beyond rawness, "sang, or rather laughed forth a song or two, his voice / creaking out slower and slower, / like the music in old music boxes, when time slows itself down in them." (Kinnell tries to keep his free verse line taut as a fishing line, paying it out or reeling it in, in accordance with pace and inflection.) Suffering, happiness, song: it sometimes seems that all of life might be summed up in a single utterance, as in "There Are Things I Tell to No One":

> Just as the supreme cry
> of joy, the cry of orgasm, also has a ghastliness to it,
> as though it touched forward
> into the chaos where we break apart, so the death-groan
> sounding into us from another direction carries us back
> to our first world.

That cry or groan—they are really "one sound"—reverberates throughout this book, often in onomatopoetic forms, as Kinnell, who has sent us to the Oxford English Dictionary as often as any contemporary poet, resorts to the most primitive exclamations in order to get to the heart of the matter. In "The Choir" some "Little beings" (either children or figures in, say, a Giotto painting) sing for joy and pain at once as they

> stand in rows, each suspended
> from a fishing line
> hooked at the breastbone, being hauled up
> toward the heavenly gases

and "their mouths gaping," say "'Ah!' for God, / 'O!' for an alphabet of O's." "Crying" begins in tears and ends in wild laughter—"Happiness / was hiding in the last tear! / I wept it! Ha ha!"—and it seems no accident that the transcription of laughter simply inverts the letters in *ah*. "Lava," a stunningly original marriage of the wacky and the deadly earnest, comprises a set of variations on that most expressive of noises. It recurs throughout in the *aa* (pronounced *ä.ä*), lava solidified in blocks and fragments, which Kinnell contrasts with *pahoehoe* (*pā.hō.ā.hō.ā*), lava flows hardened in smooth shapes. "I want to be pahoehoe, / swirled, gracefully lined, / folded, frozen where I flowed," he thinks at first, but soon he wants "even more . . . to be, ah me! aa, / a mass of rubble still / tumbling after I've stopped," a surface that anyone in bare feet would cross while "groaning 'aaaah! aaaah!' at each step." It is an eerie, wonderful music that this poem makes:

> When I approach the dismal shore
> all made, I know, of pahoehoe,
> which is just hoi polloi of the slopes,
> I don't want to call, "ahoy! ahoy!"
> and sail meekly in. Unh-unh.

He wants instead to "look back / at that glittering, black aa" he climbed across with a lover and to see and hear their revenants crying "'ah! ah!' to a heiau's stone floor" and the stone answering "'aaaaaah,' in commiseration / with bones that find the way very long / and 'aaaaaah' in envy of yet unbroken bones." Occurring twice in both the title and the keyword, the sound stands as it were in the first place for pain and in the second for joy. Indisputably, $A = A$.

The aa is to the pahoehoe much as Yeats's "blind man's ditch" is to Byzantium. If Kinnell cannot cast out remorse altogether ("I know now there are regrets / we can never be rid of; / permanent remorse"), he still finds himself "blessing the misery" and able to imagine that "the last cry in the throat . . . will be but an ardent note / of gratefulness." This attitude differs slightly but significantly from that in the *Nightmares*. The earlier book attests to what he once observed in Whitman, "the double thought of death," the simultaneous fear of and desire for it. As Whitman grew older, Kinnell thinks, "he was able to transfigure both the fear and the desire into a willingness to die and an even purer wish to live," and something of the same change has taken place in his work.

He must find himself on easier terms with mortality partly because he finds it easier to see the universe as a whole. "Can it ever be true," he wonders in the *Nightmares,* "all bodies one body, one light / made of everyone's darkness together?" Now he can answer more certainly in the affirmative. He has admired the way that "Song of Myself" takes the reader "through one person into some greater self," and he thinks the end of that poem, "where Whitman dissolves into the air and into the ground, . . . one of the great moments of self-transcendence in poetry." To put it perhaps too succinctly, to feel that the universe is a whole is to begin to transcend the self, and to go beyond the self is to mitigate the fear of death. Or even to redefine death. In "The Milk Bottle" he starts to say that a sea anemone sucking harmlessly at his finger nonetheless means "to kill," then checks himself:

> no,
> it would probably say, to eat
> and flow, for all these creatures
> even half made of stone seem to thrill
> to altered existences.

To the extent that we feel the same "thrill," we can believe that "any time / would be OK / to go, to vanish back into all things." In "The Still Time,"

> the wind blowing
> the flesh away translates itself
> into flesh and the flesh
> streams in its reveries on the wind.

The passage is no less beautiful for being itself a translation of "I depart as air . . . I effuse my flesh in eddies, and drift it in lacy jags." Whitman's lines might also lie behind the phrase "the flesh's waters" in "There Are Things I Tell to No One," which arrives at one of the volume's loveliest testimonies to unicity:

> it is not so difficult
> to go out, to turn and face
> the spaces which gather into one sound, I know now, the
>   singing
> of mortal lives, waves of spent existence
> which flow toward, and toward, and on which we flow
> and grow drowsy and become fearless again.

This view of things has permitted some of the finest poems that Kinnell has ever written. In one way or another it has let him write, in addition to poems quoted earlier, "Fergus Falling" (a little tale of death and continuity that includes a catalogue in which the details link and contrast so nicely that somewhere Whitman himself nods and smiles), "On the Tennis Court at Night," and "The Apple." Just look at this last poem's final stanza if you think it unlikely that his book can equal the *Nightmares*. Or look even at "The Gray Heron," a short, modest poem built of nuances. Kinnell goes searching in the brush for a heron he has glimpsed but finds only "a three-foot-long lizard / in ill-fitting skin." What a wonderful touch that skin is, especially in conjunction with the light rhyme of *bird* and *lizard*. At the poem's end, yet another metamorphosis begins. The implications verge on the hylozoic:

> It stopped and tilted its head,
> which was much like
> a fieldstone with an eye
> in it, which was watching me
> to see if I would go
> or change into something else.

As surely as the observing poet has merged with the bird / lizard now changing before our eyes into a watching stone,

Kinnell has changed into something else in this book. American literature is richer and stranger for the transformation. Grand as it is, *The Book of Nightmares* could only, after all, be written once. Kinnell was determined not to repeat himself but to go on, and he has gone on. It took him about nine years to write these poems, but if it had taken him thirty, none of the time could have been counted lost. *Mortal Acts, Mortal Words* might just give its title the lie. It is certainly one of the chief indications that all is well in American poetry.

Fables of Purity

Descending Figure, the title both of Louise Glück's third volume and of a three-poem sequence in the first of the book's own three parts, resonates through the whole collection. The phrase is itself almost a "figure" in a musical sense: a fundamental structural unit elaborated during the course of a composition. It takes an expanded form, for instance, in the first poem's image of "The Drowned Children," whom she imagines sinking beneath a pond's ice "all winter, their wool scarves / floating behind them as they sink / until at last they are quiet." It appears in inverted form in the last poem of the concluding sequence, which sets forth a creation myth in miniature, when she envisions the ascent of God, who "arose" and "leapt into heaven": "How beautiful it must have been, / the earth, that first time / seen from the air." But that sequence warrants its title, "Lamentations," because the divine ascent corresponds, like the rising pan in a scales, to humanity's fall, so there too she has in mind a descent.

Her title sequence, which demonstrates her exemplary brachylogy, evolves more personal definitions of the term. While it does not occur in the sequence proper, it refers in the first place to the central figure, Glück's sister, who died as a child and whom she thinks of as still descending into the underworld—or straying, like some Homeric shade given an improper burial, between this world and the next. Her sister is "The Wanderer" of the first poem, which turns from a twilight scene just past to a typical evening in the poet's childhood:

Review of *Descending Figure* by Louise Glück, *Too Bright to See* by Linda Gregg, *The Shore* by David St. John, and *Shadow Train* by John Ashbery. From *The Yale Review,* Autumn, 1981.

> Along the curb, groups of children
> were playing in the dry leaves.
> Long ago, at this hour, my mother stood
> at the lawn's edge, holding my little sister.
> Everyone was gone; I was playing
> in the dark street with my other sister,
> whom death had made so lonely.

Just as past and present fade into one another in this penumbra, however, so the dead sister and the living one, out in "the dark street" beyond "the lawn's edge," can hardly be told apart. The last line's secondary relevance to the poet as a child further blurs the distinction between the two—and so does the poem's conclusion:

> Night after night we watched the screened porch
> filling with a gold, magnetic light.
> Why was she never called?
> Often I would let my own name glide past me
> though I craved its protection.

In not responding to her parents, in resisting that "magnetic light" (wonderful adjective), she was trying on, like fascinating clothes she knew she should not wear, her dead sister's invisibility. No wonder the last sentence echoes "The Drowned Children," where the victims "hear the names they used / like lures slipping over the pond."

She pursues this relationship in the sequence's third poem. It begins by confounding past and present, time and space—"Far away my sister is moving in her crib"—and concludes with this uncanny stanza:

> Now, if she had a voice,
> the cries of hunger would be beginning.
> I should go to her;
> perhaps if I sang very softly,
> her skin so white,
> her head covered with black feathers.

If she had a voice . . . But hasn't the poet's voice become hers? She calls this last poem not "To My Sister" but "For My Sister," whose "cries of hunger" she voices even as she imagines them. Moreover, those cries are the perfect counterpart of her own. To the extent that the hunger is for the *other* world, each sister feels it in her own way. In the last lines, as Glück begins a song so soft it barely rises above its context, the two sisters move together as though to comprise the individual, with her interdependent longings for life and death answering one another. The phrase *should go* seems to veil a desire, on the one hand, and a feared necessity, on the other. As surely as if she had eaten of the pomegranate—and Persephone was one of her personae in *The House on Marshland*—she *is* going to her sister. She, like the rest of us, but unlike any of us because of her passionately unique analysis of the condition, is a descending figure.

Glück consistently practices such intense, nearly painful conciseness. She works very small areas: like her earlier books, this one is minimal in length; none of its detachable units (the poem or the section) exceeds a page; and her line usually runs between two and four stresses. She is just as committed to acknowledgment of complexity as she is to brevity. Hence the linguistic torsion: her aphoristic phrases, often oxymoronic ("the terrible charity of marriage," where the internal rhymes weld the stressed syllables); her paradoxes, little straitjackets of phrasing ("the past, as always, stretched before us"; "She is past being taken in by kindness"); and her wicked, preemptive puns ("everything fixed is marred"). Hence too some idiosyncratic devices—such as the startling proleptic title "Pietà" for a poem that focuses on the expectant Mary. She calls the second poem in the "Descending Figure" sequence "The Sick Child" and epigraphically locates its subject in the Rijksmuseum. But no painting in that museum corresponds to Glück's scene. In the one that comes closest, "The Sick Child" by Gabriël Metsu, the child looks feverishly out at the observer, while in Glück's poem "The mother . . . stares / fixedly into the bright museum." Maybe her memory is at fault; but it seems to me possible that whatever else she means, she intends to condense and to extend her complicated relationship to her dead sister. Here she turns the dying child into the mother, and in the sequence's last poem she acts as a mother to her dead sister. It is as though her sister were a self replaced by the other Glück has become. She calls the theme back in other poems, including "Tango," where she remembers how her sister "tottered toward / the inescapable body" of their mother.

As that last phrase suggests, Glück often thinks of physical existence as confinement. She could be Ariel fixed in the oak tree or one of Michelangelo's slaves struggling to shed the marble. As grimly aware as Wordsworth of the encroaching "Shades of the prison-house," she sees cribs and playpens as cages and cells. She remembers watching her sister "through the bars," and she recalls when her own son "would stand and grip the bars." If the "inescapable body" or "interfering flesh" imprisons, "bread and milk" are "laid like weights on the table" because they are the spirit's ball and chain (as well as ballast and anchor). Indeed *body* and *hunger* are two of several recurrent terms whose tangled relationships pretty much define her view of the natural world. In addition to those two, they include *need* (often sexual), *pain* (or *grief*), and—the wild card—*language*. Since appetites for food and sex tie us equally to the corporeal, they tend to merge: listening to a gull's call, she can "feel its hunger / as your hand inside me" and can recognize in both "the unexhausted / need of the body / fixing a wish to return" to the world—which for her gull is "the blue waste of the sea." If the gull's call is a "cry," sex is pain, as when she imagines her grandfather, full of his "young man's hunger," kissing his wife as tenderly as possible—"Except / it might as well have been / his hand over her mouth." It works the other way too: "the need to hurt / binds you to your partner" as sexual hunger does. Since language also conjoins, it leads back through sex to pain. In "The Return" she remembers entering a relationship on the rebound—or rather letting it enter her, like a knife reopening a wound:

> his eyes were level with mine,
> clear and grieving: I
> called him in; I spoke to him
> in our language,
> but his hands were yours,
> so gently making their murderous claim—

> And then it didn't matter
> which one of you I called,
> the wound was that deep.

Another breathtaking summary of this web of compulsions comes in "Lamentations," when the fallen Adam and Eve find they cannot

> keep their eyes
> from the white flesh
> on which wounds would show clearly
> like words on a page.

Glück's understanding of things turns on the relationship between "male and female, thrust and ache," as she defines them with heart-wrenching succinctness in "Palais des Arts." In the view that these poems disclose bit by bit, the female is the more complex and even the more representative figure. Femaleness is both the core of the woman's identity and the self divided, the spirit and the body in their own tragic marriage. As she puts it in "Lamentations": "Then the angels saw / how He divided them: / the man, the woman, and the woman's body." Maleness, on the other hand, is brutal simplicity, phallic singularity, indivisibility. It seems to be both the dominant attribute in most men and something like the essence of the world apart from the self. In "Pietà" the unborn child wants to stay in his mother's womb, "apart / from the world / with its cries, its / roughhousing," but cannot do so virtually *because* "the men / gather to see him / born." In "Portland, 1968" she turns a photograph evidently taken in the course of a spat into an emblem of male inflexibility:

> You stand as rocks stand
> to which the sea reaches
> in transparent waves of longing;
> they are marred, finally;
> everything fixed is marred.
> And the sea triumphs,
> like all that is false,
> all that is fluent and womanly.
> From behind, a lens

> opens for your body. Why
> should you turn? It doesn't matter
> who the witness is,
> for whom you are suffering,
> for whom you are standing still.

The man might as well be standing on some principle or other, or embodying some unyielding position, so that he becomes a willing martyr, a self-satisfied, self-sufficient stoic whom she both scorns and envies.

She feels both ways by nature: her women, like the ocean's waves, are doomed to be pulled in opposite directions, back and forth. They are "soft, alive," they bend and change. In view of this female duplicity, it makes sense that her poems should involve doubles and that she should find the pun an indispensable device. When she notes in "Tango" that her other sister's "bare feet / became a woman's feet, always / saying two things at once," she could as well be thinking about her poems—about, say, "Aphrodite," in effect a companion piece to "Portland, 1968." Here she says two things simultaneously about "the young wife" to whom the errant husband returns after unspecified escapades. He takes the form of a sailor and the waiting wife that of a statue on a promontory (itself a witty figuring of the mons veneris), where she has "this advantage: / she controls the harbor." In the man's absence, the woman "naturally hardens," while he nonetheless "projects" her as a "goddess." The results of the two processes converge in the final lines:

> On a hill, the armless figure
> welcomes the delinquent boat,
> her thighs cemented shut, barring
> the fault in the rock.

Since we must read *barring* both as "prohibiting entrance to" and "except for," the stanza seems to contradict itself. Glück does not tell us how to resolve the paradox, but we might imagine the young wife first refusing but eventually sleeping with her husband. The "fault," in other words, in addition to her sex itself, would refer to the fact that she *is* a woman, not a "goddess"—not as "hardened" as the man in "Portland, 1968" might be.

Glück is being uncharacteristically funny here; but if the humor is somewhat strained, that is perhaps because the woman comes near exemplifying the fickleness handled half-contemptuously, if nonetheless wryly, in "Portland, 1968." "Womanly" fluency "triumphs" in that poem, but Glück feels ambivalent about a victory that depends upon inconstancy—and even about survival, when it proves that "the losses, / one after another" are "all supportable." One of her finest treatments of this theme is "Autumnal," which opens with richly elegiac lines:

> Public sorrow, the acquired
> gold of the leaf, the falling off,
> the prefigured burning of the yield:
> which is accomplished. At the lake's edge,
> the metal pails are full vats of fire.
> So waste is elevated
> into beauty. And the scattered dead
> unite in one consuming vision of order.
> In the end, everything is bare.

The turning leaves, their "falling off" with the year's, their literal burning, and the starkness of the final scene: this little study in the futility of generation prefigures the conclusion, to which Glück links it (across some intervening lines that I omit) by a homophone:

> The word
> is *bear:* you give and give, you empty yourself
> into a child. And you survive
> the automatic loss. Against inhuman landscape,
> the tree remains a figure for grief; its form
> is forced accommodation. At the grave,
> it is the woman, isn't it, who bends,
> the spear useless beside her.

The "figure" the tree makes and the bending woman—both forms of the descending figure—reflect equivocal feelings. It is not that Glück wishes for male hardness, the capacity for resistance that the brittle spear signifies, since in order to "give" (provide) one must be able to "give" (yield). (She uses the word once for each meaning.) It is rather that she understands thoroughly the sadness of the adage, *flecti, non frangi.* She praises and yet resents the ineluctable female inclination to accommodate oneself to the world and thereby to acknowledge oneself its subject.

Other options present themselves, after all. She deals with one in a sequence called "Dedication to Hunger." The girl who believes that "a woman's body / *is* a grave; it will accept / anything" can find in anorexia a means of refusing everything, of freeing herself from the body, with its "soft, digressive breasts" that disguise the fact that we are born dying. Her self-starvation would be a slow burning away of all "blossom and subterfuge," a way of transcending appetite and becoming "like a god / for whose deed / there is no parallel in the natural world." Exactly what kept this irreplaceable poet from pursuing "The Deviation"—that slow-motion version of the meteoric suicide Plath envisioned in "Ariel"—she does not say. She does say that what compelled the anorexia also compels these poems: "I felt / what I feel now, aligning these words— / it is the same need to perfect, / of which death is the mere byproduct." The poems prove that need at every turn. "I stood apart in that achievement," she says about the illness, "in that power to expose / the underlying body"—and here she is, exposing little by little, through an austere discipline, a body of work so unadorned it might be called underlying. Or one might say that the poems reconcile the struggle within them, between the male and female principles, by sharing with the former their rigor and with the latter their complexity and increasing openness. Or one might call on "the hard, active buds of the dogwood" that she sees one day and wants "to capture." These poems have those qualities; they are taut with achievement and promise.

Like Glück, Linda Gregg prizes compression, feels an affinity with Persephone, contemns male mythologizing of women, and writes about the pain of being female. Here is "At the Shore":

> Naked women are being dragged
> down the sandstone shelving
> on their backs, very slowly.
> With ropes tied to each foot separately
> so the legs close and spread open
> as they are moved.
> When they cry out or shout down
> at the men sitting in the lifeguard chairs
> looking at them through the gunsights,
> the sounds, no matter how angry or foul,
> curve and billow like a wave: coming
> to the men on a soft wind
> caressingly, like sirens singing.

This poem will also suggest differences between the two. Gregg tends to be more linear than Glück, more narratively oriented, less dense linguistically, metrically looser. Glück would rank higher on a poetic equivalent of the Mohs scale. If Glück sometimes reminds one of the Symbolists, Gregg calls up the Imagists. T. E. Hulme would have admired her work—its laconisms, its limpidity, maybe its occasional riddle, certainly its "Classicism"—her title for a three-line poem that ironically defines that mode. "It is essential to prove that beauty may be in small, dry things," Hulme insisted; and Gregg, who calls her first poem "We Manage Most When We Manage Small," proves it anew.

Her book's fine dust jacket comports with her own classicism. Its crisp architectural illustration, taken perhaps from an art history text, shows drawings to different scales of diverse elements in a Greek temple, Corinthian order. It includes segments of column and entablature and gives measurements of features as small as flute and abacus. It serves to remind us that attention to detail and regard for the whole structure should be inseparable. We all know this. But not many have Gregg's gift, all the more remarkable in a first book, for proving it. Discrete as most of its poems are, and individually impressive as many are, *Too Bright to See* must be read as a sequence that traces a phase of a life. The poems make a whole that resists (even as it fixes) the shattering experience that motivated its parts: the breakup of her marriage. "I am moon / to what I am doing and what I was," she writes in the title poem, and "Now Destroyed" sheds some light on both:

> The girl you speak of is lost,
> managing to hold on only to objects
> with a wildness like pleading.
> Small things.
> Those she can carry with her
> and care for. She does not want a plant.
> It might die. She prefers photographs
> of the Kore with dark eyes.

The "Small things" justly given one whole line include these poems—some of which she might well have written prior to or well after or in any case without much thought of the crisis. Because she has made it the center of the volume and has arranged the poems about it with such care, however, the breakup paradoxically gives the collection its coherence.

Gregg groups her poems in three sections—"Alma," "The Marriage and After," and "After That"—on the basis of at least three closely related factors: chronology, perspective, and tone. As their titles indicate, the last two sections develop her chronological frame. For the most part, the poems in part 1 seem to deal with the same painful experiences as those in part 2, but they view those experiences from a greater distance than the later poems, which are more specific and often explicitly autobiographical. Part 3 differs from part 2 in the tone it takes as well as in the time it treats. As the poems move further away from adultery and the separation, they discover reasons for affirmation:

> There. See there. The world is good to me.
> I am finished with knife and window.
> My bed will be underground soon enough.
> I will persist in this permanence
> that flesh holds.

That ingenuousness brings with it a mild irony, but the vow to persist strikes a note missing earlier, when transience was cause for sorrow rather than irony and continuity seemed a matter of chance. "What things are steadfast?" Gregg asked at the outset: "Not the birds. / Not the bride and groom who hurry / in their brevity to reach one another . . . Fragile and momentary, we continue." Not that she has seemed self-pitying in the earlier poems. The firm rejection of "knife and window" comes as a surprise precisely because she has managed the issue with such discretion.

Among the strategies that she devises in part 1 for handling the subject she needs to write about, the most peculiar and vivid is "The Girl I Call Alma." A ghastly, protean figure, Alma seems always to be "disappearing" before the poet's eyes: she "perishes," "her hands are eaten off," her hair has been "hacked off." "She does not speak," and "Her eyes look on nothing," and she is in agony. An enigma at first, she gradually reveals herself as an alter ego—a figure like Glück's dead sister in some respects. "Tell me we are one," Gregg pleads with her—and at the same time tells us how to see the relationship. In retrospect (the book grows into a whole by means of such doublings and doublings back) Alma is the first of those images of "the Kore with dark eyes" and "The girl you speak of [who] is lost." A "girl," precisely. If she is perhaps literally or originally a childhood doll, Alma must also be the innocent self in the process of being lost—and a "moon / princess" by virtue of the purity that wanes throughout the first section. Her name means "soul" or "heart" or "essence" in Spanish; and at one point, surely punning, Gregg calls this deteriorating apparition "the sole survivor." "I take you seriously," she tells Alma with grim humor, "even if I am alone in this."

Alma lets Gregg speak of the unspeakable and transform her loss into something "steadfast." In "There She Is" Gregg could be mulling over the very devices she has been left to:

> She is silent because of the agony.
> There is blood on her face.
> I can see she has done this to herself.
> So she would not feel the other pain.

If Gregg is the chorus in "The Chorus Speaks Her Words as She Dances," Alma's dance expresses the poet's feelings—though usually it is less a dance than a series of horrible tableaux. By taking the pain on herself, if I can put it that way, Alma keeps Gregg from going maudlin—"damp," Hulme would say. And she allows such complicated wit as this:

> It is not she any more, but the pain itself
> that moves her. I look and think
> how to forget. How can I live while she
> stands there? And if I take her life
> what will that make of me?

She might eliminate Alma, whose very purpose is to give form to what she has been through; but then she might thereby reduce herself to her alter ego's speechlessness and deprive herself of a means of dealing with the experience.

"What is beautiful alters, has undertow," she hopes: "Otherwise I have no tactics to begin with." But she has a bagful of tactics, one of which is to alter her course by abandoning her tact. Part 2's first poem harks back to her earlier reserve in its title, "The Wife," but Gregg shows us forthwith that she wants the third-person here not to disguise but to mock herself. If this poem's last line—"I grow specific without consequence"—questions her new confessional directness, its first line exemplifies it: "My husband sucks her tits." The line has the power it does not just because of its bluntness but also because it suddenly gives concrete content to the anguish handled with such canniness in part 1. This poem is set in Rome, and the following several poems are set in Greece, where the separation seems to have taken place. That event goes unrecorded, but we might locate it immediately after "Alma Watching Her Husband," where the modes of the first two sections dovetail. It begins doubly in medias res: "Halfway through the scene I could not decide / whether Alma should react or go on standing there / by the window of her dark room, her back to us." What Alma is watching is her husband making love with a woman in "the apartment across the courtyard." Gregg speculates on what Alma should do—"smash the tulips, kneel crying alongside," for example, or "sit with her legs out the window watching / the birds overhead" (the germ of that motif). But in the end she knows that Alma must "just go on standing there." So we watch her watching herself watch her husband and his lover, and nothing happens—and everything does. Few poems I can think of treat as convincingly the way in which the suffering person and the expedient poet interact.

Because the two selves come together here, it seems right that the following poem, which marks the center of the book, should affirm the poet's wholeness: "Femininity is a sickness. I open my eyes / out of this fever . . . I proclaim myself whole and without blessing, / or need to be blessed . . . I belong to no one." We hear the equipoise of implications in that last sentence throughout the later poems in part 2, perhaps most notably in "Eurydice," a version of Gregg's Kore who blends pathos with a clearheaded farewell when she speaks equivocally of the entrance to the "strange world" she must now live in as "the opening which is the way in for you / and was the way out for me, my love." The last section's poems acknowledge even more confidently the virtues of "Staying On." An increasing affection for the world radiates, for instance, from "Skylord," an elegy in which a small, fierce hawk, one of the gods themselves, teaches the poet his lesson: "We learn / from you joy in the ground as you raise each / prey in your claws from the dear lost earth." She could be approving Blake's dictum, "Eternity is in love with the productions of time." But maybe it seems so only because of the influence of her "Blake," where he astonishingly "comes down, calling me. / Says this is the time," and persuades her to "Rejoice in the breaking of the light. / Rejoice when you are two and one. / In the leaving and the coming home." It includes an extraordinary Chagallian vision . . . But it would all need quoting, right up to its conclusion, with its previously empty glass "spilling light." It could hardly be more different from the early Alma poems. But anyone could see they come from the same exceptional sensibility.

David St. John's second book, *The Shore,* also reflects "the give and take of a modern-day relationship," to borrow a quaint phrase from the back cover. Perhaps because of the complications of the give and take, the course of the relationship is not easy to plot. As far as I can make out, in order to be together the poet and his lover, a painter and photographer, have left their spouses (and he has left a son, whom he still sees). Their own arrangement, however, is as "rickety" as the "House by the Pacific" that the woman owns. She has left him at least once before; and although in the early poems they are together, he fears that she will one day leave him again. By the book's end, after a trip that they take up the Pacific coast, she seems to have done so—though the separation might be temporary. In addition to the poems that outline this relationship, *The Shore* includes a few on other subjects and an autobiographical ten poem sequence, "Of the Remembered," concerned primarily with memory and imagination, which he addresses to her.

Sometimes St. John thinks of this relationship itself as a "story" ("The long story we've told of each other / So many years not a friend believes it"), and sometimes he considers it part of a larger story that we should all know the outlines of ("There is only one story, but it's told many times"). He hints that one or the other of these stories conforms to the pattern of a mythic voyage: he mentions a "story" about a hero who, at the beginning of his quest, "Must sail across the sky / To its other shore, where his father / Waits"; he recalls his lover listening to his father "read some long / Passage / Of a famous voyager's book"; and he suspects that "Homer had it right. A man sails / The long way home." He rings some of his most interesting changes on this rather mysterious theme near the end of the volume. Thus he lets us infer the condition of the relationship when he writes about a half-collapsed "Boathouse" (in effect a portmanteau term that combines the voyage with the domestic situation). Again, "Until the Sea Is Dead," which deals with the separation, includes this passage:

> From here,
> I can see the husk of the De Soto
> Someone pushed, last summer, off the cliff.

> If I'm tired, sometimes
> I'll sit awhile in its back seat—
> In the mixed scent of salt, dead mollusks,
> Moldering leather, and rust. The rear axle
> Caught on the last low rocks
> Of the cliff, the hood nosed dead-on
> Into the tentative waves of a high tide,
> The odd angle of the car,
> Make it seem at any moment the rocks
> Might give way, sending me adrift.

Especially with its eponymous explorer in the background, the old car might be a ship run aground and abandoned, the relationship on the rocks.

St. John most often gets along in a more or less leisurely manner, moving from description to anecdote to reminiscence and blazing the trail with the simplest adverbial signs, as in the second poem in "Of the Remembered," where successive passages begin "Summers, / To escape," "In spring," "Once," "Late / That summer," "A year ago," and "One night." He also likes to make little catalogues or possibilities joined by *or* and *maybe*. He wants a fluid meditation, rather than its distillates, so he has room for the gratuitous or redundant detail. Occasionally his tendency to elaborate approaches garrulousness. In "The Avenues," where he describes his visits to all-night cafeterias in those early mornings when his lover is off painting in her studio, he overextends a pleasant conceit that begins with an image of the pastry cabinets' "French bedroom" mirrors and continues through "lonely pies, / Homely wedges" lifted out, "limp / Meringues" with "Their shapely fruits and creams all spilling," and some anticlimactic "cheesecake." A little editing might have done justice to the concluding double entendre, when he imagines that by now his friend too must be out walking the streets, "looking for breakfast, or a little peace."

More commonly, he has subtle control of his casualness. The title poem, which opens the book, begins with a lovely lyrical passage whose underlying strength derives partly from the sure handling of the meter, as the initial trochees, just right in connection with the receding tide, give way to iambs and a looser measure:

> So the tide forgets, as morning
> Grows too far delivered, as the bowls
> Of rock and wood run dry.
> What is left seems pearled and lit,
> As those cases
> Of the museum stood lit
> With milk jade, rows of opaque vases
> Streaked with orange and yellow smoke.
> You found a lavender boat, a single
> Figure poling upstream, baskets
> Of pale fish wedged between his legs.
> Today, the debris of winter
> Stands stacked against the walls,
> The coils of kelp lie scattered
> Across the floor. The oil fire
> Smokes. You turn down the lantern.

Such fine writing makes it hard to break off a quotation. His comparison of the tidepools to the vitrines, attractive even as an idea, owes much of its specific force to *bowls* and *pearled,* which anticipate the museum, and he makes the transition even smoother by the repetition of *lit.* In its second use, *lit* bestows on the milk jade and the glazed vases a quality that we have dimly sensed in the earlier "pearled" stones and shells. The things in both settings give off their own rich and strange radiance. Which makes perfect sense, because St. John's real subject here is memory—moments that "the tide forgets" and he does not, like the one in the museum, which both contains and displays itself. That the present moment has its place in the museum, the poem proves—partly by mirroring the vases' "orange and yellow smoke" streaks in the "oil fire" that "Smokes" and in the turned-down lantern. Meanwhile, his left hand knows what his right is doing, and he also modulates back into the present by way of the fisherman that the woman found—as perhaps she found him.

After slipping smoothly from scene to scene through the rest of "The Shore," he comes to this passage, which closes the poem's own "soft / Parenthesis" by repeating from the first sentence that key phrase, "what is left":

> So tonight we make a soft
> Parenthesis upon the sand's black bed.
> In that dream we share, there is
> One shore, where we look out upon nothing
> And the sea our whole lives;
> Until turning from the waves, we find
> One shore, where we look out upon nothing
> And the earth our whole lives.
> Where what is left between shore and sky
> Is traced in the vague wake of
> (The stars, the sandpipers whistling)
> What we forgive. *If you wake soon, wake me.*

That "soft / Parenthesis": the shape their bodies make while they lie on the sand? Probably—and probably also this evening interlude, right out of the "dream" they share, that is a part of and yet apart from their lives (and thus analogous to the syntactical status of the penultimate line's literal parenthesis). In the rare state that these lines evoke, itself a "vague wake," sleeping and waking merge, as do self and other (either person speaks the last sentence), scene and mood. There is even something of the transcendental about the last sentence. It is almost as though these two had lain down together, perfectly content at being with each other, for the last time.

He writes elegantly of similar occasions in "Blue Waves," where he records their mornings together on the shore "In this equation of pleasure and light, / The day waking." This poem too ends on what first seems a note of subtle elation. He imagines that one day he will recall such a moment as the present one,

> will look
> Back across this room, as I look now, to you
> Holding a thin flame to the furnace,
> The gasp of heat rising as you rise;
> To these mornings, islands—
> The balance of the promise with what lasts.

In context, however, the "promise" is ambiguous, just as the memories he has set down earlier are of two kinds. As a whole, "Blue Waves" strikes a balance between his hope that they will remain together and his melancholy suspicion (hinted at in the title) that they will not. When, toward the end of the volume, the separation itself preoccupies him, St. John's elegance sometimes threatens to give way to self-indulgence. "Until the Sea Is Dead" (at six pages the longest single poem here) makes dismayingly much of a story of a Russian immigrant trader who once lived near the coast and who, when his wife left him, cut his throat. At such times one longs for a touch of Rosalind's skepticism: "Men have died, and worms have eaten them, / But not for love."

In several poems he experiments with altogether different modes. These poems range from a surrealistically slanted "Elegy" that comes too close to computer poetry for my taste ("Fog / In the attic; this pod of black milk. Anymore, / Only a road like August approaches") to an intricate, quasi-Symbolist lyric, in "Of the Remembered," which consists of vibrantly italicized, unpunctuated fragments divided into phrases by extra spaces. We occasionally glimpse bits of an actual situation—two people in bed, a fall scene beyond the window—but it is much less an exposition of events than a revelation of a process, a process that is at once external and internal, natural and linguistic: "*Now say it   now   in the dialect / Of fingers over fingers   a corporeal tongue / A script of genitals . . . word's flesh.*" Novalis's Teacher, in *The Disciples at Sais,* who "looked for analogies in all things, conjectures, correspondences," and for whom "men were stars, stones were animals, clouds were plants," might have jotted notes like these. Here is a piece of the "*music or the web*" the poem makes and mirrors:

> *Rainbows bent from a book to earth*
> *The book of leaves   newly falling leaves*
> *The corpses   veins flattened in their pages*
> *The burning manifestoes   the diaries*
> *The leaves like sheets floating*
> *Over each flat body   the smoky seamy air*
> *The ambivalent air   now say it.*

This passage loses some of its double meanings in extraction (*sheets* and *air* have musical associations), but it might still suggest the poem's extraordinary texture.

The evidence of randomness and disorder sometimes allowed to enter St. John's work has long been welcome in John Ashbery's, and in spite of the formal finickiness of *Shadow Train*—each poem has four quatrains—many of us will come to the new book expecting Ashbery once more "To relax standards, bring light and chaos / Into the order of the house." As one sits with these poems, however, and as "the sense mounts / Slowly in the words as in a hygrometer," less and less seems arbitrary or capricious—though much is ambiguous. The first poem is the place to begin:

The Pursuit of Happiness

It came about that there was no way of passing
Between the twin partitions that presented
A unified facade, that of a suburban shopping mall
In April. One turned, as one does, to other interests

Such as the tides in the Bay of Fundy. Meanwhile there was one
Who all unseen came creeping at this scale of visions
Like the gigantic specter of a cat towering over tiny mice
About to adjourn the town meeting due to the shadow,

An incisive shadow, too perfect in its outrageous
Regularity to be called to stand trial again,
That every blistered tongue welcomed as the first
Drops scattered by the west wind, and yet, knowing

That it would always ever afterwards be this way
Caused the eyes to faint, the ears to ignore warnings.
We knew how to get by on what comes along, but the idea
Warning, waiting there like a forest, not emptied, beckons.

He starts lucidly enough, though one is likely to puzzle momentarily over the evident importance to him of the banal predicament described in the first sentence. The second sentence leads us on with its little joke (dexterously sprung just after the stanza break), and the *Meanwhile* promises a narrative, so the reader settles back in the lawn chair—only to have it collapse under him. Who is this "one" compared in rapid succession to a feline "specter," a perfectly regular "shadow," and the faint beginnings of a storm? What would "always ever afterwards be this way"? And what is the "idea" that "beckons"? "Poetry," someone across the patio, having grasped at the allusion to Shelley, predictably ventures—and surely she is on to something.

The poem begins where many poems and books do, with a dead end. Since this is a specific book, we might posit for its origin a specific dead end. Ashbery's last volume, *As We Know,* featured a long poem, "Litany," a tour de force printed in two parallel columns "meant to be read as simultaneous but independent monologues." A daunting structure, it might also have been a difficult poem for the poet to go beyond, to go on from. Whether its two columns would have seemed to Ashbery "twin partitions that presented / A unified facade," that image strikes me as an apt analogy from the reader's point of view. "Litany" was no "suburban shopping mall"—but it would be like Ashbery to let an ironically deprecatory metaphor masquerade as the poem's only bit of hard physical description. "Litany" could easily have driven or inspired him to something quite different, somewhat as the *Duino Elegies* led Rilke to the *Sonnets to Orpheus.* Indeed *Shadow Train* shares with the sonnet sequence an "outrageous / Regularity"—the more outrageous for its comprising an even fifty poems that amount to an even eight hundred lines. Quite an "idea," especially for a poet given more to the cloudy and unpredictable than to the "incisive," yet perhaps a hard one for such a poet to carry on and out—an idea that might cause the waffling set down in lines 11–14 and then epitomized in that teeter-totter of a last line, with *Warning* on one end and *Beckons* on the other. But Ashbery chose the "Pursuit" that he did because of his adventurousness, so with that abrupt, perfect change of tense in the poem's last word, he's off.

Not that many of these poems can be so narrowly read. For one thing, Ashbery's "specter" or "shadow," in its later permutations, involves more than a poetic inspiration. When he tells us, at the beginning of the second poem, that "At first it came easily, with the knowledge of the shadow line / Picking its way through various landscapes" and "sorting out what was best for it," the subject looks a good deal like the process of composition (seen from the vantage point of the motivating impulse), but the image fades out at its edges into indefiniteness. We can still discern the "creeping" specter in the fifth poem's "mysterious creeping motion" that "Quickens its demonic profile, bringing tears, to these eyes at least, / Tears of excitement," but that motion is also a diffuse version, a fainter shadow of the original. Near the book's end the specter transforms itself into the "Shadow Train," a term that could designate this volume of poems; but Ashbery associates it with the "Violence" of "history" as well as with "one's private guignol." The idea of the poetic project has not been lost—Ashbery insists on preserving it in his ambiguous conclusion to the title poem: "You are half-asleep at your instrument table"—but it has been subsumed in some huge, shady, shape-shifting undertaking.

It is that process that Ashbery (shades of Plotinus) refers to as, simply, "it." These poems are shot through with ambiguities, many of which (as Paul Breslin noted in a review of earlier books) we can lay to the absence of a referent for that seemingly insignificant, increasingly puzzling, finally inclusive pronoun. In the sentence at the beginning of "Punishing the Myth"—"At first it came easily, with the knowledge of the shadow line"—the *it* absorbs the "shadow line," "knowledge," and "Myth." And such concepts do not begin to saturate it. A poem suitably entitled "The Absence of a Noble Presence" begins,

> If it was treason it was so well handled that it
> Became unimaginable. No, it was ambrosia
> In the alley under the stars and not this undiagnosable
> Turning.

"Indelible, Inedible" ends with lines no less enigmatic:

> And its enduring lasted through many
> Transformations, before it came to seem as though it
>   could not be done.

Cats were curious about it. They followed it
Down into the glen where it was last seen.

It might refer to any of a host of antecedents that blur into one another and that include an unspecified "Work," "the river" beside which the work "had been proceeding," a "mitered flashing," and an "easy spoke-movement of the hopeless expanse." From one point of view, this *it is* hopelessly ambiguous. But surely Ashbery means to suggest that *it* is such transformations as we have just witnessed in the poem. In that case, that "it was last seen" in the glen means only that it, being indelible and inedible (and highly metamorphic, as the title's nice *trouvaille* tells us), has gone on through other as yet undetected "transformations." Ashbery asks in his penultimate poem whether *it* can be "the context" and answers with customary obliquity, "No, it is old and / Sometimes the agog spectator wrenches a cry / From its own house." But if it is not "context," it is not in exactly the way it is not "this undiagnosable / Turning." Both terms come close to naming it—*context* in a literal sense (an interweaving) and *Turning* in several interwoven senses (transforming, changing, versing)—but it is finally as unnameable by nature as Stevens's first idea.

How Ashbery must tire of the pairing—which, however, seems inescapable. Like Stevens, Ashbery conceives of poetry as a means of engaging enthusiastically in this ceaseless process of transformation. As he advises us in regard to "impurity," we should "Help it along! Make room for it!" "You accept it so as to play with it / And translate when its attention is deflated," he explains in his last poem. Two of the three Fates or Graces or Muses in "Oh, Nothing" are "Love" and "fear," but "the youngest and most beautiful sister / Is called Forward Animation," and this impertinent presence generates change: "Of her it may be said / That what she says, she knows, and it will always come undone / Around her." Some of us may choose to "move on, untouched" by her. Or so we might imagine. But even as we "move on," she, the very spirit of movement, reflected in the "glassy, / Chill surface of the cascade," will be "de-defining" us. So whether we take her for a muse or not, we shall be "amused" by her—and thus "immortal, as water gushes down the sides of the globe." As for Ashbery, because he has committed himself to Forward Animation, she lets him "hear," of an autumn afternoon,

> The patterns of distress settling into rings
> Of warm self-satisfaction and disbelief, as though
> The whole surface of the air and the morrow were scored
> Over and over with a nail as heavy rains
>
> Pounded the area, until underneath all was revealed as mild,
> Transient shining, the way a cloud dissolves
> Around the light that is of its own making, hard as it is
> To believe.

This passage in "Tide Music"—its storm in effect anticipated by the cloud implicitly responsible for those "first / Drops scattered by the west wind" in the opening poem—is pure transition, a cycle of metamorphoses that unites earth and sky, emotions and their cause, weather and metaphor, and reveals the whole as a "Transient shining."

Such volatility characterizes these poems at every level. "These, these young guys / Taking a shower with the truth," he complains with good-natured irony, "can disentangle the whole / Lining of fabricating living from the instantaneous / Pocket it explodes in." Since he cannot, the imagined and the real turn into one another in the most graceful ways through the volume. Past and present also frequently merge, by virtue of tense shifts and a cagey use of those quasi-logical terms *then* and *now*. And—more surprisingly perhaps—so do the poet and virtually all of the other figures referred to pronominally in this sequence. "All men are ambiguous," he once phrases this principle. He means, to put it one way, that any moderately experienced person represents humanity; that is, "if you have curled and dandled / Your innocence once too often, what attitude isn't then really yours?" This proposition leads to his pluralizing of the self: "We are overheard, / As usual. We're sorry, I say." It also leads to his interchanging of *you* and *I*. *You* is sometimes a means of self-address, but it frequently refers to someone the reader has been led to believe is another person—sometimes the reader himself. "Here Everything Is Still Floating" ends with these beguiling lines:

> Still I enjoy
> The long sweetness of the simultaneity, yours and mine, ours and mine,
> The mosquitoey summer night light. Now about your poem
> Called this poem: it stays and must outshine its welcome.

Of course it is the reader's poem to the extent that Ashbery means it to be read. But his exchange of places with the reader (a maneuver he repeats rhetorically in the metathesis in "stays and must outshine") argues a sense of a more fundamental connection, a radical unity—the sort that he perhaps also alludes to in one of his persona's claims, "It was me."

But in spite of his intuition that the universe resembles an active imagination in which all things relate, he knows full well that the individual often has only himself to talk to—that "we are alone up here"—and so a sadness shadows the sequence. In "Night Life," for example, an evocation of the modest beginnings of a relationship concludes when he allows that he likes

> the way
>
> Your hair is cropped, it's important, the husky fragrance
> Breaking out of your voice, when I've talked too long
> On the phone, addressing the traffic from my balcony
> Again, launched far out over the thin ice once it begins to smile.

As this beautifully unfolded passage gathers momentum, the poet's isolation increases with every phrase, as "your voice" turns into his own, his chat with a virtually physical presence becomes first a phone conversation and then a monologue, and finally he seems banished from the human environment altogether.

But that irrevocable solitariness has its other side, which we glimpse here in that odd "smile" (which shows up from time to time in the sequence and which in this instance belongs as much to the voice that has willy-nilly become his own as to *it* in the dangerous form of the thin ice). In "The Freedom of the House" he admits that "being alone / Is the condition of happiness," that "we can split open / The ripe exchanges, kisses, sighs, only in unholy / Solitude, and sample them there." If that pertains to writing as well as to remembering, it also has to do with reading—at least when the poems have as much to sample as these do. Take that ripe exchange at the end of "Here Everything Is Still Floating." Its last phrase, *must outshine its welcome,* carries the not unreasonable hope that the poem will shine longer than the human welcome can—as a star outshines its life. At the same time, since Ashbery would have in mind the archaic sense of the verb, he means that the poem should shine forth its own welcome. And indeed this whole sequence does.

Bright Sources

Dark Sayings

John Hollander's *Kinneret,* darkly brilliant, a short sequence recently published in a limited edition, is one of the richest inventions yet by a tireless experimenter. Hard as coral, intricate, hard as oracles, it sounds like nothing else, though it has something in common with the kind of Chinese verse that confirmed Pound in his ventures in superposition and something in common with Fitzgerald's *Rubaiyat.* Unique as it is, however, *Kinneret* could almost have been projected on the basis of Hollander's previous collection, *In Time and Place.*

Although its title pretends to locate it firmly, this earlier volume is in transit from its first poem, with its promise that its

> measured lines
> Shall wander yet, slowly to mark
> A journey through a kind of dark
> In which a distance faintly shines.

A "distance," we notice, not a destination. When in this volume's transitional second section, "In Between," the speaker picks up "an odd volume of Emerson lying on a chair," one imagines that volume might contain "The Poet," with its celebration of "fluxional" discourse, since Hollander characteristically works "In Between," in gaps, in interstices, in "the House of Distance." Is there anywhere else to work? Perhaps not, but

---

Review of *In Time and Place* and *Kinneret* by John Hollander, *The Sunset Maker* by Donald Justice, *Palladium* by Alice Fulton, and *The Gold Cell* by Sharon Olds. From *The Yale Review,* Autumn, 1987.

he makes us especially aware of Emerson's principle that "all language is vehicular and transitive, and is good, as ferries and horses are, for conveyance, not as farms and houses are, for homestead." Even when, just before his coda, Hollander envisions "the finished structure" that he has been at work upon, he stipulates that "it will always have to keep its own distant appearance." In this "tower," he knows "one must be . . . amid what has always been, and will be, beyond."

Thirty-five poems, all in tetrameter quatrains but of various lengths, compose the first of the collection's three parts, "In Time," whose "Steady Work" is the love and pain and memory in the aftermath of a marriage's breakup. The quatrains rhyme *abba,* and as usual with Hollander, the form expresses the experience, which in this case repeats the situation of the poet, by nature separated from the remembered or the desired and always making "nets of love and lack." His rhymes, Hollander observes, are

> An emblem of love's best and worst:
> *Marriage* (where hand to warm hand clings,
> Inner lines, linked by rhyming rings);
> *Distance* (between the last and first).

This quatrain comes from a virtuosic performance on precursors in this form, this "suite of rooms," or stanzas, "A bit worn by now, with crowds of word." No doubt. But a line such as that last, which lets us feel how *words* can be packed unseemly into *crowds,* even as the chiasmus of *wor* and *ow* sounds repeats the rhyme's pattern, is a rejuvenating gem. Still, a certain stuffiness seems inescapable in these chambers, and Hollander is especially refreshing when he laces decorous diction and urbane allusion with vulgar figure. In "When Song Will Not Do," having just overheard a lyric from *Die Schöne Müllerin,* he writes his own addition to Schubert's cycle, which includes these mixed and mixing stanzas:

> In the dim song of distances
> The river slowly unwinds,
> Your soft mill tirelessly grinds
> The mixture of your joys and his;

> I hear the laughing overshot
> Wheel and its merry, whispered splashing,
> The moan of softening, the mashing
> Pestle gentle in your pot.

The painfully canny enjambments in the second stanza are such discoveries as make Hollander our past master of the prosodic trope.

So it is all the more impressive that the last section of *In Time and Place* is written in a consummate prose. "In Between" makes witty use of an old notebook and some invisible ink (made of dried tears, sweat of anxiety, some fine white wine that has turned, and a few drops of remembered rain) in its prose meditation on writing and absence (the broken relationship is still in the background), but to my mind the highest achievement of this volume is "In Place," a sequence of prose poems. They "start out to be stories," as Hollander puts it in a note, "but get lost, amid other things, in the telling." Some of them are parabolic, and some are like the bullets in "Keepsakes," detached from all narrative frames, grown ever more inward and more intensely themselves as they "lay in whatever box it was, creating more and more of their own purity." Passage after passage is meticulously shaped, whether aphoristic, as in "Action is so epigrammatic, discharging its meaning like a joke," where the last word fires off the paradox, or quasi-narrative, as in the following example from the first prose poem after the prologue. After a plague in the city, "village life had broken down":

> Those who huddled in the house during the long rain, and rekindled the stubs of blue candle until there was power again, were not going to tell old stories to pass the time as they sorted odd seeds in what light there was, or silently sat out the important thunder. It was as if they could not be prelude to any narrative that would not be twisted out of shape as it awkwardly sidestepped the embarrassments of its own unfolding, or strove to avert its hearing from the creaking of hinges as its own doors opened and shut.

This is altogether alive, from "the stubs of blue candles" that light up the scene at the outset, through the passing allusion to the old story of Psyche that outflanks the refusal to tell "old stories," and the resonance of *important* and *embarrassments,* to the evasive syntax and the escape by means of the double negative into this section's skewed world, as its own doors open and shut.

These prose poems keep teaching us to read, each in its own way. Take "Crocus Solus." Among the three experimental writers to whom it is dedicated is Raymond Roussel. Because Roussel wrote a novel called *Locus Solus,* it is fitting that he should have a place in this sequence entitled "In Place," which is always about the solitude in which writing is done. It is also fitting that Hollander should write in place of Roussel's *Locus* the word *Crocus.* That substitution itself is in effect the starting point of this prose poem, since such a procedure would follow Roussel's method of composition as he outlined it in *Comment j'ai écrit certains de mes livres.* Roussel's works characteristically had their origins in a common word or phrase that through wordplay would yield others. Thus his *Impressions d'Afrique* began in "Parmi les noirs," a story that originated with the metagrams *billard* (billiard table) and *pillard* (plunderer), each of which then generated, in reciprocal relationship to the other's terms, its own phrase: "les lettres du blanc sur les bands du vieux billard" (the white letters on the cushions of the old billiard table) and "les lettres du blanc sur les bandes du vieux pillard" (the white man's letters about the hordes of the old plunderer). The story set out at the one point and arrived at the other. Any mature Roussel work includes an unknowable number of such transformations, though usually the primary phrases have been suppressed in composition and only the least likely meanings appear in print.

Hollander's prose poem evokes the single flower: "A sigh? No more: a yellow or white rupture of the cold silent winter ground, the exclamation of such effort. Yet unaccompanied by the echoing multitudes that hope surveys; one only, and whether an accident or an example, too important in its uniqueness to be considered important for its meaning."

From the alpha that it begins with, however, this prose poem about its writing involves Roussel, and "the cold silent winter ground" that the crocus ruptures probably translates Mallarmé's "vide papier que la blancheur défend"—so both the singularity and the uniqueness of the crocus are called into question immediately after the tip of the pointed *A* has emerged. "Language is the rupture within totality itself," Derrida puts it in his essay on Edmond Jabès, and the appearance of the word—*sigh*, say, which figures the crocus—creates between itself and any signified a distance that is also the locus (indefinitely expandable) of other words. Like a word processor in insert mode, language is always pushing its object in front of it. No sooner is the original sigh "No more" than it is "yellow or white," where the alternatives testify to the linguistic rift. Willy-nilly "the echoing multitudes" have been called into play, and we are amid what Michel Foucault—in *Death and the Labyrinth*, his fascinating book on Roussel—calls "the proliferating emptiness of language."

Since language, with its "wealth of poverty," in Foucault's phrase, has too few signifiers for the possible signifieds, it borrows shamelessly from itself, and in the process it fosters further discontinuities. *No more*, for instance, carries with its negation the positive injunction, *Know more*, which is not so much spelled out as complied with by the rest of this prose poem, though the crucial homophone does turn up in the next sentence: "O, spring will come, and one time it will not, but what we are to know we will know from all the various emblems crying, out of the grass, *vivace assai*, and waving in the soft wind, *ô Mort*." Moreover, as the grass's voices suggest, to Hollander's keen ear, we will also "know *mort*," so that the first *more*, like a birth, bears fatality within it. But by the same token, *No more* can be read back against itself as "No *mort*" and as an affirmation of spring—just as the tentative and costive opening, "A sigh? No more," yields a music that is plenty (*assai*) lively. As Foucault says of Roussel's work, the tenuousness of language here confronts its richness. "One flower points to nothing but itself," Hollander asserts later. Yet this "flower" points to all these possibilities and to Roussel and to Mallarmé's "Brise marine" (and very likely to "Crise de vers":

"I say: a flower! and, out of the oblivion to which my voice relegates all contours, there rises musically something different from all known blossoms, the one absent from all bouquets, the sweet idea itself"), and by the end of the prose poem, the opening words have produced a homophonic phrase that is understandably their contrary: "A sign? O, more . . . "

Kinneret derives from both the melancholy verse about the lost love in "In Time" and the more abstract, parabolic treatments of absence in "In Place." Here, too, disjunction and distance are part and parcel of the form, whose extraordinary possibilities dovetail with Hollander's extraordinary gifts. The form is the Malay *pantun,* which in a note Hollander distinguishes from "its fussy, refrain-plagued French derivative, the *pantoum.*" In the former, we learn, "the first and second lines frame one sentence, and the next two another, apparently unrelated one. The two are superficially connected only by a common construction, scheme, pun, assonance, or the like, and, below the surface, by some deeper parable." The paradigm that he provides in the note is entitled "Catamaran":

> Pantuns in the original Malay
>   Are quatrains of two thoughts, but of one mind.
> Athwart these two pontoons I sail away,
>   Yet touching neither; land lies far behind.

In its ingenious and crystalline definition, however, "Catamaran" is in the style of *Rhyme's Reason,* Hollander's self-demonstrating prosodic handbook, rather than that of this penumbral sequence. In its ten sections, each of which consists of four pantuns, the poet mulls over his life, especially his childhood and an absent figure the reader associates sometimes with the wife of "In Time" and sometimes with the Muse, and his language; and he makes a moralized landscape of the Sea of Galilee, or Lake Kinneret, a name that derives from a word that perhaps meant "harp." Throughout the sequence, Hollander switches among levels of discourse as he focuses now on one subject, now on another. At the same time, each more or less self-contained stanza bears on others within its section and reflects facets of stanzas in other sections. Furthermore, Hollander shuffles his pronouns, so that the speaker appears also in the third person while the other figure appears in both the second and the third person, and on occasion he shifts from the somber musing that is his home key into tones ranging from the rancorous to the quietly elated.

The effect is prismatic, somewhat cubist. If I do not understand all the details, that fact does not trouble me. Somewhere behind this meditation set on the shore of "the harp-shaped lake" is Psalm 49: "I will incline mine ear to a parable; I will open my dark saying upon the harp." And who would not agree with Frost (who was chewing on Emerson): "I don't like obscurity and obfuscation, but I do like dark sayings I must leave to the clearing of time." Meanwhile, the last pantun in the eighth section can stand for what I mean by "prismatic":

> A kingfisher flashed by them on their lee
>   To lead their thoughts toward a blue yet once more.
> My tears blur world and water and I see
>   Each seed of flickering lake, each drop of shore.

The current regret cuts across the recollected idyll. But for thousands of years Kinneret, fed and drained by the Jordan but salty because of hot springs, has been a health resort, and as soon as the disjunction appears, the poetry, which constitutes its own kind of restorative, begins to redress it. The sonic pattern of "lee / To lead" leads to that of "see / Each seed," and the *blue* slurs into the *blur*, while the "flickering lake" reflects the flashing kingfisher. The two sentences merge as "world and water" do in the last line, where the subtle chiasmus muddles the two elements as though they were past and present. Here the grief that is the result of separation is also, thanks to the rhetorical formulation, the partial solvent of boundaries.

If one burden of the poem is language's affiliating power, this power is the other side of language's inevitable slippage, its necessitous economies, the gaps and overlaps that make for wordplay. Hollander himself has insisted, in an essay about Daryl Hine, that "if for minor writers word-play is an evasion of depth, a mere rippling of surface, for a true poet" it is a means of contending with matters of fundamental importance. In *Kinneret* what is at issue is the relationship between affinity and difference—the matter of relationship itself. By implication, this poem figures love in terms of the operations of language and vice versa. But this trope is not so much the subject of the poem as it is something more pervasive, latent in the medium, whose potentialities (for adhesion, division, propagation) the rhetoric focuses and frames.

Hollander's terms often relate to one another through what he calls the "Off-color language [that] gives the world its hue." I think he has in mind primarily neither the slipperiness of our names for colors nor the sort of venerable pun that crops up when he foresees that "Some husbandman will plow where now I row" but, rather, the sort of wordplay that happens in his first and third stanzas:

> As the dry, red sun set we sat and watched
>   Them bring the fish in from the harp-shaped lake.
> At night my life, whose every task is botched,
>   Dreams of far-distant places, by mistake.
> . . . .
> We played unknowing for the highest stakes
>   All day, then lost when night was "drawing nigh."
> The dark pale of surrounding hemlocks makes
>   Stabs at transcendence in the evening sky.

It is a "mistake" that the phrase *dark pale* is oxymoronic, since *pale* here first designates a fence that imprisons and derives not from *pallere,* to be wan, but from the completely separate *palus.* Not even in Proto-Indo-European are the terms meaning "fence" and "whitish in color" related. Yet they *are* related— and the pale that is a fence is thus off-color—in that they participate equally in this "mistake" that language makes. Or that Hollander (who tacitly admits his stake in a mistake that can conjoin contraries) gives it the irresistible opportunity to make. Again, the tall hemlocks, pointed like the sticks in a pale, themselves qualify as "the highest stakes," so that one might say that if the stakes have been lost with the lover in the first sentence, they return transformed in the apparently disjunct second, albeit along with the dividing and divided pale. In several different ways, then, even as barriers are acknowledged, separations are challenged, or "hemlocks"—there is another mistake in the second half of that word, as well as in the first—are expertly picked.

The warp and weft of the poem are connection and severance:

> They tunneled through the mountains to connect
> The raging ocean with the inland sea.
> Dreaming of you, I wander through some wrecked
> Historic region of antiquity.

In a rhyme like *connect* and *wrecked* the poem makes its own "Stabs at transcendence" of difference and divorce. But then relationship asserts itself everywhere in *Kinneret*. "The harp-shaped lake" resembles the poet's "dark guitar," and he is said to "harp on" his "flowing" themes. With perfect topographical justification, the lake becomes a "heart," and then in the poem's last line (since "Resemblance turns our language inside-out") the musical instrument always being played upon is "lake-shaped." The *lee* in that eighth section (as we are led to discover by Hollander's earlier analytical pun, "galley on our lee") is a drop in "Galilee." Many other words bear traces of the sea in the form of sounds that consort with the German *Meer* and the French *mer*. The fifth section's *Immermeer*, a kind of eternal sea that the lover or Muse dreams of, combines these terms, which are also echoed throughout in *mirrors* and in versions of *mere*, as in "The sea's a mere mirror wherein you see." The "Tears [that] merely glistened in my childhood's eye" are truly seeds of the sea, which finally seems, like resemblance itself, to be everywhere from first to last.

Or everywhere language is. And as Hollander makes us see, at least for the moment, the world is language. Or rather it is languages, and "languages are imperfect because multiple," in Mallarmé's phrase. If one of the poet's "flowing themes" is "still / Water," still water runs deep, and the other is "jagged disconnectedness." The pale separates, and Hollander's "Stabs at transcendence" must remain just that, though *Kinneret* closes with one of his most telling: "He broke the thrumming surface of his sleep / As if some lake-shaped instrument had sounded." *Sounded* itself is an echo chamber. We have to think of him both as diving in, in response to a summons, and as surfacing, after having touched bottom and struck the chord he wanted to strike. The sentence signifies return and emergence, loss and recovery of self. In doing so, it is true to the experience of ongoing displacement that poetry is. Because *sounded* also echoes a theme in the second section, the reader might look up only to plunge back in for these lines: "Beauty? the dolphins leap. But for the truth / The filtering balein of the great whale." Whether from sentence to sentence or across the whole of *Kinneret,* Hollander's leaps of thoughts are often spectacular. What is wonderful is that they are so many and so nicely judged that they make a fine mesh as well.

Shades of Things

The beguiling jacket of Donald Justice's first volume since his *Selected Poems* eight years ago is a painting—watercolor and sepia, I think—that bears the title *Tea Dance at the Nautilus Hotel* (1925). It pictures little groups of people at and among garden tables set beneath palms and prettily striped umbrellas. The people are in twos and threes or alone, dancing, talking over tea, looking on. What are perhaps the three most important elements of the volume, tantalizingly entitled *The Sunset Maker,* figure here. There is first of all the elegiac quality of this lightly washed late-afternoon scene from another era, which forecasts a tone even more strongly valedictory than that of Hollander's recent work. In addition to a number of poems about Justice's youth and a number of others set in the first half of the century, several are explicitly elegies. The volume's first line ends on *past,* and its last word is *passing.* As for what is "to come," that is not Justice's concern—except to the extent that it too will soon be gone.

Then there is the music in the air. This book is a little anthology of forms and genres—including sonnets, sonnet sequences, a ballad, several poems in forms of Justice's own devising ("Nostalgia of the Lakefronts" reads like a miniature canzone), a dramatic monologue in blank verse, and two stories—but it coheres, in large part because of the influence of its prose memoir, "Piano Lessons: Notes on a Provincial Culture," which reminisces about the importance of music to the young Justice. The material in the memoir reworks or is reworked by six poems and gives rise indirectly to the title poem and to a story. I suppose that one might even say that this whole complex emanates from a six-note musical phrase that a note tells us derives from a composition Justice wrote for Carl Ruggles, his piano teacher when he was seventeen or eighteen.

Finally there is the painting itself. The date is the year of the poet's birth—and the painter's, for as we learn from the credit, they are one and the same. "I always wanted to do everything, everything there was to do," Justice says in an interview reprinted in his *Platonic Scripts,* a bracingly incisive and entertaining collection of his interviews and prose, and while he is talking about poetry, it appears he could be talking about art forms. That we meet Justice first as a painter is as it should be since as a poet he has something of the visual artist about him. In this he is like Elizabeth Bishop, the other poet I can think of whose watercolors have appeared on her dust jackets—and whose poems he has greatly admired. ("Marianne Moore perfected," he calls her in one interview.) By comparing Justice to a painter, I mean no more than the obvious: he sometimes draws upon the vocabulary of painting in the service of description, and he sometimes presents scenes as though they were descriptions of paintings, or as though he were doing a painting in verse. His images are often crisply visual, seemingly static, and accompanied by a minimum of interpretation.

Here is "October: A Song":

> Summer, goodbye.
> The days grow shorter.
> Cranes walk the fairway now
> In careless order.

> They step so gradually
> Toward the distant green
> They might be brushstrokes
> Animating a screen.
>
> Mists canopy
> The water hazard.
> Nearby, a little flag
> Lifts, brave but frazzled.
>
> Under sad clouds
> Two white-capped golfers
> Stand looking off, dreamy and strange,
> Like young girls in Balthus.

As Justice has said about the sequence printed here as "My South," this poem "can only aim to be transparent." As clear as it is, however, any reader will sense its depth, the result of Justice's superb control and judgment. In the end these qualities have little to do with the painterly, since it is not so much that this poem is like a painting as it is that it uses the idea of a painting as the ground for its "mysterious precisions," to borrow a term that Justice has used in connection with Rafael Alberti. I am thinking, for instance, of the delicate relationship between the advance of the year and that of the birds. If the latter change position and diminish almost imperceptibly with distance covered, the days draw in ever so gradually with time's passage. Nor are we uninvolved, since Justice discreetly sets the cranes in motion toward a goal that is first of all the golfers'. We might say that, for all our ambling down the fairway, for all our own unthinking, moment-to-moment presumption of the longevity cranes have always been associated with, in the end no shorter order exists than our own movement toward the "distant green" and the hole. The "little flag" itself, which awaits the pair of golfers, seems already to have been carried—and thus as though by them—through a long campaign and planted at last on its plot of ground.

The poem, that is, envisions life's passage in a scene that does not move. Or that hardly moves. For this is precisely *not* a description of a painting, though at points the scene seems timeless. Isn't that one reason that the golfers are "dreamy and strange"? It is as though they were contemplating, as the poem invites the reader to contemplate, how time passes in such different ways at once—unnoticeably, breathtakingly. They are all the dreamier here because of their characterization in the poem's most relaxed line—the only one with four (or five) stresses, it doubles the opening dimeters—and because of the splendid oddness of that rhyme of *golfers* with *Balthus*.

That rhyme approaches a musical effect, and it might remind us that, its visual distinctness and its oblique verbal exactitudes notwithstanding, this is "A Song" and music is at the heart of this volume. In "Piano Lessons: Notes on a Provincial Culture," Justice tells us something of the matrix of his sensibility. The moods induced by Chopin's nocturnes and ballades, "dreamy and bittersweet," have their natural successors here, and the eerie dissonances that his childhood piano, ever out of tune, produced to his fascination live on in passages such as that which concludes "October: A Song"—and this at the end of a poem in the four-part portrait of Tremayne, a deft caricature of the poet himself:

> Tremayne takes note of one more spring—
>
> Mordancies of the armchair!—
> And finds it hard not to be reconciled
> To a despair that seems so mild.

How disquieting the chord struck, with its overtones of both Stevens's luxurious "Complacencies of the peignoir" and Hugh Selwyn Mauberley's velleities.

It seems Justice got his penchant for "method and exactness" from Mrs. Snow, his first piano teacher and one of the volume's dedicatees, so we owe in part to her a poem like the volume's first, "Lines at the New Year":

> 1
> The old year slips past
>   unseen, the way a snake goes.
> Vanishes,
>   and the grass closes behind it.

2
No clouds—and the grayblues
   subside into saffron.
Delicately they subside,
   into the saffron.

Everything here asks us to hush and pay attention. We are so enjoined, for example, by the first line's expeditious monosyllables and by the coincidence of the snake's movement with the enjambment and the indentation—their insinuation. Meanwhile one senses without noticing that the snake's disappearance comports with the rhyme of *goes* with *closes,* occluded by the extra syllable in the latter and the words that close the stanza behind it. But we hear that rhyme anyway, partly because of the poem's mysterious precisions—for example, the way it insistently pairs up its terms. Even as each of the two parts consists of two sentences, the second part contains the identical rhyme on *saffron,* as well as the doubling of *subside.* The last two sentences play subtly off one another, as the slight variation and the adjustment of the line break conjure the subsiding, the settling of the evening sky's "grayblues" down into the sun's glow. (Justice gets intriguing if quite different effects from relineations in "Nostalgia and Complaint of the Grandparents," where he adapts a phrase from a song by Duke Ellington and Bob Russell and rings the following unsettling changes in his refrain: *"The dead / Don't get around much anymore"; "The dead don't get / Around much anymore"; "The dead don't get around / Much anymore."*) Partly because of the repetition of *subside,* which by means of a characteristic economy of displacement supplies us also with the sinking of the sun, we understand that this *is* a sunset, rather than a dawn. But we know that also because of the title of the volume this poem introduces, the relationship between sun and snake, and the falling meter of the concluding adonic, which has such elegiac overtones in English. ("Tenderly ending" is Hollander's self-exemplifying description in *Rhyme's Reason.*)

Justice's materials are sometimes sternly limited. Anthony Hecht, quoted on the dust jacket, compares him to Wallace Stevens, and the observation makes its point, but it seems to me that Justice is quite unlike Stevens, whose "whirroos / And scintillant sizzlings" pay tribute to the power of enthusiastic invention, in that he tends to rework or to recycle detail rather than to bring it blazingly forth. In fact, like the Canon Aspirin's sister, Justice sometimes paints "The way a painter of pauvred color paints" as he gets down his painstaking, often iterative constructions, including two villanelles. A number of memorable modern villanelles are elegiac, from Dylan Thomas's "Do Not Go Gentle into That Good Night" to Elizabeth Bishop's "One Art," and Justice here contributes to the tradition one good poem, "In Memory of the Unknown Poet, Robert Boardman Vaughn," and one marvelous one, "Villanelle at Sundown." The latter, which admittedly demands of its first refrain only that it end in the word *yellow,* and which takes as its second refrain the line "Why this is, I'll never be able to tell you," seems to echo W. H. Auden's villanelle, "But I Can't" (which turns on the refrains "Time will tell you nothing but I told you so" and "If I could tell you, I would let you know"). Since echo recovers even as it revises, it harmonizes with the formally recursive and the elegiac, and Justice also calls up Verlaine's "Art poétique":

> The smoke, those tiny ears, the whole urban milieu—
> One can like *any*thing diminishment has sharpened.
>   Our painter friend, Lang, might show the whole thing
>   yellow
>
>   And not be much off. It's nuance that counts, not
>   color—
> As in some late James novel, saved up for the long
>   weekend,
>   And vivid with all the Master simply won't tell you.

As Verlaine put it, "Car nous voulons la Nuance encor, / Pas la Couleur, rien que la nuance!" To be "not . . . much off," in Justice's characteristically judicious phrase, is to be right on. The shades of things intrigue him. In this case, the *yellow* is rescued from itself, if I can put it that way, by the off-rhyme, by the shading off in Justice's own "off-color language" of *yellow* into *color.* Nuance counts too, as always in Justice's poems, in the earlier rhyme-word *value,* when he asks, "Or does more distance lend a value / To things?" *Value* here designates "merit" or "worth," but here at sundown it has a touch of another of its meanings: "gradations of tone from light to dark." "Rien que la nuance": the value is in value. Verlaine's desideratum is answered also in the modulation, as smooth as that from French to English in *milieu* or *nuance,* from Verlaine to James, off whose golden bowl the slanting light must also gleam. "Turn your head," this poem begins, and it keeps making us do so. As we hark back for instance from *tell you* and *yellow* to *Villanelle* itself and hear the rhyme toll, the poem, like its river, "seems enriched thereby, not to say deepened."

Where do such echoes and enrichments end? One thing that the Master did tell us is that they don't: "Really, universally, relations stop nowhere," he notes in the preface to *Roderick Hudson,* "and the exquisite problem of the artist is eternally but to draw, by a geometry of his own, the circle within which they shall happily *appear* to do so." Justice completes his circle when his envoi's second line ties into that word *deepened* in his first stanza:

> How frail our generation has got, how sallow
> And pinched with just surviving! We all go off the deep
>   end
> Finally, gold beaten thinly out to yellow.
> And why this is, I'll never be able to tell you.

To convert *deepened* to *deep end* this way is to go to a poetic extreme that makes fun of the final extreme, the distinguished thing. The humor complements perfectly the *frisson* that comes with the disintegration of the sallow, aging skin into the atmosphere's yellow cast as the sun goes off its deep end at sunset. Dust to dust. The end is really just six feet deep, after all, and *shallow* is the ghost rhyme in the last stanza. Here also in the shadows is the master of the shudder, John Donne, whose own indelible circle-drawing poem, with its "gold to airy thinness beat," James also might have had in mind. Justice's final line, even as it admits that he will be beyond telling of the deep end after going off it, blends a gleam of wit with a "mild despair." In that respect, as in its progressive deepening of its subject (the main problem posed by the form is how to avoid mere repetition), this villanelle recalls Bishop's, which so movingly balances dead seriousness with gentle irony, a sense of devastating loss with an acknowledgment that things go on.

Among Justice's own clear-eyed recognitions of death and continuity is "Psalm and Lament." A stringently beautiful elegy for his mother, wrought into a lucid intricacy out of the commonest reiterated materials, it is characteristic of his work also in its handling of emotion. Justice has long feared that contemporary poetry is "awash in a great ruck and welter of sentimentality," and he does his best to keep his work high and dry.

> The clocks are sorry, the clocks are very sad.
> One stops, one goes on striking the wrong hours.
>
> And the grass burns terribly in the sun,
> The grass turns yellow secretly at the roots.
>
> Now suddenly the yard chairs look empty, the sky looks empty,
> The sky looks vast and empty.
>
> Out on Red Road the traffic continues; everything continues.
> Nor does memory sleep; it goes on.

The doubling of *one* seems to encourage a lingering of the effect of the first line, in which the emotion has been displaced in order to protect itself through a certain pseudo-lugubriousness, so that we see how the poet too, has stopped—yet gone on, however disoriented. The phrase *goes on* itself goes on later to reveal its other side. If it means "continues," it also means "vanishes." Everything goes on going on. Memory may go on like a light in the last line quoted here, but "This long desolation of flower-bordered sidewalks / That runs to the corner," as his mother would have run as a child,

>   turns, and goes on,
> that disappears and goes on
>
> Into the black oblivion of a neighborhood and a world
> Without billboards or yesterdays.

(How touching that *yesterdays* is, where the lesser poet might have written something banal and inexact like *tomorrows*.) Because the cemetery has been forming itself between the lines at least since the "flower-bordered sidewalk," we know where to locate the last distich, with its echoes of the opening: "Sometimes a sad moon comes and waters the roof tiles. / But the years are gone. There are no more years." Now it is the moon, "sad" with a savingly blatant conventionality, that replaces the poet—and comes to water the flowers on the grave. (The dark star of a rhyme here, with *years,* is *tears.*) Just as one clock has stopped at the beginning, so there are no more years at the end. She has stopped. Having made a miracle out of nothing, the poem stops.

This book might remind us how varied are the poems we describe as elegiac. The tone of "Psalm and Lament"—a stony, deep grief—is sharply different from the graceful, slightly arch regretfulness of "Villanelle at Sundown," the stormy romanticism of "Nostalgia of the Lakefronts," and the Dantean gallantry and understatement of "Purgatory." Then there is the mellowness of "The Sunset Maker," a poem of about the same scope and openwork texture—and of exactly the same length, if the musical phrase does not count as a line—as "The Idea of Order at Key West." The speaker, the heir of the papers of a fictional composer named Eugene Bestor, sits on his terrace at sunset looking out over the Gulf of Mexico and thinking about his dead friend, forgotten by all but a few people, and his no-longer-played masterpiece, "Little Elegy for Cello and Piano," which the speaker once heard in the Phillips Collection in Washington, in a gallery that also housed Bonnard's painting, *The Terrace.* He recalls how the painting's woman and sea are tied together by color and how the two musical parts are interwoven ("who could call back now the web of sound / The cello and the piano spun together"), and at the same time he entangles the "Elegy" and the painting ("It may be mixed by now /

With Bonnard's colors"), music and thought ("Or feeling, should we say?"), and finally the arts and nature:

> Hear the gulls. That's our local music.
> I like it myself; and, as you can see,
> Our sunset maker studied with Bonnard.

This radiantly wistful poem seems almost to consider the whole of the world "a web" of color and sound, as though the two instruments were imagination and nature. By its light, transience seems a hue in the larger composition. The loss of human-made beauties is sad, the poem admits. It is all the sadder when we realize that these beauties teach us to see the world. But the relationship is reciprocal, and, moreover, the sense of loss itself is a feeling to value. After all, Justice has dreamed up Bestor's masterpiece in order to let it be neglected. But then the poet himself wrote the piece we have only the fragment of—a piece that the fictional version of this poem suggests its composer wrote "in a sense, for himself." "The feeling was one of rich complications and balances," Justice has said of the emotions behind this volume's "On the Farm," but he might as well have been thinking of "The Sunset Maker." It is for this kind of passionate but unblinkered response, scrupulously executed and subtly shaded, that one must come, again and again, to Donald Justice.

Light Light

Reading Alice Fulton's poems I am reminded that *work* and *orgy* come from the same root. Fulton revels in her findings, in the artisan's sense of the term, and the poems in *Palladium* are prepossessing and formidable partly because of the delight and obsessiveness with which she scrabbles around through the language. Especially next to Justice's classical style, her work is remarkable for its flamboyant diction, the wide range and acute particularity and vibrant color of it. "There were / dictionaries," is her way of conjuring one of the wide-eyed discoveries she made when, in one version of this volume's most important experience, she put off "control" and "edged toward expansion." "Mercury vapors," "cyanotic blues," and "arabesques of argon violet," "smudgefires," "twitchy lights," and the "lunchpail's spuds," "a warm glogg" and "a blub-blub of vinegar," "acroliths" and "Carborundum-bladed saws," "denobrium" and "ass / unintentionally flashed," "scumbling" and "clabber," "penetralia" and "billspike" are all unabashedly here. She breezily invents words and forms—"shawleries of morphine," "guilt . . . lickspittled from [babies'] lives"—and relishes the ravishing or jarring phrase: "flirtatious affidavits," "a dead bass / in the Bill Blass Broiler." She cherishes labels and brand names, but she does not invoke them to represent a society of frenetic consumers and tawdry pleasures. When she characterizes a local Michigan wine, made "from grapes grown in the Motor / City, going by its nose of Pennzoil and Prestone," the nasals and the long *o* and the alliterative twinning make their own sourly twanging music. She recalls that in one town where she lived she would often see

> a woman bareback on a springy Arab
> by the Dairy Queen on Shankpainter,
> mane flaggy, sienna
> coat dappled as if containing
> a hardly contained fire.

This constellation of terms makes me think of the passage in his notebooks where Leonardo remarks that any object in a still life should take on tints from colors of contiguous objects. The woman would be altogether different if the Dairy Queen were a Baskin Robbins or a Robin Rose. As for *Shankpainter*, which also rhymes by way of *mane* with *containing* and *contained*, it already has a touch of *sienna*.

Fulton is everywhere alert to the colorations that words have in proximity to one another. Like her scientist in "Peripheral Vision,"

> Her mind works
> toward the marginal,
> what's tentative but ready
> to take on sound and color.

She loves puns and polysemy (her title has an astonishing number of aspects, a few of which she lovingly reveals at the beginning of each of her book's six sections), and I suspect that she also enjoys making up evocative names. "Elijah's / Hellenic Den," whose door opens on a waiter carrying a platter of flames, and "Ursula's Body Shop," which fields a women's lacrosse team, if not the flagrant "Kissamee Springs," a honeymooners' resort, must owe their very existences to Fulton's lexical zest. The same ebullience produces her series and lists, lively as jumping beans. In Hell, it turns out, "Things are permanently crooked, / out of kilter, whack, on the fritz and blink." An experienced stripper's moves include

> the hook and eye
> and switch and mince, the wrench
> kicks, heavy-duty ratchet
> dips, the chops, the hits.

One poem disdains "Twitchers, fainters, cringelings," and another finds the poet in a seaboard town "half-prepared" to discover "hostile mermaids, pilot whales, stranded / miscreants clad in moss and furs" washed up on the beach.

Because of Fulton's energy and passion for specificity, there is hardly a dead line in *Palladium*. Here is the opening of "Days through Starch and Bluing," a description of her grandmother's routine some decades ago:

> Mondays, sweating the flat smell
> of boiled cloth, Octagon soap,
> washday moves in. Stirring work-
> clothes with a stick,
> chafing grime against the washboard's crimp,
> labor-splurging to coddle the particular
> Mrs. Westover's preference for blue and white paper-
> ruled pinafores done just so, she knots
> cubes of Rickett's bluing in small
> knapsacks, swirls them through rinse water
> till the tub mirrors a periwinkle
> sky for her dingy whites.

The fifth line, with its careful choices and its vigorous trochaic pentameter, says it all: here cliché is anathema, every line will be as taut as a good clothesline, and each word on it will be bright with the attention paid it. If I have a reservation, it is that Fulton's language threatens to betray her subject. In this case, what of the sweat, the aching back, and the raw knuckles? True, later in the poem her grandmother's "fingers are stiff as clothespins" on this cold morning, but that simile's exquisite but limited aptness upstages any pain suggested, much as the wittily oxymoronic phrase *labor-splurging* does in the excerpt quoted earlier. But this is perhaps to cavil, to charge perversely a persistence of virtue rather than a defect, especially since one can well imagine that the point here is to have things "done just so," blued and starched to a *T,* in tribute to the grandmother.

While Fulton's details are usually impeccably executed, her wholes are sometimes loosely organized, and a poem like "Men's Studies: *Roman de la Rose*" is a chain of charming observations. A couple of other poems are so capriciously associative that their moments are nearly interchangeable. These whimsies, however, seem part of a strategy to counter the very neatness that poems like "Days through Starch and Bluing" are prone to. In "Palladium Process," Fulton harks back to a period in her life when she was timid and "islanded": "Each day became a vacant lot / I trimmed with safety / scissors, blade by blade," she admits, and

> It took angers, lovers,
> to enfranchise me. There was this difficult rip-
> cord! Then control scattered
> as I edged toward expansion.

What most of these poems testify to so energetically is the power of "expansion"—the movement from some kind of constriction to some kind of freedom, as "News of the Occluded Cyclone" moves from a frightened retreat to "the dead center of the living / room," at the height of a night storm, to dawn, "calm free- / falls of sun," and the day that "lets color be /

color and light light." The line breaks will suggest the agility, virtually balletic, that characterizes *Palladium*. If that lightness sometimes blurs into a "happiness" that she likens to "a terrier's in a blizzard, chasing / every dizzy flake," even the most extravagant of her headlong, "improvident / constructions" is worth it.

"Susceptible / to connections," Fulton coaxes us into being so, too. "Aunt Madelyn at the White Sale," a dramatic monologue from a section of the book that deals with Fulton's family, drifts from the setting indicated, "Here in the kingdom of irregulars, / land of no-two-alike," where in spite of bursting linen closets the speaker hunts furiously for new goods, through thoughts about her own neuroses and difficulties and those of some relatives, to a glimpse through the department store window of snowflakes that "lift, float sideways" and fall "never to rise at all" among "the calm bustle of shoppers." Without insisting, floating sideways itself, the poem lets the unmatched towels and sheets, the singular snowflakes, and the family's affectionately rendered eccentrics form their pattern. Something related but more complex occurs in "Aviation." A brown study induced by the loneliness of people "at work or play," it compasses "bingo-playing ladies," ice fishers, a snowshoe maker, and finally a women's lacrosse match:

> Knowing nothing of the sport,
> I was surprised at how important it seemed,
> a ball going win or lose
> from net to net, flimsy webs
> against the shifty air.

What is such a poem, we have to wonder, if not a comparable sport, whose "flimsy webs" reach from bingo prizes of "macramé plant cradles" through the fishers' lines and some boats' "complicated ice-bound / ropes" to the lacrosse sticks. The snowshoe maker "would have no use for me," the poet tells us, but in fact, just as Fulton shares a good deal with the bingo players who "hover, intent as air controllers, / above their cards in social halls," so she has something essential in common with this "plump woman in brogues." "It takes shoes like blow-ups / of lace, of butterfly veins, / to suspend hunters and lovers" (how *much* of the world her details open up to disclose) "above the delicacies of snow," and that suspension is what this stunning poem achieves, as it focuses our diverse lonelinesses and thereby connects us up.

One of the poems that treat confinement and escape, "Risk Management" is an equally finely adjusted meditation that combines amplitude and exactness. Set at a "convention" of "venture / capitalists," it concerns itself indirectly with "conventions" in the other sense and with the natures they mask. Its opening demonstrates the graceful sureness with which Fulton works between the words and lines:

> Relentless escalators bore us
> to this convention where we wander, homogeneous,
> sinking into easy chairs
> as if our hearts were made of butter. A contained fire
>
> triggered the sprinkler system yesterday.

Because of the latent pun on *bore,* which the line break brings up, and because of the juxtaposition in the fourth line, the *contained fire* (the same phrase that appears in connection with the bareback rider, as Fulton, whose poems often gloss one another, well knows) will also be inside the conventioneers, "Dressed in checks / and balances." The line break matters there too, as it does when we hear that the speaker and her colleagues fold "classic jackets over / our bodice-ripping / novels." The books' "jackets" link up with the "checks" and thus suggest, along with the poem's fourth line and the line break before *novels,* that it is also the conventioneers' *hearts*—in this instance of simultaneous revelation and attack—that are unconventionally "bodice-ripping." By such means the poem prepares for the speaker's dry fantasy of propositioning the man beside her and the laying down "in the great arena opposite the lobby" of "half / an inch of ice for tomorrow's hockey game," an image that restates at once her themes of containment and vicarious fulfillment. (Mindful of minutiae as always, Fulton informs us that the ice recipe calls for two hundred gallons of white paint to seven thousand gallons of water.) The poem concludes, unpredictably and perfectly, with two other scenes, one of a foundry worker, seen by the light from his blast furnace's own contained fire, who moves "with a ballerina's ease / and strain . . . somewhere between risk and safety," and the other of majorettes in a parade, their "suits molten as new pennies," whose soaring batons "catch the light and twirl / before they're caught." Between them the foundry worker and the majorettes act out the poet's means of responding to the lure of risky propositions. If she, like her speaker, wants "to rise above the drudge / work" and "ballet, croquet / [her] days away in light that burns / . . . to the hidden quick," her poetry lets her do it—though the escape entails its own "grunt / work" and can only be momentary, since in the end the twirling baton or ballerina or figure of speech that "catches" the light must in turn be "caught."

Fulton writes several different kinds of poem. In addition to these ostensibly wayward meditations and the dramatic monologues and portraits, there are compressed lyrics, including "Scumbling," "Palladium Process," "Fierce Girl Playing Hopscotch," and "Terrestrial Magnetism," all among the best things in this very impressive volume. In these poems Fulton's intensity is less often mitigated by jauntiness, her meditative leaps and loops give way to an impressionistic introspection, and her poetic logic tightens up. "Fierce Girl Playing Hopscotch," which enables the mature poet in the form of a kind of phantom to observe herself as a child, opens with this combination of nostalgic crooning and intellection: "You sway like a crane to the tunes of tossed stones. / I am what you made to live in / from what you had: hair matted as kelp, bad schools." The same fetching chord is struck at the end:

> Lost girl, playing hopscotch, I will do what you could.
> Name of father, son, ghost. Cross my heart and hope.
> While the sea's jewels build shells and shells
> change to chalk and chalk to loam and gold
> wheat grows where oceans teetered.

Such a passage has negotiated inclusion of whatever it needs: the promise almost drowning out the exact statement of the case in the first line, the sweet chant of the little girl in the second, the soft jingle of the final sentence, and the accuracy with which it traces the metamorphic process that figures the poet's development. And there is the fine moment in the penultimate line where at first the chalk seems to turn into gold— and so it does turn into gold, to the extent that there is an alchemy involved according to which the poet's memories have become her essential substance. At the same time, the sentence must be read as a fragment, a dependent clause, in which *gold* is not a noun that might have been followed by a comma but an adjective for *wheat*. If only because of the two readings it demands, this last clause does its own teetering. That final word, on which the poem refuses to come to rest, is also an admirable choice because of its rhyme with *wheat* and its reference back to the hopping girl, unsteady on one leg, and chiefly because of its jolting conjunction with *oceans,* a word that the poem has worked (ever since the first stanza's *kelp*) to justify in its own right. The options exercised in these last lines are risky in the only sense that poetic decisions really can be risky: Fulton takes the chance here of seeming clumsy in order to make her point as fine as possible. This is the kind of choice that, when made as often as it is in *Palladium,* Fulton's second book, augurs the arrival of an exceptional poet. We can be grateful for what she calls at the end of the last poem in the volume, "Traveling Light," "the nothing / [she] will always have / to fall back on." By such resourceful means she keeps making something memorable of it.

Luminous Bodies

"We're here to learn / the earth by heart and everything is crying / *mind me, mind me!*" That is Fulton's Rilkean credo in "Everyone Knows the World Is Ending." In "Little Things," in *The Gold Cell,* Sharon Olds has her own version:

>
> I am
> paying attention to small beauties,
> whatever I have—as if it were our duty to
> find things to love, to bind ourselves to this world.

How divergent their means of minding and binding are, a couple of poems about early sexual experience will suggest. Fulton's "Scumbling" is a lustrous, dreamy lyric, one of her poems of inwardness, all discretion and reticence. When she writes that "My reserve circled, imperial / as the inside of a pearl," the beautifully turned sentence traces the contours of the poem as well as that of the night with her lover. As she recalls it now, Fulton watched her

> feelings hover
> over like the undersides
> of waterlilies . . .
> topped by nervous almost-
> sunny undulations,

and the repeated sounds ripple like small waves through the passage. The conclusion's tentativeness is the light's and her body's and her language's:

> I had to
> let myself be gone
> through, do it in the arbitrary light
> tipping and flirting
> with seldom-seen surfaces.

In "First Sex"—how different even the titles are!—Olds, too, acknowledges that she "knew little," but she "took it as it / came, his naked body on the sheet." Here the surfaces are well-lit,

> the tiny hairs curling on his legs like
> fine, gold shells, his sex, harder and harder under my
>   palm
> and yet not hard as a rock his face cocked
> back as if in terror.

At the end of her poem,

> he gathered and shook and the actual
> flood like milk came out of his body, I
> saw it glow on his belly, all they had
> said and more, I rubbed it into my
> hands like lotion, I signed on for the duration.

There is nothing "off-color" here. Downright, with a sensibility like a strong appetite, Olds characteristically shoulders nuance aside and goes straight at her subjects. Her work is chockfull of striking metaphors that are rarely delicate, never precious. With the exception of her habitual use of the run-on sentence, a technique that lends a poem a breathlessness more satisfying on some occasions than others, her syntax is purposeful and unmannered. Her verse is free and even resistant to prosodic effects. As she splices sentences, so she enjambs lines; but whereas Fulton will bring semantic pressures to bear by wrapping a phrase over a line ending or poising it there, one foot on either level ("be gone / through"), Olds breaks her lines with studied disregard of the sense—often after an article, a conjunction, or a preposition—so that the endings seem erased rather than judged.

This lack of prosodic integrity is in keeping with the narrative urgency of these poems. While the poems do not always involve much in the way of event, they unfold as though under the pressure of a tight plot. They are usually not divided into stanzas or sections, and they usually describe a single continuous arc. True, a poem might go off like an errant firework at a tangent, but that is a different matter. It is hard to excerpt her poems effectively because she works cumulatively and persists in a line of thought until it has built up such a momentum that it takes on a special luminosity from the friction of passage, at which point she is likely to shunt it off in a new direction. In "Gabriel and the Water Shortage" her nine-year-old son devotes himself to conservation. "He will not / flush the toilet, putting the life of the / water first." "He befriends" the water until he is "glazed with grime, and every / cell of dirt . . . is a / molecule of water saved." Gabriel has "given his heart to water," which at poem's end turns out to be

> so much like a nine-year-old—you can
> cut it, channel it, see through it and
> watch it, then, a fifty-foot
> tidal wave, approaching your house and
> picking up speed as it comes.

And so the poems move.

The starkness of Olds's language agrees with her abiding concern, the ground of her three books to date, the physical body. At the end of *Satan Says*, her first volume, she asked in "A Prayer," since answered, that she continue to "be faithful to the central meanings," presented in terms of sex and birth. She advises us in "This" not to "ask me about my country or who my / father was or even what I do, if you / want to know who I am, I am this, *this*," and what Sharon Olds means is not the word on the page but the "body / white as yellowish dough brushed with dry flour" that put it there. Indeed, her gold cell, whatever else it is, is the corporeal essence.

This gold cell is almost as protean and recurrent as Fulton's palladium. The full term appears just once, in "The Quest," in the phrase "every gold cell of her body," which refers to her daughter, but there are traces of it throughout, sometimes in casual allusions ("small cells of their faces," "pleasurable in every cell"), and sometimes in dramatic passages. (In "What if God," God is imagined as "a squirrel reaching down through the / hole" that her desperately lonely mother broke in her childhood shell, a "squirrel with His / arm in the yolk of my soul up to the elbow, / stirring, stirring the gold.") The gold cell takes the form on the handsome dust jacket of a gold ball encircled by a serpent, an image that assumes special meaning in light of the poet's preoccupations and especially in light of "201 Upper Terrace, San Francisco," which is the address of the house in which Olds was conceived and in which she lived until she was three years old. Driving up to visit it decades later, she looked at it—the phrasing is pointed—"as you'd / gaze on a cell where you had been kept, with / awe and terror" and imagined her mother standing at a window after making love with her father. Then comes this startling passage:

> and I
> whipped my tail and sailed up and
> saw the egg like a trap door in the
> side of the jail and I pushed through it
> head first, my tail fell off I be-
> gan to explode in ecstasy re-
> leased, released, and in nine months they
> lifted me up to the view.

If among other things the gold cell is the gamete, it can also be understood as the very principle of life. In "Greed and Aggression" Olds compares herself during lovemaking to "a tiger lying down in gluttony and pleasure on the / elegant heavy body of the eland it eats." The elaboration of this image seems to me to come very close to defining the center of her fierce creative vision:

> Ecstasy has been given to the tiger,
> forced into its nature the way the
> forcemeat is cranked down the throat of the held goose,
> it cannot help it, hunger and the glory of
> eating packed at the center of each
> tiger cell, for the life of the tiger and the
> making of new tigers, so there will
> always be tigers on the earth, their stripes like
> stripes of night and stripes of fire-light—
> so if they had a God it would be striped,
> burnt-gold and black, the way if
> I had a God it would renew itself the
> way you live and live while I take you as if
> consuming you while you take me as if
> consuming me.

As this passage will suggest, whatever thoughts Olds has of the sacred are bound up with the corporeal. "The Pope's Penis" is surprisingly free of satire and snigger:

> It hangs deep in his robes, a delicate
> clapper at the center of a bell.
> It moves when he moves, a ghostly fish in a
> halo of silver seaweed, the hair
> swaying in the dark and the heat—and at night,
> while his eyes sleep, it stands up
> in praise of God.

And in "Love in Blood Time," as the poet and her husband lay in bed,

> your lower lip
> glazed with light like liquid fire

> I looked at you and I tell you I know you were God
> And I was God.

This intuition is another reason for the jacket illustration. The credit acknowledges Jung's study *The Archetypes and the Collective Unconscious,* where the source turns out to be the section entitled "Concerning Mandala Symbolism," in which the plate is described as "an Indian picture of *Shiva-bindu,* the unextended point," or Shiva in the primordial state, encircled by Shakti, the snake that "signifies extension, the mother of Becoming, the creation of the world of forms." At the moment that Shakti embraces the unextended point, known also as the "golden germ" or "golden egg," creation begins—and as Jung reminds us, Indian thought does not distinguish the divine essence from the human.

Between cosmos and gamete comes another aspect of her gold cell, never explicitly addressed by Olds. "I have been trying to think of the earth as a kind of organism," muses Lewis Thomas in *The Lives of a Cell,* "but it is no go. . . . It is too big, too complex, with too many parts lacking visible connections. . . . If not like an organism, what is it like, what is it *most* like? . . . It is *most* like a single cell." A sense like Thomas's of the kinship and interdependence of things on earth permeates *The Gold Cell.* Olds is an active member of PEN, and a year ago in an essay in *The American Poetry Review* she described her first exchange of letters with a Turkish political prisoner. "The day I received his reply," she tells us, "the world became much smaller. I felt how connected we are." Taking a characteristically surprising direction, the poem succinctly entitled "In the Cell" begins as the poet, "Sitting in the car at the end of summer" with her children, notices that "the hairs are sparser on my legs, / thinning out as I approach middle age," then swerves off, by way of the "vigorous hairs" on his skin, to a young man torturing information from a political prisoner:

>   he is
> taking a man's genitals off as
> slowly as possible, carefully, so as
> not to let him get away.

Rather than overt outrage, the poem's response to this man's "undoing" the means by which "he himself was made" is the assertion of likeness, of "the / innocence of his own body, its / goodness and health," which make for relationship—as among the family in the car, or even between the torturer, "the hairs like sweet / molasses pouring from the follicles of his forearm and / cooling in great looping curls," and his victim. In "On the Subway" the white poet and a young black man face each other across an aisle. They are on "opposite sides," but the other figures tell another story:

> He is wearing
> red, like the inside of the body
> exposed. I am wearing dark fur, the
> whole skin of an animal taken and
> used.

These last two poems are in the first section, which has to do mostly with the world as we know it from the newspapers. The next three sections turn to the poet and her family: her childhood, her adolescence and her marriage, and finally her children. These three sections slide into one another like the sections in a collapsible telescope, and the first fits as well when one considers the poet's representation of her father. Her love for him is never in doubt, but neither is her early terror of him, and she makes his cruelties touchingly clear. In "San Francisco" she recounts her father's wicked glee in driving her ever more slowly up one of the city's steepest streets and scaring her so that finally "I would break, weeping and peeing, the fluids of my / body bursting out like people from the / windows of a burning high-rise." The home situation is powerfully mythologized in "Saturn," where he, as usual passed out and snoring on the couch, is understood to be "eating his children." The family's own lives, Olds puts it in a phrase that combines the unstoppered bottle and the open mouth, "slowly / disappeared down the hole of his life."

> My brother's arm went in up to the shoulder
> and he bit it off, and sucked at the wound

> as one sucks at the sockets of lobster. He took
> my brother's head between his lips
> and snapped it off like a cherry off the stem.

Especially compelling when she evokes appetencies and obsessions, Olds tells us that

> he knew what he was doing and he could not
> stop himself, like orgasm, his
> boy's feet crackling like two raw fish
> between his teeth.

He is no torturer, to be sure, but he is a guarantee that the torturer is not, alas, utterly alien. Her closest connection with evil, he is a key figure in this volume, whose poems keep asking us to think—as though nothing else could save us—in terms of relation. When Olds brings him and Mussolini together in "History: 13," the odd effect is not so much, as it might be in Plath, to revile the former as it is to rehumanize the latter. "The Chute" recalls that her father would hold one of the children upside down in a laundry chute three stories deep and "pretend to let go—he loved to hear / passionate screaming in a narrow space." He was no torturer—but "how could you trust him?" Olds asks.

> And then if you were
> his, half him . . .
>   . . . how could you
> trust yourself?
>   . . . How did the
> good know they were good, could they look at their
> hand and see, under the skin, the
> greenish light?

Her father never would have dropped one of them, and in the end, "although it's a story with some cruelty in it, / finally it's a story of love / and release"—and even of rebirth, "the way the father pulls you out of nothing / and stands there foolishly grinning." Much the same might be said of the volume as a whole. Tough-minded as Olds is, she has an optimistic streak (as her almost dismayingly frequent use of the word *goodness* suggests). After he has been cajoled out of his suicide attempt, the man in "Summer Solstice, New York City" is leaned against a wall and given a cigarette by a tall cop:

> they all lit cigarettes, and the
> red, glowing ends burned like the
> tiny campfires we lit at night
> back at the beginning of the world.

In the essay on Turkish political prisoners she asks—in simple earnestness, I think—"What do you do to a boy that makes him, when he grows up, want to put a man and a woman on hooks on a wall and give them electric shocks in front of their small children?" In "Late Poem to My Father" she moves back beyond what he did to his wife and children and calls up his own difficult molding,

>   that
> child being formed in front of the fire, the
> tiny bones inside his soul
> twisted in greenstick fractures, the small
> tendons that hold the heart in place
> snapped.

Because of this long view, Olds can respond with love and pity: "I like to think I am giving my love / directly to that boy in the fiery room / as if it could reach him in time."

So too with her mother. "What if God" is a severe indictment, and it mounts indignantly to the point that it invokes a just and angry God—but then look what happens:

> she said that all we did was done in His sight so
> what was He doing as He saw her weep in my
> hair and slip my soul from between my
> ribs like a tiny hotel soup, did He
> wash His hands of me as I washed my
> hands of Him? Is there a God in the house?
> Is there a God in the house? Then reach down and
> take that woman off that child's body,
> take that woman by the nape of the neck like a young cat and
> lift her up and deliver her to me.

The way Olds slips from one question to another on the "tiny hotel soap" is inspired. But this passage's real strength is its concluding sentence, where the voice of wrath curves touchingly into pity, and Olds embraces her mother as her mother once embraced her—or as the serpent on the jacket, the mother of Becoming herself, embraces the gold cell. I have said that Olds subordinates nuance, but what a richly shaded term *deliver* is in this context, with its allusion to giving birth and its root in freedom. I think that this is how we bind ourselves to this world.

Versions of Maximalism

I am grateful to Rei Terada, author of *Derek Walcott's Poetry: American Mimicry*, for introducing me to the term *maximalist poetry*. While I suspect that I did not take the term in the way that she offered it, I soon discovered its utility. It would have something to do, one saw immediately, contra much of this century's aesthetics, from T. E. Hulme through Paul de Man to Neoformalism, with the virtues of elaboration as distinct from those of economy, with purpleness as distinct from precision, indulgence as distinct from incisiveness. Not Dryden, not Jonson and Johnson, not Hemingway and Carver, to turn to the collateral prose line, but Lyly, and Browne and Burton, and Barnes and Barth. Not *le mot juste* and a weeded garden of French tropes and other proofs of perfection would be the aim, but periphrasis and an English garden of roundabout phrases and runes rampant and other manifestations of multiplicity. And not monism or atheism but, say, hylozoism or pantheism or omnism would be the implied theological context. The ludic would be valued over the apodeictic, of course, and (if it came to that) catalogues and networks would be preferred to nuggety aphorisms—especially catalogues of the sort that Borges appreciates in a perhaps apocryphal Chinese encyclopedia known as the *Celestial Emporium of Benevolent Knowledge,* where animals are divided into "(a) those that belong to the Emperor, (b) embalmed ones, (c) those that are trained, (d) suckling pigs, (e) mermaids, (f) fabulous ones, (g) stray dogs," and so on. Not the Dickinson of legendary succinctness but the Dickinson of poem

---

Review of *Rapture* by Susan Mitchell, *To Put the Mouth To* by Judith Hall, *Sub Rosa* by Susan Prospere, and *A Gilded Lapse of Time* by Gjertrud Schnackenberg. From *The Yale Review,* Winter, 1993.

1129, where "Success in circuit lies," would be the guiding light, and the Dickinson of poem 1405: "Bees are Black, with Gilt Surcingles— / Buccaneers of Buzz. / Ride abroad on ostentation / And subsist on Fuzz." ("Fuzz" precisely, I hear someone muttering.) Not the Blake of the manner of *Songs of Innocence* but the Blake of the substance of *Proverbs of Hell* would be the standard bearer: "Exuberance is Beauty," and "If the fool would persist in his folly, he would become wise."

It has occurred to me that this tradition is disproportionately represented in the later twentieth century by women writers. Luce Irigaray and those who concur with the views put forward in *This Sex Which Is Not One* (especially in the chapter "The 'Mechanics' of Fluids") would think so. And indeed much of the new poetry that I admire for its ebullience and fervor and abandon, its viscosity and lavishness, is written by women. As soon as I say that, I think of exceptions—Louise Glück in *The Wild Iris* and Linda Gregg in *Sacraments of Desire* continue in the austere, classical vein that we have come to associate with them, while John Ashbery and Galway Kinnell and Ronald Johnson (in his *Ark* series) continue to go off in their different directions like Roman candles. Yet the Neoformalists, for instance, seem to be predominantly male, while the mavericks of extravagance are frequently female—Alice Fulton, Jorie Graham, Mebdh McGuckian, Harryette Mullen. . . .

Among the latter I would have to include Susan Mitchell. Having somehow missed her first volume, *The Water inside the Water,* I was surprised by the luxuriant vigor of her second, *Rapture.* A lover of literal purple—as well as violet, magenta, blue—Mitchell is a maximalist in the sense adumbrated earlier; in her work we find what Cyril Connolly identified as the baroque impulse to exhaust the impulse, as well as the compulsion to include rather than to delimit (the criteria of propriety and correctness would be anathema to her), and the reckless rehabilitation of that rhetorical pariah, the adjective. A naturalized Floridian, Mitchell is unabashedly florid, knowingly excessive, and everywhere heterogeneous. Her mixogamous diction will range within a quatrain from Caedmon's "hwaethwugu" to the teenager's "eensy-weensy" ("Rapture") and within five lines from the academic's "a *summa,* a *speculum naturale*" to the Midwesterner's "*pi'jamma,*" a regional pronunciation of *pajama* ("Night Music").

Mitchell treasures arresting etymologies, both more and less verifiable *and* more and less fanciful, so she will know that her title, *Rapture,* comes from the past tense of the Latin *rapere,* "to seize," and that it is one of those words that Roland Barthes calls an *enantioseme,* a word that harbors contrary meanings, like *ravel* and *livid. To cleave* (*to*)—which even now means both "to cling (to)" and "to divide"—is one of the most common surviving examples. Li Young Lee has written a rich poem that springs from that semantic bifurcation, and Mitchell follows him in her aptly entitled "Self-Portrait with Two Faces." The Proto-Indo-European *rep-* is the root not only of Mitchell's *rapture* but also of *rape* and *rapacity.* And a violent severing from a source is indeed one of her recurrent topics, set forth, for example, in the image of the cut flower (she draws on Goethe's two songs about plucked blossoms, "Das Veilchen" and "Heidenröslein") and in that of the broken branch. In fact, forcible removal—exile, alienation—gives her the subject of perhaps her strongest single poem, "Cities," which conjures Dante as a figure of banishment (from Florence), as a symbol of inconsolable loss (of Beatrice), and as the author of *Inferno,* canto 17, where he learns that suicides, who take the forms of trees, can speak only when their limbs are broken and they bleed. A piercing, complex piece of work, "Cities" is about one's ineluctable loss of home, represented by "the city where I was born," which seems to be New York, and the "distractions" that one responds to homelessness with, represented by "long gloves of champagne suede with pearl / buttons that take forever to fasten / into delicate loops / and cafés with marble tables." As that sumptuous image itself implies, it is therefore about the loss of one's original idioms and the invention of the tropes that are the poet's chief surrogate. The former, in recollection, are "the languages undressed to lamb's wool and perspiration," which is to say, to high school sweaters and the sweat of youthful labors and of loves that end in (for instance) "*I be seeing you some time, adios, ciao*"; and the latter, the tropes, are "the languages" dressed or redressed in such terms as *suint,* which "lamb's wool and perspiration"

121

defines but which Mitchell omits as too arcane, as it were (though she *uses* this term in "From a Book of Prophets"), as well as such elegant locutions as

> columns of
> women in floor-length gowns, their lithe arms irriguous,
> faces shot through with metallic iridescence
> of recently excavated Roman glass.

But it is the Anglo-Saxon *scop* Caedmon whose experience of being inspired (however reluctantly) is at the heart of Mitchell's title poem, and it is Saint Teresa's ecstasy (rather than her terror) that pulses through "Mosaic, Mostly Narcissus." The experience of "rupture" asserts itself, to be sure, but "rapture," with its connotations of union and *jouissance,* prevails. The central figure in the Picasso painting reproduced on the book's cover, a woman, seems almost a variation on Bernini's Saint Teresa or perhaps Danaë. So *Rapture* is a matter primarily of celebration and lyricism. Birds and birdsong recur eerily, doggedly, almost obsessively throughout these poems, from the opening "Havana Birth"—"the song a bird pours itself / into is tough as a branch / growing with the singer and the singer's delight"—to the last lines of the last poem, "Sky of Clouds," where as a bird drinks its "throat muscles are moving," as though to forecast its own singing. While other motifs appear through this unified book, this one predominates, even to the extent that it is the subject of the volume's longest unbroken poem, "Aviary," a tour de force based on the theme of the mockingbird's imitations. Once a student of piano, Mitchell aspires to a kind of music in her poems: "I can't help it, I have to / get in the car and play toccatas and fugues," she confesses, and her own poems are often fugal in the broad sense that they are built of interlacing themes. Her characteristic lyrically meditative mode, if diagrammed, would look something like a map of part of a narrative by Ariosto: she initiates a theme, digresses from it, and follows the new direction (which might become another theme) into a mazy way back to it. The confidence with which she lets her themes evolve and branch and dovetail makes for a loosely if deftly woven verse that can accommodate a wide range of memories and musings.

"Havana Birth" moves with virtuosic ease among reminiscences of a scene in her childhood, memories of a childhood daydream about life in Cuba, and reflections on the nascence of the imagination. Mitchell teaches in Boca Raton, and this poem (like others here) suggests that she has read Elizabeth Bishop, another poet with strong ties to "The state with the prettiest name," with admiration. In "Havana Birth" it's Bishop's peerless story or memoir, "In the Village," that one calls up. Like Mitchell's poem, Bishop's story has a child's point of view, a dressmaker with pins in her mouth at the foot of the child's mother, and a male figure in an apron who represents the hard, physical world (though Nate the blacksmith is a looming figure, while Mitchell's butcher puts in just a brief appearance). If in Bishop's story the grandmother's hair is "full of music," because the child has been playing tunes on combs that are then stuck into it, in Mitchell's lines

> I was about to have
> my hair combed into the new music
> everyone was singing. The dressmaker sang it,
> her mouth
> filled with pins. The butcher sang it and wiped
> blood on his apron.

But the influence, if that's what it is, is wholly absorbed, and in the end it is the difference between the two sensibilities that is most interesting. What Mitchell calls "The song the world sings" appears in Bishop in analyzed form: in the "beautiful pure sound" of Nate's hammer on the anvil, and the minatory, melancholy ringing of a buoy at sea, and "A scream, the echo of a scream, [that] hangs over that Nova Scotian village. . . . Flick the lightning rod on top of the church steeple with your finger and you will hear it." (So much for the *sweetness* of unheard melodies.) In Mitchell, we are more aware of the allure of the world than of its immanent horror. What the allure consists of is not simply that "syrupy music" that the child associates with

Havana, where "the air / is chocolate, the sweet breath of a man / smoking an expensive cigar," because after all one of Mitchell's points is that the child, unlike the mature poet she has become, could not imagine the terror behind the sun-glints on the workers' machetes in the sugarcane fields in Batista's Cuba any more than she could envision the real life of "a prostitute in a little *calle* of Havana" who "dreamed / the world was a peach and flicked / open a knife." But for all its notional assent to evil, the poem has none of the *frisson* that runs through Bishop's story.

In fact, Mitchell often makes one think of Wallace Stevens—yet another poet with a Florida connection—in the hedonistic mood that produced, say, "Sea Surface Full of Clouds." (In her "Sky of Clouds" she invokes "the clouds, / fat ladies on their couches, the green / and gold tassels of a sumptuous life / that keeps changing its liqueurs and girdles, / the slow slide of its trombones. Over the ocean.") When Mitchell refers on occasion to Ezra Pound and his mentors, the troubador poets, she must have in mind the Pound of "Alba from Langue d'Oc," with *its* beautiful imitation of birdsong, not the anguished, pathetic author of the *Pisan Cantos*. In "Women in Profile: Bas-Relief, Left Section Missing," the figures on a piece of broken marble are ingeniously coaxed into fleshly existence and placed in the middle and then on the edge of a festive occasion. The last lines, which Mauberley would applaud, epitomize her jeweler's taste and touch:

> Or perhaps it's they
> who have broken off, suddenly freed
>
> like guests departed, their pockets stuffed
> with cake wrapped carefully in paper
>
> lace, turning one last time to toast
> the musicians who have started up again, the pianist
>
> playing the small bracelet of light someone
> dropped in a corner, its endless variations.

But if her verse is reliably soigné, richly decked out and scented, its speaker seemingly in search of a flute of oenomel in the rooms whose colors are keyed to the shades of their peachblow porcelains, this is nothing that Mitchell herself doesn't know. Her criticism of her own sensibility is a minor compulsion throughout this volume. She reminds herself that "Nietzsche understood, that there are no beautiful surfaces / without dreadful depths," and she frequently sneers at some lovely aquarelle she has just shown us: "If the way I said that made it sound / pretty, I'm sorry." After sketching "a sky / floating its jets and fountains, its flimsy / chiffons of spray," she admits, "I'm a sucker for beauty." And at the end of "Self-Portrait with Two Faces," following a nearly visionary insight into the universe, its "pulsars, crowns, supernovas, / long strings humming . . . hot young stars frothing / into intergalactic space. . . . Starstuff," she tries to sum up her feelings over drinks "at the revolving bar where I met with reps / from the other company":

> But as soon as I said it
> the looks on their faces
> told me this was something kids
> shove into your hands at airports, cheap
> rose smelling of incense.
> I threw it away.

These lines look very much like an attempt to have one's sugary words and to eat them too. In "Mosaic, Probably Narcissus" she prohibits all extravagance—but the prohibition itself smuggles in the contraband:

But now I reject that

the way one changes one's mind about dessert
the can of free-stone peaches left unopened on the kitchen
    counter
the pie of tropical fruits untouched, its finish

without fingerprint, its slices of kiwi untoppled, the
    sugarplum
pediment shellacked, chocolate buttresses unbroken,
    marbled
creams, cinnamon whispers, lusciousness.

Or is she being ironic about that change of mind? In either case, she often wants more than she wishes to repudiate: "I'm in the mood for something fuzzy and pink / I'm goose pimply for a drink / no longer in fashion, a Manhattan, the maraschino cherry." Writing of Isidore of Seville and his tireless pursuit of what he took to be the relations among words, she notes that she hasn't his "patience":

> I skip to the parts I love best, the vowels
> steeped like peaches in brandy, the hard sweet
> suck of the pit, the wasp building up its
> galls, nipple-tipped, velvety,
> in spring a riot of reds and greens.

One imagines her relishing the banquet stanzas in "The Eve of St. Agnes." One imagines her poring over Pater, though burning with a soft, amber-like flame. But it is when this side of her is no stronger than the side that yearns for "my crooked teeth, language / before orthodontia, the sounds unbarred . . . / [the] tongue crushed, slummed in," and when consequently we hear "the buck / and buckle and overlap" of desires, and when "the slow raptures of now" of *back then* are "pressed mouth to mouth" with the longing "thens" of *now,* as in "Cities," that she sounds like no one else.

Other singular poems here include "Night Music," a little invention that weaves together quotations from Coleridge and Chaucer and a paraphrase of a story by Chekhov into a kind of love poem, in which the beloved is the world at large, as understood through birdsong and great literature—and for the purposes of this poem, literature that focuses on nightingales. Mitchell invokes Chaucer's "Prologue" (its "smale foweles" that "maken melodye" and "slepen al the nyght with open ye") and Coleridge's "conversation poem." (Though the minimalist reviewer would note in passing that Mitchell pluralizes Coleridge's *twig* and splices two widely separated phrases into what she calls a "passage"—which would not be remarkable except that she gets considerable mileage from a very close reading of Coleridge's text, including the *y*s in *blossomy* and *giddily*.) The interactions are dense—dense enough that I am reminded of the birdsong in "Aviary," where "it would take a machete / to cut the music"—and the poem concludes—no, *stops* with an implicit comparison of a friend's throat's vibrations, when she speaks certain words in her dialect, to a nighingale's warbling and the poet's own ambitions:

> I could feel what pulsed
> and pushed under the skin of that
> music, and I would love to learn how
> to do that, taking it from a bird's
> mouth directly, the way Middle Eastern men
> will kiss you after they have had a sip
> of an aperitif you've never tried
> so you can lick each sweet drop from their tongues.

"Middle Eastern men"? Iraqi, Iranian, Lebanese, Israeli? No matter; this is *melos* and *meli* at once.

The preceding quotation reminds me that I must not understate the eroticism of *Rapture*. It is here at every juncture, and nowhere more vividly than in "Wave," which recounts a sex act from a woman's point of view—specifically, or so I take it, masturbation of her male partner and then fellatio. The poem's degree of—discretion? insinuation?—is exceptional; the subject manifests itself as gradually as arousal does and grows to a climax at the same time that the speaker maintains a bemused detachment from the scene in which she is involved. The speaker is both the "I" and the "you" of the poem (the man is in effect a third person, though it is fascinating that "he" never appears), and that very division bears witness to the distinctive combination of remoteness and engagement that the poem addresses. The opening lines refer back to the title of "Wave":

> I don't mean this as a command, though
> if you want to wave to someone
> there's no reason why you shouldn't.
> I'll go on looking out this window, pretending
> you're not here, not doing something
> as ridiculous as jerking your hand
> up and down.

This window gives on the Atlantic and a "cat's-paw, a purpurate / empurpling into which I yearn / violently to be dipped, / rubbed against," an image that allows a crucial transitional passage—"I envy birds of prey, how they don't / waver as they come in close"—that culminates in concluding lines that invoke

> that holding back
> to make it linger,
> the pillow play of lip,
> all that plumping before
> it breaks.

The purpleness of these lines, the plosives and the playfulness, make the writing and the reading of them sensual experiences.

In Judith Hall's first book, too, the aesthetic and the erotic lie down together. *To Put the Mouth To:* the title seems weird, or quirky, then careful, yes, and even finicky . . . but probably memorable, and certainly sensual, as the first and last words seem almost to kiss, and maybe above all inviting, in the way that a flute or a clarinet reed is inviting to one who picks up the instrument. In any event, Hall's book—it was Richard Howard's selection for the National Poetry Series for 1992—is at once a debut and no beginner's book at all. The poems are for the most part small, exquisitely detailed, not obviously maximalist, full of surprises, absorbingly cohesive as a volume, and also steeped in psychological wisdom. Much time and much labor, of recollecting and deep analyzing on the one hand and of crafting and revising on the other, have gone into this volume. Hall's lines are made of some substance that we thought was still in the R & D phase: coruscant, capable of extreme attenuation, but with a very high tensile strength. The poems take sleek but intricate yet openwork shapes that elicit a concentration of mental energies commensurate with that which produced them. Each phrase and every line break, every "h, hă, he, hŏo," and each punctuation mark has been laser fused into place and tested. The goal is not so much to contain the poet's experiences or to frame them as to outline them with such tact that the reader has to pick up each weightless, perdurable piece, turn it this way and that in a good light, set it back down into its own constellation of poems, and promise to return to it later.

To Put the Mouth To is organized into five sections, the second and the fourth of which each consist of one longer poem: "A Fluency in Blame" and "Cameos," respectively. The first section, "Fragments of an Eve: Scraps from Her Album," presents itself as a selection from a sequence of sonnets—only ten of at least thirty-six sonnets are included here—interspersed with five other lyrics. Though less unified than the first, the third and fifth sections are also distinct groups of poems, stitched here and there into the others. The fifth section, for instance, is entitled "Momentum: Waving Back, Turning Away," and even as Hall's title adumbrates a theme from the penultimate poem in this section, "Again, I Write to You about Tomorrow," it responds to "Her Epithalamium," in the third section, which ends "as Father waves, / Smiling, waves and turns away." In "Again, I Write to You about Tomorrow," it is the poet's mother who "turned away," while the poet pleads with her unnamed correspondent, who is perhaps also the reader of the book, "Don't turn away, before / You learn more than I did: More than brief / Accompaniments." If we do not turn away, we will recall, among much else, the volume's epigraph, from Blake— "Tell me where dwell the thoughts forgotten till thou call them forth?"—the implication of which is that the poet did turn away for a time from certain of her own thoughts and memories. They would be like her "dawn redwood" (*Metasequoia glyptostroboides*) in the prefatory verse, "Untitled," that was "discovered again / After having long been considered extinct."

Every facet of the sonnet sequence reflects some bit of these thoughts and memories—which are nowhere fully set out. The twenty-six omitted (repressed? unfinished? hypothesized?) sonnets would doubtless make things clearer. "Is more narration needed?" she asks in "Pictures of an Exhibition." The answer has to be yes, but as the book's epigraph might be made to suggest, these poems take place against a background that includes Beulah, "where Contrarieties are equally True"; and it must also be no, precisely because it is of the very essence of these spare, multivalent, neosymbolist poems that they evoke rather than name. Blanks, interstices, teasing glimpses, wincing allusions, "rubbing innuendoes" constitute part 1's narrative, which sketches the poet's life from about her fifth year until she is a teenager. It is a family drama, featuring the father, the brother, and her, the daughter. The mother, however much a part of the *donnée,* is a background figure ("The mother enters, / Balancing plates and forks, the leftover cake, what / The neighbors say"), and her ignorance or blinkered vision provides a lightly ironic counterpoint to a situation in which knowledge itself must have been blinding. The speaker has undergone a trauma:

> At first I could not see past *that*—that
> Shivering green flared around bits too bright
> For color. I had nothing to say—shy,
> Perhaps, or nauseous from the perfumed blasts
> Of simple shapes above.

Or rather a series of traumas. They are sexual, and they involve her brother; though it might not be until part 2 and the following lines (and even they are superficially equivocal) that we acknowledge the circumstance:

> I could tell her how I slept
> With my brother, bathed with him that summer,
> When nights held the long-
> Accumulated heat.

What especially complicates the matter is that the brother is in collusion with the father, though that collusion might be more or less unconscious and might even involve deadly enmity, as in Freud's *Totem and Taboo.* Be that as it may, one of the interludes in the sonnet sequence, "Pictures of an Exhibition," recounts with a startling directness the poet's experience of being photographed, naked, by her father. (I take it that the "I" in these poems is the poet—or "is" the poet—even though, as Hall reminds us in "Dear Reader," the grammatical distinction between the first and the third person can be misleading.) Looking back, the poet calls that photography "pornography." "Only if I were art would I avert my eyes," she says in a touchingly paradoxical flash. Either the poem is somewhat ambiguous or the photography covers a number of years; at one point, the child model seems to have breasts and pubic hair, and at another, "I am five. He loves me with his camera." But the gist is unmistakable:

> And I would faint in such desire.
> Or vomit, tear myself apart the way he looks at me.
> He holds me and I know his silhouette.
> Afraid to press him back.
> I wanted a bed with bars.

At the same time, the child was ambivalent—in Freud's sense of the term—about her father. "If this happened long ago, you would know / I was the one accusing him of loving me / Like a god. I wanted a god," she writes elsewhere. No accident, evidently, that Blake's line quoted as the epigraph is followed in its context (which turns out to be "Visions of the Daughters of Albion") by these lines: "Tell me where dwell the joys of old! & where the ancient loves? / And when will they renew again & the night of oblivion past?" And we note in passing that these pictures are not "in" or "from" but "of" an exhibition; and "The laugh [in a photo] is half a licking of my lips." In sonnet 4,

> he rubs me on his skin, rubs me under—
> "Wake up," he says. Then I—; then he—; but
> Do I know what I want? His hands under
> My arms, lifting me up?

We are not told the identity of this man in sonnet 4, but it must be the father—just as that "dawn redwood" must be both paternal and ithyphallic. Yet isn't it she who is like the tree in needing "to drink" the rain that finally "comes," and isn't it her old self who is "discovered again" in these poems? The implication is that these two are deeply joined—or, as her father claims in another poem, "You are like me." *To drink* is itself "to put the mouth to," and both terms participate in the insistent motif that includes phrases like "the sucking litter" of a group of sounds and "pulses / Sucking" and, in part 3,

> Distant women still hear a sucking
> Sound: Men who touch, who will be touched,
> Or let them suck and cuddle and rock.
> This is not a conversation for the shore.

Something of the fineness of Hall's textures might be indicated if I ravel out a related motif in "Her Plainsong": "We eat all day and by aroma—pears, / Apples, happy when we do not think about it." The *it* is not specified in this villanelle, but we may look back through the preceding speculation that "Ideas parallel and may / Refrain" (one of several verbal kinks in the volume that suggest that Hall has Berryman's "Homage to Mistress Bradstreet" in her blood) with its pun on *Refrain* to "We eat all day and by aroma: pear- / Liquid on chins." The "parallel" ideas must be those of eating and sex, or of a pear devouring and a devouring pair—as the first syllable of *parallel* itself suggests. The "Apples" also give us a foretaste of "In an Empty Garden," a pantoum (Hall's compulsiveness draws her to such iterative forms), where we find the following passage:

> I handed him a place to put his tongue,
> A place where we knew why we kissed.
> Like a snake, turning his skin into a skeleton,
> I turned the air to kisses, golden nipples,
>
> Any place. I knew why we kissed.
> Another apple, another, another tongue.
> The air will turn to kisses, golden nipples.
> He wanted me to say I did it. Touched
>
> Another apple, another, another tongue.
> I will not tell you what we whispered.

The little sonic overlap in *apple* and *nipples* echoes that in *Apples, happy* as well as a passage in sonnet 8:

> Am I happy—*hap*—*chance*—a random
> "Passion," a variant of touching,
> He said. Am I happy if only lucky,
> Only happened to be here, apprehended
> From a bone? He called a rib my ancestor.

132

Both the *hap* motif and the "rib" pun (all but invisible) connect in turn with sonnet 6, from which I quote the opening and closing lines:

> "How did it happen?" he asks; the grass
> Unflattens as he turns.
> . . . .
> At least his hands
> Lead along the lip of *tell me,*
> Along the rib of *hold me,*
> Along the //, the calligraphic weeds, the *we.*

Whatever else the "//" means, it makes the sign for the *parallel* in "Her Plainsong" even as the pair of *l*s appear here in *calligraphic*. (Similarly maximalist wordplay is at the heart of "A Letter," in part 3, where the subject is "W: [double you]," and its ramifications lead us quickly to Middle English, or "ME.") The "//" also sketches the "weeds" within which—within the grasses and within the word itself—we find the wild *we* of this poem ("I am heated / Under words like *animal, sister, his.*") and others. The theme of parallelism recurs in sonnet 28, with its dance of one and two:

> Voluptuous
> Touches—no one body or two—no one way to
> Touch . . .
> . . . .
> . . . A love awake, of words and hands—
> How flesh meets flesh through rinds of I am, I am.

If one *I am* is hers, the other is his, and so, as in some Metaphysical lyric, the two prove and reprove their separateness and their union. And meanwhile this figure of two-in-one acquires connotations of a transcendence achieved.

Hall's third section, "Cameos," is a long poem, 150 lines, that is as seductively diaphanous as "Fragments of an Eve" is sensuously detailed. It is a tone poem that marries two kinds of structure: an alternating of three- and four-line stanzas, unrhymed, and a weaving together of about a dozen themes, each a few words long. It is not much like any other poem I know, though here and there its lush abstractness reminds me of Wallace Stevens, and because of its subtle thematic use of its tenuous materials it suffers in quotation. A thoughtful, mysterious, musical meditation, half-resentful and half-eulogistic, it dwells on women in a world seemingly dominated by men: especially on "painted women" in both senses, made-up and depicted (or made-up by themselves and remade-up by men); on cosmetology and art; on mirrors and artists' models; on beauty as power and as the object of power, as fantasy and as the object of fantasy; on the deep enchantment of surfaces at the museum and at the garden party alike. It restlessly defines and redefines the genre it creates, and one of my favorite definitions is "A song of protest / Improvising the inarticulate / Tangle of loveliness and rage." Finding the *art* in the "inarticulate" is its captivating achievement, or a part of it. "Cameos" and "Fragments of an Eve," when combined with the other lyrics here, make *To Put the Mouth To* one of the most *painstakingly* eloquent first volumes since W. D. Snodgrass's *Heart's Needle* (1959).

If Judith Hall's first book throws light into some psychic crevasses, Susan Prospere's wafts us into exotic reaches of the imagination. Much of Freud's *Totem and Taboo* (where we read that the "interest of creative writers centers on the theme of incest") and some of Otto Rank's work can be read alongside Hall's undertaking; and Hans Christian Andersen's tales and Lewis Carroll's stories are almost prerequisites for Prospere's *Sub Rosa*. The lights that Prospere sees by are characteristically crepuscular or paludal, will-o'-the-wispish. A piece of rotting wood's phosphor provides a lantern for the mole and his beloved Little Thumb in one of her adaptations of fairy tales. In another poem some pears by night are phosphorescent, and in another at night in Mississippi "you could see the green hay / begin to smolder in the barn," and in a third the landscape is lit by lightning bugs hardly distinguishable from stars. Angels and ghosts, mermaids and other chimerical or rarefied presences, float through these poems—these Prosperean or even Arielian poems—which have something of the ambiance of a romantic production of *The Tempest* or of *Les Sylphides*. Prospere prefaces one poem with Lewis Carroll's rhetorical question, "Life, what is it but a dream?" And when *she* chooses an epigraph from Blake to show the linkage of her youth with her career, she takes it from *Europe a Prophecy*, where Blake addresses the limitations of what he knew as "the female will," the impulse toward the corporeal, the reproductive, the natural world that is both nourishing and narrowly moral, as distinct from the joy of apotheosis and recognition of unicity: "Forbid all Joy, & from her childhood shall the little female / Spread nets in every secret path." Prospere implicitly appropriates Blake's irony and wryly acknowledges her surreptitious involvement—as an artist—in the external and therefore illusory world.

At the same time, its epigraph notwithstanding, there is nothing secretive about the language of *Sub Rosa*. The diction, syntax, and plots are nearly as straightforward as Andersen's. True, the volume's title implies a clandestine communication, and so does the title of its third section, "In Petto," in which we in turn find a poem called "Heart of the Matter," at the center of which there is yet one more locked cabinet:

> It was a woman's hand, I think,
>   that turned the key
>   to lock away some token, hidden perhaps
>   in her underclothes, lying under
>   her corset, its hooks
>   and eyes open.

But for all the evident attraction to Prospere of the concealed and the whispered, there is remarkably little that is cryptic or esoteric about her medium. Its powers, especially when it comes to transitions, are those of metamorphosis—and in this respect Prospere recalls Mitchell and resembles Gjertrud Schnackenberg. Here is the end of "Party per Pale," which can represent Prospere's frequent preference for an open-field prosody and for pastoral topoi too. The title, the heraldic term for a shield divided in the middle by a vertical band, reframes Prospere's immediate subject, a freemartin—a beautiful but sterile female calf born the twin of a male—that must be sold for slaughter:

>   Of milk, curd, butter,
>   dung, and urine, she gave us only waste
>   and beauty. My father shipped her
>   somewhere he wouldn't tell us
> though my brothers played out the scene
>   over and over,
>   linking their cars together
>   on their 00 gauge railroad—
> the locomotive, the coal tender, the stock car—
>   the plastic cattle huddled
>   behind the lattice, unloaded
>   at way stations, whistle-stops, crossings,
>   until they were lost
>   in a romeo slipper or cardboard boxes
>   in the back of a closet. Years later,
>   rummaging through the attic,
>   my mother found one,
>   holding it in her palm, hardly remembering
>   how happiness was composed. *I swan,*
> she said, looking across the rafters—
>   as if astonishment were a bird
>   heading out over open water,
>   its wings spread wide, uplifted.

This passage, delightfully mercurial, is quite moving in its own right—and all the more so in view of other poems that testify to the speaker's childlessness on the one hand and to her lack of "Joy"—to call back Blake's term—on the other. And yet the callous reader might feel that it is somewhat colored by sentiment. ("Sentimentality," Stevens warns in a wise paradox, which the minimalist has thumbtacked above the desk, "is the failure of feeling.") This reader might think that the opening of "Heart of the Matter" is similarly tinted: "How forlorn and lost / they must have looked, the mahogany deer / carved on the cabinet, / peering forth from the trailing vines and foliage." Again, "Farm Life" incorporates these interpretations of a dogwood about to flower:

> It is afraid of our disapproval,
> or that we will be merely obtuse
> in not seeing its analogies,

> the petals rusted as if nailed shut all winter.
> They are wallflowers,
> so I assure them again that they are invited.

It is almost no surprise that this poem ends with an image of the mimosa, the famous sensitive plant.

There are other indications that Prospere is no dry precisian. In "On Thin Ice," a poem exemplary in its deft borrowing of fairy tale, she conjures Andersen's Snow Queen with her frozen lake, fractured into pieces so uncannily like one another that their assemblage is a superhuman accomplishment, in order finally to praise the "formal variance" of "each particulate grief" in life, each snowflake-like pain, and to redeem the apparently nearly tragic circumstances of a brother who once

> put down the ragged pieces
> of a life he couldn't fit
> together. It's by sheer will
> he's come back.

Perhaps because she distrusts the cold, perfectionist impulse, Prospere tolerates some loose writing here and there—as when she commits the following rhetorical snarl:

> At night we listen from the screened porch
> as the trees ice over and break,
> their branches cannonading as the angels load them
> with their terrible artillery.

And when she permits this ramshackle syntax: "Crossing our paths, here's to the deer / captivated by our flashlights." The phrase *an ombres chinioses* will be an awkwardness combined with a misprint, but the facile irony and slack phrasing of the following lines are a matter of choice:

> though for the lightning bug,
> even death is glorious and predetermined,
> whether collected in jars,
> or smeared on sidewalks.

137

And what is one to do with the fancy image in "Sophronia and the Wild Turkey" of two women "sitting under the morning glories, open like a showroom of Victrolas"?

I can imagine a rejoinder that would be based on "Peonies," where the address is to a masculine figure who views the poet as "brutally feminine,'" even as she envisions "the Sirens / bending over—their tendrilous locks flowing / over the ovolo moulding, their rosebud / mouths open, open, singing." Certainly we do not have to believe that the feminine entails the soft and the floral to recognize that the musicality of these open vowels reproves the addressee and the philistine reader alike. One has to admire passages like that and also to admire this quite different passage, concerning a tourist outing by the poet and her lover in Oxford—a passage that, by the way, has a direct relationship to the volume's title:

> "In this tomb lies Rosamond, the Rose of the World, the fair
> but not the pure": Rosamond, the mistress of Henry II,
> lies in Godstow Nunnery, and she seems
> to have been given into our company, the frill
> of her clothing brushing past as she follows us
> along the path by the tea-colored water of the Isis.
> By the end of summer you will discover
> that you love your wife.

The rustling rhyme of *follows us* with *Isis,* the barest ruffle of *thrill* in *frill,* the almost inaudible clink of *ice* in *Isis,* the irony of the weak overtones of *tea-colored* in this context of the name of the Egyptian fertility goddess who was wife to Osiris: these all make for an elusive rightness, also characteristic of this book, that overshadows its occasional gaffes and mawkishness.

Any younger poet who wants to study endings should look up Prospere's work. Her conclusions are neither predictable nor tacked on. They swirl up like meteorological phenomena. I have in mind, for instance, the end of the first poem, "Passion," and the end of the penultimate poem, "Moving Pictures," and the end of "The Company We Keep," about the memory of a love affair:

> Let's meet once at the equinox in this kitchen
> to take the brown-shelled eggs from a carton
> and balance them on end for thirty minutes.
> You will explain that the greatest show of physics
> is what we know: the way we travel in life
> through multiple dimensions, or stand, as I stood once
> in Houston, haunted by a small tornado
> that crossed the house, flattened down the banana trees,
> and opened the kitchen door and all the kitchen cabinets
> to release forever a world of household spirits.

That last line's sad equivocation on *release* also contains in little much of the poignancy of *Sub Rosa*.

Rosa gallica, the old French rose, a deciduous shrub known for its redolence and its often vivid colors, is the first specific rose to appear in Prospere's book, in the well-made opening poem, where it grows in the lot of a burned-down house where her father as a child in the 1930s shot marbles. At the end of the poem, when one of the poet's brothers gets an electrical shock from a lamp the shade of which has roses printed on it, we understand that a certain current of "Passion" (that is the poem's title), as dangerous as it is illuminating, flows from one generation directly to the next. The same variety of rose turns up in another poem rooted in the 1930s, and again in the context of the passage of generations, at the end of Gjertrud Schnackenberg's third book, *A Gilded Lapse of Time.* That similarity is odd but trivial, and the difference in compass is fairly breathtaking. Prospere's poem is a family poem in the "confessional" tradition; Schnackenberg's poem, a profound, sweeping, emotional tribute to Osip Mandelstam, the Russian Jewish poet who died in the gulag probably in 1938, though springing from the end of the poet's life, characteristically views things as though sub specie aeternitatis. I quote from section 7, where Schnackenberg seems at first almost to speak for God:

> If I could begin again,
> I would measure time in the generations of
> Roses, and not the succession
> Of rulers of men,

> In that fragrant clambering
> Across the cliffs between millennia,
> In the world without us,
> Roses linking their chains among outcroppings
> Of stone and shale
> . . . .
> One of the varieties of damask rose
> Killed off, they say,
> By the eruption at Pompeii,
> Depicted on the walls of plastered bricks,
> Unscented as music, and
> The gallica roses, established
> After the fall of Rome wherever
> They had fallen.

Like Lévi-Strauss in the paragraph in *Triste Tropiques* that records the "miracle" that is the "master meaning" of his book—the coexistence within inches on either side of a fault line of plants that originated in widely separated geological eras—Schnackenberg sees how "the living diversity of the moment juxtaposes and perpetuates the ages." Partly because *A Gilded Lapse of Time* is so committed to "the living diversity of the moment," it is not for the faint of scholarly heart or the wan in intellectual spirit. It is thorny with classical history (Tacitus and Suetonius, Livy and Dio Cassius and Gibbon), Jewish tradition and literature (from the Talmud and the Bible through Rabbi Johanan to the Mandelstams), and medieval Christian documents (notably Dante's *Comedy* and Augustine's *Confessions*). At the end of the book there is a long set of "References" (keyed to the lines in the poems) like these: "This is an ironic paraphrase from Michael Psellus's encomiastic description of the dying days of Emperor Michael IV (1031–41), in book 4 of the *Chronographia,* translated by E. R. A. Sewter"; and "According to the fifth-century Greek historian Socrates Scholasticus in *The Ecclesiastical History,* translated and with notes from Valesius."

There are three parts to the ambitious, spacious architecture of this volume. "Part One / A Gilded Lapse of Time," which totals approximately nine hundred lines, is itself in three sections, each set at a medieval site in Ravenna (the mausoleum of Galla Placidia, the church of San Vitale, and Dante's tomb) and each comprising several subsections. "Part Two / The Crux of Radiance," a touch longer than the first part, consists of seven poems, three of them based on Piero della Francesca's frescoes in Arezzo's church of San Francesco, one on a canvas by Andrea Mantegna found in his rooms in Mantua after his death, one on an epitaphios recovered in Thessaloniki, and one on a story in Eusebius' *Ecclesiastical History*, while the remaining one draws on diverse sources ranging from the Greek historian Thucydides to the pro-Roman Jewish priest Josephus. These seven poems are arranged in the chronological order of the events they describe, beginning with "Annunciation" (which culminates in Gabriel's appearance to Mary) and extending through the death of Jesus to Constantine's prophetic dream of the existence of the True Cross in Jerusalem—a dream that legend tells us took place before his defeat of Maxentius near the Miluvian Bridge in Rome in 312 and that in Schnackenberg's rendition of it (or in my reading of that rendition) adumbrates the founding of Constantinople (324), the building of the Church of the Holy Sepulchre (326), and the end of the Roman Empire. Finally, "Part Three / A Monument in Utopia" is the nine hundred–line tribute to Mandelstam.

Such a précis might suggest the vast scope of this volume and its structural scrupulousness. And it might at least intimate that Schnackenberg's movement from Dante back to Jesus and forward to Mandelstam in our own day reveals how passionate she is about exile and alientation, pistological dilemmas, the transience of the world, and the comparative permanence of art. But it cannot begin to reveal the labyrinthine meanderings of the poems, especially in those first two parts, where personal reflections, visions and dreams from various sources, ecphrastic descriptions, and allusions to far-flung historical events all commingle in the course of long, looping, hypotactic sentences. (One sentence in "A Monument in Utopia" is 146 lines long—and I am not at all sure that it's the longest in the volume.) Though veneration of Dante is evident throughout, we are not directly involved with that kind of Dantean imagination that produces—however daedalian the

141

cosmology and however intricate the prosody—what the Italian poet called "transparent speech, precise and plain" and what T. S. Eliot referred to as a gift for "*clear visual images.*" Regardless of *The Divine Comedy*'s spectacular effects, we always know which circle we are in, but in a poem like "The Dream of Constantine" we might well feel a vertiginous disorientation, as scenes and speculations swirl together in sentences that delay their verbs and wind through parallel and dependent clauses and prepositional phrases. Here one is always something of an explorer, working under a hot, bright sun (or lamp), trying to follow this path and that. Nor are there many lyrical clearings: there are no berceuses, no albas, no lighthearted roundelays here among the intense and erudite periods.

Stevens's dictum that "Poetry is the scholar's art" has rarely seemed so pertinent. The "References" not only help, they are often indispensable—so much so that one sometimes wonders why more of the necessary information was not worked into the verse—and yet they seem occasionally insufficient and occasionally whimsical. In "Tiberius Learns of the Resurrection," why is Capri so long identified only as "the island"? Why does a note to "Christ Dead," which is based on the painting by Mantegna (last half of the fifteenth century) and which uses the phrase *uncarved block,* direct us so laconically to Lao Tzu's *Tao Te Ching* (fourth century B.C.)—where that term is not only important and recurrent but also ambiguous? Another note to this poem, glossing *bitter bread,* refers us to Shakespeare's *Richard II* and its "bitter bread of banishment"—a reference all the more puzzling for its aura of anachronism and incongruity, since the same term occurs, also in the context of the experience of exile, in a well-known passage in *Paradiso,* canto 17.

But enough grousing about the edges. This is an extraordinarily energetic, impassioned, zealously worked-over volume. Because it makes such a long music, so to speak, it is hard to excerpt, but some of its more or less local effects have qualities that (if it weren't for Dante) one might imagine had to derive from contemporary camera technology. Here is a passage following a description of Mandelstam's arrest in 1936 and the police search of his apartment, which was full of rare, suppressed, old editions whose pages were interleaved with obsolete money and papers:

> These books, dumped out,
> Are still drifting down somewhere between
> The autumn of 1900
> And the later fortunes of a region
> That hurled itself into a terrifying dream;
> They still are falling through the air,
> Still fluttering out across the century
> And have not hit bottom.

Although this image is much richer in context, where it calls into play other paradoxical images of mortality and continuity—which include falling snow and flaking gold leaf and falling rose petals—it stands or rather floats on its own. There is something holographic about it; it reminds me of the "depth" that Schnackenberg sees in Dante, although when she runs her "palm over the page / Those hovering magnitudes evaporate, / leaving flat paper." Then there is the zooming in and out of the poet's lens in the title poem, where she climbs a ladder up to the scaffolding in a dome to join a restoration team at work on a mosaic. At first she seems to have been lifted into Paradise itself—

> I hear a rope wobble, lashing
> The globe back and forth in a scourge of gold snow
> That parts on the sight of other ceilings,
> Other chains, other heights from which
> Other worlds hang

—and into "that ancient time when God" controlled the cosmos. Then suddenly, even as she describes the hand of an ineffable God reaching down "to interrupt the sacrifice" of Isaac, she realizes that back then

> We'd not yet driven Him into the high gilt corner
> Of a tesserae-shattered wall where a workman
> Touches a flake of gold leaf in the hem
> Of His threadbare gown with a tweezers woefully small.

God's hand reappears in the "San Vitale" section in lines that delicately anticipate the passage about Mandelstam's arrest quoted earlier and that gather up numerous preceding phrases, ranging from the opening of "The Mausoleum of Galla Placidia" ("When love was driven back upon itself, / When a lapse, where my life should have been, / Opened") to scattered images here in "San Vitale" ("the celestial globe" in the "gilded apse," "the guilt of poetry," and a "flooded, inaccessible crypt, / A radiant blur" that inspires the declaration that "We are water that is spilled on the ground"):

> God's hand hangs empty above
> The depiction of frightful laws
> As if He tried to plunge
> His hand into a bank of gold snow
> Covered with grime,
> To grasp at least a handful
> Of Creation, to remember it by,
> But what He touches thaws,
> And starts to trickle through itself,
> Then streams off through His hand,
> Downward, through the gilded lapse of time.

One thinks of Blake's insight, "Eternity is in love with the productions of Time." The interlaced, unobtrusive, but meaningful rhymes of *laws* with *thaws* and of *Grime* with *time* are characteristic of Schnackenberg's verse—as is the accumulated richness of that last line. The heart of the poem might even be located in the single word *lapse,* evocative at once of the Fall that introduced time into the world, the decline of the religious spirit since "that ancient time," apostasy, and—with a gleaming irony—the seeming disappearance of time between past and present (and the consequent linking of both eras) in the mosaic. As Schnackenberg herself puts it, allowing for both change and continuity, "the *verbum visibilum* really does / Flicker in the gilt fog of the apse / Where once it burned." And it does so thanks to her power, which is partly that of an ardent nullifidian visionary. Hers is a maximalist poetry with a mission.

Wild Plots

Harryette Mullen's *Trimmings,* her second volume of poems, so far nearly invisible on the literary horizon, is an ebulliently feminist, black and bluesy, bebop, wicked, scatty, addictive sequence of mazy prose poems, ostensibly about wardrobe accessories and the ramifications thereof, and in fact about language and semiotics in general. The poems rely heavily on wordplay and paradox and make us think harder about gender and racial issues. Compact, sometimes no more than eight or ten words, they are as loaded as chocolate truffles and the finest Vegas dice. Several of them allude to Gertrude Stein's *Tender Buttons,* without which *Trimmings* would not have been possible. Mullen's title acknowledges the debt, since it means both "sartorial decorations" (to comport with Stein's *Buttons*) and "garnishings" (to supplement Stein's "Food" in the third part of that work). Not that Mullen sounds very Steinian, even when she is paying homage:

> Girt, a good old girl got hipped. They thrive with wives, broad beams. Most worthy girth, providing firm. Foundations in midriff. Across (between) girdled loins, tender girders. Gartered, perhaps, struts. Stretching, a snap crotch.

A tribute to Gert, a "most worthy," hip, and hippy writer, who "got hipped" instead of hitched, who underwrites Mullen's enterprise and with whom Mullen hereby joins in partnership

---

Review of *Trimmings* by Harryette Mullen, *Clamor* by Ann Lauterbach, and *The Wild Iris* by Louise Glück (from *Partisan Review,* April 1, 1994); and *Sun* by Michael Palmer (from *Poetry,* August, 1989).

145

to make a "firm," this poem goes off forthwith in its own directions—under the influence or the gaze, as it were, of certain other construction workers, who build their architectural structures of "broad beams," "girders" and "struts," and meanwhile hope for smiles from a passing broad, whose loins however are girt or girded, and who has built her own redoubt of garters, girdles, and other foundations, a body suit, and a saucy walk that is at once seductive, defensive, and jazzy (her own structures "firm. Foundations" being established and shaken at once as they are mid-riff). As one of the earlier poem puts it, "Dress shields, armed guard at breastwork, a hard mail covering. . . . Whose armor is brassier." One probably doesn't need to recall that the euphemistic origin of *brassiere* is *arm guard* or need to have seen the bustier that Jean-Paul Gaultier designed for Madonna to recognize the brassiness—the boldness *and* the armorlike quality—of the brassiere sported by this poem. If soldiers can "Dress arms," women can "Dress shields," even as their dress protects but arms them.

One of Mullen's points is that in our culture feminine dress is often a version of nakedness—a means not only of covering but also of revealing. One could design a seminar around this volume, *Tender Buttons,* Ann Hollander's scintillating *Seeing through Clothes,* which argues in part that in any given era the haute couture informs our idea of the ideal female body as much as our sense of that body dictates the lines of fashionable clothing, and Vera Lehndorff's "*Veruschka*": *Trans-Figurations* (done in collaboration with painter and photographer Holger Trülsch) in which the eponymous figure, famous as a model in the 1960s, appears in body paint only. The recent cover of *Vanity Fair* that showed Demi Moore in a body-painted man's suit is precisely a superficial rip-off of Lehndorff's profound work. It is exactly the sort of rip-off that Mullen's book is *not* (of Stein) and that Mullen might very well scorn. As coy as Mullen's book is, it is also a scathing attack on the sexist culture, epitomized by *Vanity Fair,* that is its matrix. Here is a poem, the likes of which we are not likely to find next week in the *New Yorker,* in which the wealthy capitalist woman's clothing is equated with the power of her nakedness, which is to say exposed as a species of merkin:

Animal pelts, little minks, skins, tail. Fur flies. Pet smitten, smooth beaver strokes. Muff, soft, "like rabbits." Fine fox stole, furtive hiding. Down the road a pretty fur piece.

At bottom—though after pondering this book, one cannot take any such phrase for granted—Mullen is fascinated by what she calls in her postscript (entitled "Off the Top") "language as clothing and clothing as language." Its many other coups—its invocations of Josephine Baker and Manet's "Olympia," its Joycean *trouvailles* and *jouissances*—I have to leave to the reader.

Mullen's use of clothing allows me to note the beautiful jacket on Ann Lauterbach's third volume, *Clamor*. It represents a fragment of a fresco by Giotto, the whole of which—or so the credit informs us—is known as *Vision of the Ascension of St. Francis*. Not one to wrangle over such matters with a poet who has been a painter and a director of art galleries here and abroad, I must still record that a friend has shown me that in fact the jacket reproduces a painting in Florence's Santa Croce, usually called *St. Francis Appeals to Bishop Guido and Vision of a Dying Friar*. Is this difference inadvertent? (The fresco of St. Francis's ascension, in San Francesco at Assisi, has a similar structure.) Or meaningful? Because much of the cover's allure is the absence at its center, where the figure that would be St. Francis has itself been lost, it is possible that the mistitling is meant to identify that loss with the ascension of the saint, or vision with vanishment. In any case, the image is an appropriate emblem for *Clamor* because these poems are riddled and raddled (doubly riddled, doubly raddled) with "elaborate absences." They are shot through as samite with threads of the proverbial golden silence. They are thunderous with sunderings, with omissions, distortions, vacancies. "There are holes in the fabric," as one poem puts it. And there are unobstrusive wholes too.

One corollary to the elisions and lacunae in *Clamor* is continual surprise. "In [this] parade's deft narration," to borrow again, "Anyone could join the party"—and "What comes up comes up." At any moment in this postmodern surround "Someone moans through thin walls / Between the sonata and the football game." The idiom is dependably strange, or vivid, or rebarbative; and one poem could be describing itself when it notes that

> The wild words obey their primary intelligence,
> Forget their settings, forget their images,
> Come riding across the road like hard things
> Without hindrance, making a subtle new noise,
> Making an angle.

Lauterbach has read John Ashbery closely, and Ashbery's and Mullen's great example, Stein. Like Michael Palmer, or rather unlike him because utterly in her own way, she has studied the Language poets yet never sounds imitative. Relentlessly errant, intensely thought, uncannily reflexive, coruscant with wordplay (as she overlaps terms like *partition* and *parturition, rupture* and *rapture*), and compositionally innovative, her maximalist poems are "Lavish, syntactic, new in the natural key / But frugal and obscure in translation." They are "unstuck, estranged and original." One section of one poem ends each strophe on the words "shed, and." "Prom in Toledo Night" creates an esoteric, intricately recursive form, which invites the reader either continually to hold one sentence in suspension while working through another or to photocopy the poem, cut it up into lines, and reorder it into its "original" narratives—only to return reeling to the poem as it is on the page, with its intercalated segments of thought. These poems are rich and eldritch at once.

Throughout *Clamor* there is a "girl," who, like Stevens's "hermit in a poet's metaphors" in *Notes toward a Supreme Fiction,* "comes and goes and comes and goes all day," a "girl materializing like a path along the ridge," then vanishing, like St. Francis ascending, then reappearing at the next turn. She is bewitching; she is the poet and is not—or the muse, the poet who knows that the "similar" always "Harbors difference in its midst," and whose poems blaze a trail into a whole new climate, wherein we come to expect, amid tinted fogs and shafts of light, emulsions and apparitions, shards of references in rainy abstractions, "a naturalism of the obscure."

Louise Glück's *The Wild Iris* characteristically contains no poem longer than thirty lines, and many of the poems gleam with the knifing ironies and the burnished paradoxes that have always marked her work, while some show a new visionary fire; but there is a strong sense in which this, her sixth volume, is really a single, rhizomic sequence, a complex structure that we can now see has been evolving at least since her third volume, *Descending Figure,* and which is embodied, in a less integrated form, in her fifth, *Ararat.* Glück wrote these fifty-four poems in ten weeks, a period that lends the book an organizational element: the poems in its first half are set mostly in the spring, while those in its second half occur in deepening summer. At the same time, Glück moves from morning to evening, since the lyrics in the poet's voice in the first half are mostly called "Matins," while the corresponding poems in the last half are "Vespers." Taken together, these poems from the poet's point of view constitute one of three kinds of poem in *Wild Iris.* Poems of a second kind see things from the vantage of nature—or, to be more specific, flowers and other vegetation in the family garden. The remaining poems, whose titles usually designate a time of day, a season, or a weather condition, are in the voice of God—here a "father," a "master," a figure of "authority," and primarily Judaic, regardless of the crepuscular Catholic coloring of "Matins" and "Vespers." The presence of this third point of view puts Glück's compelling sequence in a venerable and recently quite vigorous but ever startling genre that reaches in English from George Herbert through Blake and Yeats to John Berryman and Ted Hughes and James Merrill.

The jacket copy's exigent prose tells us that the volume creates

> an impassioned polyphonic exchange among the god "who disclose[s] / virtually nothing," human beings who "leave / signs of feeling / everywhere," and a garden where "whatever / returns from oblivion returns / to find a voice."

In fact, things are both more and less complicated than that. For instance, it is precisely "polyphonic exchange" that never occurs. The different speakers usually don't hear and never truly understand or respond directly to one another, and they rarely (if significantly) speak in unison—and their different isolations give the sequence much of its reverberating pathos. As God puts it in "Sunset," when addressing the poet:

> My great happiness
> is the sound your voice makes
> calling to me even in despair; my sorrow
> that I cannot answer you
> in speech you accept as mine.

As that passage will suggest, Glück's strategy entails certain nagging epistemological difficulties. For one, God speaks to the poet in words that she cannot understand but can somehow transcribe in the language that she writes and that we read. Or can we elude that paradox by drawing a hard distinction between the "poet" and the human "speaker" of the "Matins" and "Vespers"—in which case, the invisible "poet" knows the language of God but her "speaker" does not? If so, as the dust jacket puts it mighty casually, we have here a "ventriloquism," whereby the poet throws her voice into God and garden as well as into her own stand-in. Or perhaps we are to infer God as the source of all voices and the rest of the speakers as dummies. But the speaker in one of the "Matins," for *her* part, finds the proposition that God "must be all things" entirely "useless." Maybe we should not posit a source at all; maybe we can know only that we are enmeshed in a network of desiring voices deaf to one another. The possibilities are intriguing—the more so because each of the points of view is contradictory. Thus while God claims transcendent attributes, he is ordinarily all too human (petty, pitying, vindictive, impotent). Similarly, the voices from the garden are sometimes imperious and unfeeling ("The Hawthorn Tree" and "Lanium"), sometimes wonderfully passionate ("Trillium" and "The Jacob's Ladder").

My best guess is that we are dealing with conflicting projections of a single, solipsistic, human sensibility, to which each moment has its own flaring, lyrical life and transitory, dramatic truth. Something like this motivates Berryman's "Homage to Mistress Bradstreet" and Merrill's "From the Cupola" (*The Changing Light at Sandover*, by contrast, resembles *Paradise Lost* in that God is a character in an epic pageant, rather than another importunate lyric presence), but in each of these other poems the conflict is sharply defined and part of the crucial issue from the outset. It is not clear to me that such a psychomachia is sustained in *The Wild Iris*—though I must say that Glück's final poem brings the different voices together in a fashion reminiscent of the closes of those earlier twentieth-century masterpieces and that it works best for me when I imagine that it springs from and momentarily resolves such a drama. Here is the last stanza:

> Hush, beloved. It doesn't matter to me
> how many summers I live to return:
> this one summer we have entered eternity.
> I felt your two hands
> bury me to release its splendor.

"We," exactly. The title "The White Lilies" suggests that this voice is that of the flowers, speaking to the poet/gardener; but the lilies symbolize resurrection and thus blur into the incarnate god, who could be speaking to the poet; while the elated poet herself might deservedly feel that this part of her has been planted like a bulb in the autumn by a gardener/god. In any event, *The Wild Iris* is a perennial.

Wilder than Glück, much closer in spirit to Lauterbach, is Michael Palmer. "This notebook . . . claims to have no inside / only characters like A-against-Herself, B, C, L and N, Hans Magnus, T. Sphere, all speaking in the dark with their / hands." So goes a winning passage from the last sequence in *Sun*, the sixth volume by Michael Palmer, one of the most widely known of the group of poets associated with the Language movement. The stuffy reader's response to this claim— "All too true"—has been foreseen throughout the volume, as when "some father says / Your words are not connect." Foreseen and abruptly cut off, just like that, as by a slammed window. Like the work of most of the Language poets, whose name is now legion (for generous samplings see *The L = A = N = G = U = A = G = E Book* edited by Bruce Andrews and Charles Bernstein and *In The American Tree* edited by Ron Silliman), Palmer's is an adversarial poetry, self-consciously subversive of the usual codes, meant precisely to bring the phallogocentric sensibility up short.

Palmer works hard against the grain of conventional coherence, closure, decorum, and the logic of identity and noncontradiction ("A-against-Herself" is well named). Even superficially the volume declares its independence. The titles of its six parts, all but the first of which are sequences or series, are "Fifth Prose," "Baudelaire Series," "C," "C," "Sun," and "Sun." "Fifth Prose," in spite of its title, is in lines; "Baudelaire Series" includes a couple of prose poems as well as free verse; and the second "Sun" is either in long lines or—it is impossible to say—chunks of prose. Throughout the volume, elision, anacoluthon, solecism, and non sequitur are the staples. Oddly enough for a poetry written in part against bourgeois academicism, it is itself bookish, with cliquish overtones (writers whom I take to be Mei-Mei Bersenbrugge, Bernadette Mayer, and Michael Davidson are all referred to by their first names), rife with inkhorn terms (*dystopic, alea, inframaculit, tesseract*), and preoccupied with the concerns of recent theorists and philosophers of language. Thus one of its key terms is *Trace*, which would have come to Palmer by way of Heidegger and Emmanuel Levinas and Jacques Derrida and which, as the yin of the yang of Derrida's concept of *différance,* indicates the inexorable residue of the Other or the otherwise absent and consequently implies a rejection of a humanist metaphysics founded on notions of simple presence and origin. "Day One is called Trace" is the succinct paradox in which Palmer formulates this crucial principle of postmodern decenteredness. Commitment to it enlists him also against the poetry that he thinks of as consumer goods, the poetry that he supposes is produced in university workshops and that (as he has said in an interview) "can stand as a kind of decor in one's life" because it treats issues in terms "utterly defined and closed." His aim is to "open up these terms, to examine the sign itself—the mystery of how words refer and how they can empty out of [*sic*] conventional meanings and acquire meanings that threaten the very way that we talk to each other." Such opening up means that apparently constrictive habits like discursive continuity, narrative, and description—whether of emotions or "things"—must give way. "Today space is splendid / The mountains have come loose / Let's unmake something," he proposes in "Baudelaire Series."

In Palmer's poetry the liberation of the signifier demands on the one hand the author's own self-effacement before the language and on the other the active complicity of the reader. His thought must derive in part by way of Roland Barthes from Mallarmé, who in "Crise de vers" argued not only that poetry had the power "de nier les choses" but also that pure poetry entails the disappearance of the author, who grants precedence to the words themselves in the faith that their reciprocal illuminations will replace the effects of lyrical inspiration and a distinctive voice. In Palmer's terms (in the interview) "language inhabits" the poet, who "learns to listen to the poem as it unfolds." Indeed, there is a whole "variety of selves and nonselves which propose themselves as language on the page." At one point in *Sun* "The persons in the poem say this / between liquid spirits and sense / A broken jar says this," and at another point the poem's discourse emanates from "We, the center." In a revealing revision of Pound's well-known lines in his most personal work, the *Pisan Cantos*, "*ego scriptor* gets blotted out."

The corollary to this abnegation of the traditional lyrical self is a radical disjunctiveness that invites the reader's participation in the act of the poem. Such disjunctiveness itself has a tradition, as *Sun* everywhere implies. One suspects that the title of "Baudelaire Series" alludes to the dedicatory preface to *Le Spleen de Paris*, where Baudelaire writes to his friend Arsene Houssaye that he is sending along "a little work of which no one could say, without injustice, that it has neither head nor tail, since on the contrary it is all simultaneously head and tail, alternatively and reciprocally. We can cut wherever we like," he adds, "me my reverie, you the manuscript, the reader his reading, because I have not kept the latter in suspense by means of the threads of some interminable and superfluous plot." The same might be said of Palmer's assemblages, in which some poetic version of the quantum leap replaces transition. The poems often make one think as well of the vestiges of Archilochus and Sappho and of Hölderlin's discontinuities—and so it is no surprise to discover on the copyright page an acknowledgment of the latter's *Hymns and Fragments* in Richard Sieburth's translation. When in the first "Sun" Palmer writes:

> sky a painter's house
> No yes
> You churn hymns into fragments
> No then yes
> Asleep you set fire to this house,

he at once borrows an intriguing scrap from the German poet ("Und der Himmel wird wie eines Mahlers Haus / Wenn seine Gemählde sind aufgestellet"), touches on an element, fire, that is crucial for both of them, and recognizes his own procedure. In his introduction Seiburth proposes that to read Hölderlin now, given the "radically open and processual character of his poetry" in the manuscripts, is "to practice an aesthetic of the fragment" and to encounter "above all works in progress, neither beginnings or endings but becomings," and one sees why Palmer would respond so warmly.

Palmer's aesthetic involves a fascination, as he has said elsewhere, with different "units of enclosure" or "levels of identity," ranging from "the particular shape of a particular poem" to the overall form of the book itself. So what does a "particular shape" look like in the case of a poet so disdainful of the conventionally crafted poem? "Fifth Prose," which provides a kind of preface, affords the smallest example of a firm infrastructure. Because of the poem's fitful logic and broken syntax, it is hard to see at first that it has in spite of itself a certain concinnity. It is in fifteen distichs in which the first three distichs, a syntactical unit introduced by parallel dependent clauses beginning in successive lines with *Because*, are balanced by the last three, which are introduced in exactly the same way. It's rather satisfying, then, to find at the center of the poem, introduced by the only other *Because* clause in it, "Hassan the Arab and his wife / who did vaulting and balancing"; those are the very activities the poet engages in. As one re-reads the poem and grows accustomed to it, parallelisms and repetitions of subtler sorts disclose themselves and lend it a tentative coherence even as we begin to catch its drift: the urge to dismantle or to transform the "house" built by the Father, since it is at bottom "words only" and can be "taken limb by limb apart," or to leave the house and join a strange kind of circus. But the poem stubbornly retains its rifts and gaps and requires that its readers take chances—that for instance she and he associate themselves with Hassan and his wife, and also with

> Lizzie Keys
> and Fred who fell from the trapeze
> into the sawdust
> and wasn't hurt at all

(this kind of risk taking is not after all physically perilous), and take the hint as to how to respond to this kind of work.

The sequences and the text as a whole bear witness to the same ambivalence toward structure. A local form obtains, for example, throughout the "C" sequences, where each poem is seven lines long, though the grouping of lines is different in every case except the last two, in both of which the pattern is seven isolated lines, so that the length of the strophic unit is always fluctuating within the set limit. One's impression of a "unit of enclosure" is mitigated, moreover, by an internal disjointure summed up in the subtitle of the second "C" (which duplicates the following poem's first line but in a characteristic gesture appears first in quotes, as though to mock the idea of origin): "('Paper universe of primes')." Prime numbers, being divisible without remainder only by themselves and unity, figure Palmer's phrasing, so often irreducible or nonconvertible. At the "level" of the whole text, form is a matter of such things as systematic variation of length. It turns out for example that the six-part *Sun* is almost symmetrical, since it opens with the short piece called "Fifth Prose" and ends with a short piece that might as well be in prose, locates its longest pieces in second and penultimate positions, and centers on the two short "C" sequences.

Beyond such matters, the coherence of *Sun*, such as it is, derives from internal echoes, often of the strangest sort. I take Palmer to have this volume in mind in these lines (from the first "Sun"):

> We spoke in the zero code
> system of assemblage and separation
>
> arcuate scar, shadow and necklace
> doubled by their reflections
>
> then redoubled in the lens
> 34,000 words spread out before me
>
> words like incarnadine, tide and cheer
> asymptote, locus, tear and tear.

In *Sun* revision is extension, elaboration erasure. "The lines through these words," as Palmer puts it in a cleverly equivocal phrase, "form other, still longer lines." That idea itself doubles the sense of another observation: "Words pass backward / onto the tongue / are swallows." And it is redoubled in the first "Sun" sequence when we read that

> A word is beside itself
> A word twists backward
> peeling its skin up over its face
> A word looks behind itself.

Just as *backward* looks back a word to *word,* so *incarnadine* in the earlier passage looks behind itself clear back to "Fifth Prose": "Because there is a literal shore, a letter that's blood-red / Because in this dialect the eyes are crossed or quartz." While *shore* means "littoral," so that each of these words is truly "beside itself," the letter that's blood-red or incarnadine must suggest multitudinous seas. Are they related to the inland C's in *Sun?* In any case, a C will be an "arcuate scar," and "This notebook contains shadows / nothing else" (first "Sun"), and any one of these sequences is a "necklace." When we are asked in "Baudelaire Series" to "consider the lace in necklace," we might well discover in the OED that the first meaning of *lace* is net, noose, or snare. Such "reticular figures" (second "C") confront us everywhere in *Sun,* until it seems that "We are facing the nets" at every turn ("Baudelaire Series") and that the volume itself consists of "desire in a net" (first "Sun").

So it goes in this dialect in which, instead of the i's being dotted and the t's crossed, "the eyes are crossed" and a certain double vision is produced. Crossing is itself one of Palmer's motifs. "X / we are called," he notes at one juncture, where he perhaps has in mind our inescapable formerness and our unknowability as well as our hybrid natures. "X, name of X / we are," he remarks near the end of the first "Sun," where he also proposes that

> It is our fortune to have been born
> at the crossroads of a chiasma
> in a land known as How to Laugh
> and How to Die.

Time and again poet and reader find themselves in a labyrinth: "We entered the forest, followed its winding paths, and emerged blind" (second "Sun"); and

> I was aware of things those
> things were me amazing the forked branch
> spilling names I had been-not I
> had been not-lost I had seen you once
>
> (first "Sun")

As we go through this labyrinth from which we cannot emerge, we come upon evidence of a quite different version of Daedalus' story in the form of piece after piece of broken "thread."

As Barthes has observed, the postmodern text's characteristic metaphor is the *réseau,* and the intelligence and the verbal ingenuity behind Palmer's labyrinth or network are impressive. Moreover, his decreative method has a salutary, purifying effect. It even has political implications, if all too little direct impact. As Herbert Marcuse pointed out many years ago, the intersection of avant-garde literature and the power of negative philosophical thinking comes in "the effort to break the power of facts over the word, and to speak a language which is not the language of those who establish, enforce, and benefit from the facts." The perennial problem is that "as the power of given facts tends to become totalitarian, to absorb all opposition, and to define the entire universe of discourse, the effort to speak the language of contradiction appears increasingly irrational, obscure, artificial"—as Palmer's poetry attests. Still, his efforts continue Stevens's project, to throw off the received language, "like a thing of another time, / As morning throws off stale moonlight and shabby sleep." In *Notes toward a Supreme Fiction* Stevens defines his project in terms Palmer might have recalled when titling his book: "There was a project for the sun and is. / There is a project for the sun." Palmer's own difficult work makes us think anew that meaning is not a question of commodification but of metamorphosis and activity, that it is a process occurring in a zone of energy whose limits are beyond our ken, that it is more a ludic than an apodeictic activity. Perhaps even these days we are wont to think of a text as a Book—as a fortress to be breached and pillaged, rather than as a playfield. If so, Palmer's work will serve as a corrective, provided that his readers already have a certain venturesomeness, and patience, and a high tolerance for disorderliness.

At the same time, for all the "play" in Palmer's text, there is precious little playfulness. There is hardly any good laughter, hardly any unattenuated sadness. The poems are short on affect altogether, partly because they have "only characters like A-against-Herself." The drama is limited to interchanges between anagrams, or between a more or less abstract form and formlessness. The work is so nearly ascetic in its fierce narrowness of focus that one is inclined to recall (especially since he often refers to his "name") that *palmer* can refer not only to a magician or conjurer (one who might travel with that troupe in "Fifth Prose") but also to a pilgrim from the Holy Land (and indeed "shreds of palm / leaf lie / here"). As far as

I can tell, such narrowness does not follow necessarily from the nature of his enterprise. Stein's *Tender Buttons* combines a similar decreative passion with the affective and even the dramatic. But in any case there is no doubt in my mind about the integrity or the intensity of Michael Palmer's undertaking.

Sensuous and Particular

The eye-filling cover of Sherod Santos's *The City of Women,* his third book of poems, reproduces a painting by William Bailey, its structural components elegantly interlocked in what I suspect are golden section ratios, entitled "Three Sisters." The painting's geometrical and tonal subtleties are beyond the scope of this discussion; perhaps it suffices to note that the three nude women look enough alike to be triplets, and that the one on the viewer's left holds an open book, while the one in the middle casually covers herself, and the one on the right sits beside a table with a coffee mug. The Charities or Graces, their positioning would suggest. Or perhaps the Fates? The goddesses Paris judged? Chekhov's *Three Sisters?* In any event, Santos's volume is itself in three parts, involves women who sometimes seem almost interchangeable (hence one possible adverse criticism), and tells the story (to borrow from the first poem) "of my life / In love, the buried life I know little about, / Perhaps nothing at all." The echoes of Matthew Arnold's "unspeakable desire / After the knowledge of our buried life" and his claim that "I feel a nameless sadness o'er me roll" are purposeful in this often lovely and unremittingly melancholy "Sequence of Poems and Prose."

The streets (so to speak) in Santos's city, meandering and unexpectedly intersecting, often abruptly dead-ending and sometimes picking up again, are the poet's relationships with a number of women: Zoë, L. the poet's mother, the Virgin, a

---

Review of *The City of Women* by Sherod Santos, *Stained Glass* by Rosanna Warren, and *The Invention of the Zero* by Richard Kenney. From *The Yale Review,* April, 1994.

maid, Baudelaire's *reine de péchés*, Eurydice, a girl who pees on a path, women never seen before or again. . . . It's a fruitful idea, this notion of moving mentally among the loved ones in one's life, and it provides for all kinds of echoes and parallels, the more satisfying in this case for the book's formal variety. Changing his modes as he does his subjects, Santos writes now in blank verse sections (twenty-three of them, usually from ten to twenty lines long) and now in prose (thirty-seven sections, most of them less than a page long) and draws on various genres, including journal entries, vignettes, meditations, dramatic monologues, narratives, conversational exchanges, and assemblages of gnomic fragments. As the poet shifts among these different modes, he moves in and out of diverse, mostly erotic relationships as though they coexisted in time—as of course they do, in the poet's mind and, consequently, in the reader's.

The volume opens—after a prefatory verse—in a characteristic manner:

> She is seated somewhere—I can't recall where
> Exactly now, the young Algerian shopclerk
> From a bookstore Mother frequented those days—
> And she is seated alone, in a café, let's say,
> Looking out onto a crowded square in Châteauroux,
> On a market day in the early fall, a shifting
> Fretwork of pushcarts, string bags, makeshift stalls,
> The gutters a rubble of spoiled fruit, rinds,
> Bread crusts, dung, stray dogs sniffing at
> The entrails too bruised to lay out in pans,
> An acrid smell of the *pissoirs,* and the dizzying
> Zigzag horseflies make in the airless crush
> Of those afternoons.

These are marvelously gauged lines, from the initial pronoun that epitomizes the volume's subject, through the deft transposition of *where* and *Exactly* with its attendant ambiguities, to the shuffling of present and past in the midst of the labyrinthine richness of the marketplace. A kind of Beatrice, the unnamed woman or girl sits at a café table:

> though it had rained,
> Earlier, off and on, the sun's come out, the sun's
> Reflected off the window she sits staring from,
> So that her image deepens behind the pane,
> Advances as if out of flame and then recedes again
> Into a glossy incandescence our desolate world
> Would crisscross for a moment before the next
> Cloud came and shadowed her back.

So "she" appears and disappears throughout the sequence.

Images harking back to the opening poem recur, as when the poet finds himself in the midst of a carnival in a Catalan seaside town:

> A spray of streamers from the quaysides
> And restaurants, the sail-shaped whitecaps
> Blooming onto shore, soft salvos, and then,
> At the sound of some imaginary gong,
> Throngs of townspeople parading up the sand,
> Bull-horned, goat-headed, mantled in foil,
> And fueled by the racket of countless handmade
> Carnival horns, a local fantasia advancing fast
> On the filled, flung-open terraces and bars,
> As though the riddling past had reversed itself
> Through the make-believe of a crazy dream.

Against the backdrop of this version of Arnold's "world's most crowded streets," there appears on a balcony "a carved, life-sized, / Palanquined Virgin." Reminiscent of the figure in the first poem, who is sealed off from "all the heaped activity" by a "stillness that surrounds her," the icon emanates a "calm, almost / Impersonal aloneness." As in Arnold's poem—where the poet must ask, "Are even lovers powerless to reveal / To one another what indeed they feel?"—this isolation of selves is a nearly inevitable condition. Indeed, the last image in Santos's book is of a lone "middle-aged woman who has paused momentarily to stare at the sky—a bright contrail swept by on high stratospheric winds—on an evening walk in December." True, this last section in *The City of Women* comprises a miscellany of images, some of which recall Arnold's rare moments when

"Our eyes can in another's eyes read clear," as in "The SHARED EMOTION of a radio song"; but that sentence's small caps (a recurrent device that suggests an inflection somewhere between italics and quotation marks) undermine the central phrase, and over the sequence as a whole the theme of solitariness overwhelms the instances of connection.

Our understanding that Santos is dealing with a basic human estrangement (Arnold's people are "alien to the rest . . . and alien to themselves") mitigates if it doesn't cancel the possible charge that the book is reductive or essentialist. If it's hard to remember the differences between Zoë and L., and if the matter is further embrangled by the occasional representation of each in anonymous terms, Santos has not set out to do life studies. His sequence has more the quality of George Meredith's *Modern Love* than that of Robert Lowell's *The Dolphin* or John Berryman's *Sonnets*. Santos is often chillingly particular, but the particulars have to do not with personalities but with ungendered interpersonal structures. The psychological transpicuousness sometimes makes one think of Proust:

> When I begin to explain, with a wave of her hand she dismisses it all as ANOTHER OF LIFE'S NATURAL HAZARDS. At that my shame resolves itself into a sudden, moribund anger, as though the issue were no longer *the actual danger* I'd placed her in, but *the imagined slight:* That she'd forseen all along my petty burden of vengefulness and guilt.

Meanwhile, there is much finely tuned writing in this sequence. The transitions can be wizardly:

> The story of a woman who will leave a man.
> A man who thinks in metaphors. A woman
> Who thinks the reason she'll leave has less to do
> With him than her. Some flaw. Some ache for things
> That end. A second nature inside of her: A land
> That's seized by absence just as some lands are
> By snow: the furious snows of late December,
> Powerlines down, streets deserted, the bright
> Abrasions the wind has scored against the loudly
> Ticking windowpanes. At a complete loss

> For what to do, the man's been walking through
> That snow. His eyes are wet. His hair is wet.

The conciseness is exemplary: "In our strict cosmology, it was crueler to say 'I'm tired' than 'I hate you.' 'I hate you,' in fact, had sometimes signaled an argument's end, as though one had actually confessed one's love." Santos usually writes with an unostentatious specificity, but he also composes the richly wrought description:

> a middle-aged
> Couple in evening clothes has cut across
> An abandoned lot behind a car repair: a scatter
> Of shattered window glass flung in looping
> Zodiacs, the pitted asphalt onyxed with oil,
> A floor fluorescing in the streetlight like the scud
> Of memory—a high school dance?

His use of gaudy rhetoric in the service of such settings is comparable to his turning upside down of romantic conventions like *die ferne Geliebte*. And he has a gift for the vivid conclusion.

Rosanna Warren's preceding book of poems, entitled with distinctive flair *Each Leaf Shines Separate,* was for me one of those rare first books that startles, thrills, clarifies, and demonstrates withal that it is not only "promising" but truly precocious, proof of a talent already ripe. Wallace Stevens's *Harmonium* will have been the model of that kind of book for some people, along with Elizabeth Bishop's *North and South,* as in my own experience W. D. Snodgrass's *Heart's Needle* and Geoffrey Hill's *For the Unfallen* have been. The aura of fullness and yet imminence about Warren's first book was epitomized near its conclusion in poems like "Orchard" and "Painting a Madonna," which were reminiscent of Keats's "Ode to Autumn," and of Hölderlin's "Erntezeit," where the mature fruits, before they are even picked, are already dipped in fire, precooked—*precocious* precisely.

Warren's *Stained Glass,* the winner of the 1993 Lamont

Award from the Academy of American Poets, is even more heavily autumnal, harvest oriented, elegiac. The book's epigraph from "Il Penseroso"—"And made Hell grant what Love did seek"—ironically foreshadows Warren's obsession with loss in its reference to Orpheus' brief moment of triumph in Hades and implicitly invokes Milton's "sad Virgin" and "Goddess," "divinest Melancholy" in her "robe of darkest grain," who encourages the speaker "To walk the studious Cloister's pale" with its "storied Windows richly dight, / Casting a dim religious light." Indeed, the mood of "Il Penseroso" mediates between this book's dust jacket, with its reproduction of a gorgeous stained-glass window at Chartres that shows the healing of a blind man, and the first poem's echoes of "Lycidas." Instead of Milton's chiefly delicate, vernal flowers ("The tufted Crow-toe, and pale Jessamine, / The white Pink, and the Pansy freakt with jet"), however, Warren's "Season Due" appraises September's rugged survivors, "chrysanthemums, brash / marigolds, fat sultan dahlias" ("Pansy / freaked with jet be / damned"); and, instead of Milton's finally prevailing resurrection and harmony, Warren closes with "radiant bitterness" and the "last acrid flood / of perfume that will drift in the air once more, / yet once more, when these stubborn flowers have died." *Radiant bitterness* is her summary phrase—and it is the shadow title of this volume.

"Song," set in a cemetery, begins on a note of Jonsonian tenderness with "A yellow coverlet / In a greenwood" and with the gravestones' expressions of faith ("'Meet me in Heaven'") but ends in a stunningly fierce rejection of consolation, a savage relishing of mortality:

>   I turn away.
> I shall meet you nowhere, in no transfigured hour.
>   On soft, matted soil
>   blueberry bushes crawl,
> each separate berry a small, hot globe of tinctured sun.
>   Crushed on the tongue
>   it releases a pang
> of flesh. Tender flesh, slipped from its skin,
>   preserves its blue heat
>   down my throat.

It is characteristic of Warren both that she writes under the auspices of the tradition—in this case the "veiled Melancholy" is Keats's, "seen of none save him whose strenuous tongue / Can burst Joy's grape against his palate fine"—and that she makes the transumptions consonant. Characteristic too is the concinnity of the diction and images. In somewhat the way that *tongue* and *pang* rhyme (they are then englobed and rhymed again by *sun* and *skin,* in a kind of miniature version of the whole poem, whose last couplet rhymes with its first line), the living and the dead converge in the moment, which is a moment after all of communion and transfiguration, though the transfiguration itself is worldly. The subtle irony in *preserves* returns us to Warren's home key of *radiant bitterness.*

The elegiac theme is so sustained through these poems that Warren can parody it in "Necrophiliac," a masterful neo-Metaphysical sonnet that also ends with a gustatory image:

> Death, since you nourish me, I'll flatter you
> inordinately. Consumers both, with claws
> cocked and molars prompt at the fresh-dug grave,
> reaper and elegist, we collaborate
> and batten in this strictest of intimacies,
> my throat an open sepulchre, my tongue
> forever groping grief forever young.

The wickedly witty inversion of the image of the "open sepulchre," the last line's painfully sarcastic twisting of Keats ("Ode on a Grecian Urn" this time: "For ever warm and still to be enjoyed, / For ever panting and for ever young"), and the self-disgusted exactness of *collaborate,* which brings together the work of mourning and the labor of death, are all inspired touches.

Warren's deepest affinities are with the Greek poets, with Latin literature, and with French and Italian work. As well as being a poet, she is a passionate scholar and translator (section 3 of this book consists mostly of translations from Alcman, Pierre Reverdy, and Max Jacob), influenced not only by Jonson and Marvell, but also by Archilochus and Sappho, Carducci and Baudelaire. Yet her learning is worn as lightly as any

Hellenic chiton—and indeed, what might strike one first about her poetry is the sensuousness of its vision or the texture of its language. She was trained as a painter at Yale, and she is one of our most painterly poets. It's not just that she sometimes writes about art, though ecphrasis is one of her métiers, nor just that the poems gleam with the delightfully specific colors of the painter's palette, but also that her consonants and vowels are worked like oils, so that we get audible impastos, sonic scumbles. Here she is sketching "Girl by Minoan Wall":

> This solid
> sun-browned girl, pad and pencil in lap, cheek
>   on palm, already
>
> burns. Her flesh, like the town wall, quavers
>   in the heat-smite
> of noon: by evening her very frame
>   will melt, as mountain-hulk,
>
> marketstalls, kiosks, Cyclopean
>   masonry melt
> into indigo, into the promise
>   hovering above
>
> the harbor. It is not water,
>   weed-slung, scummy sloshing, that
> survives. It is, in water, the jeweled plummet lines
>   of reflected light.

She loves the natural world's details as well as the literature that praises them, and she moves gracefully from one register to another. As flatly lovely as her poems are, however, they hide nothing from us—let alone from her. Her sensuousness combines readily in this book with what Warren has spoken of elsewhere as "the central barbarity of the deepest art," a phrase that helps to define the raw rightness in "Necrophiliac" and other poems here. In her first book, describing a Renoir painting, she wrote that "Flesh is fruit, whispers the brush, and sunlight / Wine." But here is a related theme at the opening of "Science Lessons" in *Stained Glass:*

> The human body is superfluous.
> Rochester knew it: lurching home
> from a night of swiving and sluicing,
> ballocks crumpled, loins wrung out,
> fingers dripping and pungent, he was consumed
>
> by knowledge. Having caressed
> the soft slippage of flesh from rib and hip,
> foreknew rack, gibbet, kettle, all the precise
> instruments of quest including
> the final, eloquent shudder.

If one thinks of a painter at this remarkable juncture of consummation and consumption, it's surely not Renoir but rather Francis Bacon, for whom flesh is paint and sunlight is candor.

Richard Kenney's wonderfully entitled and mazily, fugally complex *The Invention of the Zero* is dedicated to James Merrill, "who candled earth first" in the sense that his epic enterprise *The Changing Light at Sandover*, with its amalgamation of recent discoveries in physics with occult sources—the latter ranging from Egyptian lore through Gnosticism to Yeats's version of Madame Blavatsky—gave Kenney a precedent for his book. I note also that Merrill's lyrically dense narrative "Santorini: Stopping the Leak" is explicitly echoed in the first line of Kenney's first major section, as its mode is implicitly echoed throughout. Not that Kenney's volume or sequence—at its heart a sort of quaternion, to borrow an antiquated term, framed by "A Colloquy of Ancient Men" on the one end and an intimately related "Epilog: Read Only Memory" on the other, with choral interchanges intercalated all along the way—is imitative. If Merrill's work was sui generis, Kenney's is no less recherché, punctilious, ambitious, and sonically sophisticated—all in extremes. An idiosyncratic masterpiece, from time to time it will call up or toss up Whitman, Hopkins, Dylan Thomas, Hart Crane, Berryman, and W. D. Snodgrass's poem on Van Gogh's "Starry Night," as well as Merrill, H.D., Milton . . .

Kenney's wisely postponed "Notes and Acknowledgments," Swiftian and archly overwritten, provide useful afterimages of "this book's four narrative chapters." Each of these "chapters" is written in a loose iambic pentameter that easily expands to hexameter and that is thickly, delicately, ingeniously rhymed and prefaced by a quotation, three of which derive immediately from the "Colloquy." The first of these four narrative chapters, "The Invention of the Zero," is based in part on eyewitness accounts of early A-bomb experiments in the New Mexican deserts; the second, "The Encantadas," records the experience of "an Army Captain commanding an antiaircraft battery in the Galapagos Islands in 1944 and 1945"; the third, "Typhoon," which Kenney calls "my father's story," recounts "shipboard events surrounding the notorious typhoon of December 18 and 19, 1944, which caught the United States Third Fleet unprepared, and devolved into one of the worst naval disasters" of World War II; and the fourth, "Lucifer," sets down, among much else, the travails of a Navy SEAL attendant on his first parachute jump. According to the jacket copy, "All of the narratives are based on detailed testimony of friends of the author," and taken "together they give us a sense of the world in which man's attempt to control nature and natural violence displays both its heroic and its comic side." Their titles also allude to other rich works—Melville's stories, Conrad's novella, and so forth. The verse paragraphs in "Typhoon" are accompanied by marginalia reminiscent of those in Coleridge's "The Ancient Mariner," though these purport to be transcriptions of terse messages in naval shorthand. In addition to the prosody, these four chapters have in common apocalyptic vision, richly proliferating catalogs and metonymies, a no-holds-barred approach to diction, a headlong syntax, and a Dionysian abun-dance of wordplay. This passage, near the beginning of "Typhoon," will suggest something of Kenney's usual narrative manner:

> But why anticipate? Sidereal
> considerations got us to this fix, Dear
> Reader. You know how it all comes out: we won:
> *The End.* And there's a fine beginning, star drill
> on stone—straight to the point, for once,
> the period I'm writing in, its true plot, terse
> and open and dimensionless as O, the pierced cipher

falling through its own true nature, *poof*, as stars
are said to do. What stands to reason? *Entropy?*—
it goes against all sense, what's this, *the end*, per-
force, Ferris wheeling back in mind, a whorl of faces,
freed of personality, in time, maybe; but tears
stream inward, still, against the wind, centripetal.
You'll do your own recalling, friend. This periphrasis
isn't mine, it's the curve of the volume of things: the
    moon's
swing, earth's, the stars in curving space, the petals'
whorl, the double strand, the eye of this typhoon.

That is a lot of apparatus and aspiration—and that's the half of it. To wit: at the beginning and at the end of the volume, and alternating with the named sections specified earlier (the "Colloquy," the four narratives, and the "Epilog"), there are untitled lyrical sections written in a self-conscious synthesis of a pun-fraught futuristic mode and "a worn-out poetical fashion" (Eliot). Here is an instance of this lyrical manner:

> Mind minted *thee*,
> old dah-dit,
> encanta'd orbiter, O,
> antedated Ike dime
> turned, re-
> turned again
> against the sky's
> flecked velvet—
> but reflect: echolocate
> *x, y, z: The End*.
> Send, child,
> that I may receive.

The point of view in this stanza is that of a figure often addressed as "Lord" and "Father," who reminds one of Merrill's God Biology. The "orbiter"—who or which seems to be a kind of satellite computer / Holy Ghost / space scout or perhaps Earth itself reporting (according to its shifting lights) to an otherwise blind overseer on the status and history of the universe—has the other point of view, and these two figures exchange messages throughout the interludic sections. In the table of contents, instead of titles, each of these sections is represented by a brief synopsis (compare Merrill's procedure in "Mirabell's Books of Number").

The Homeric "Colloquy of Old Men," near the beginning of the book, consists chiefly of quotations, from diverse scientists and writers, each of which has been tactfully, musically deranged. In most of its seven sections, for instance, each quotation begins with the same word or a variant of it. Kenney's procedure involves opening each quotation in medias res at the point at which this word occurs—and then appending the precedent "remainder," so to speak, at the end of the excerpt, with the result that startling "enjambments" occur between excerpts. Enjambments also occur between sections, at the same time that the initial word changes. In illustration I quote the end of section 3 and section 4 (in which MP is Max Planck, BLF is Bernard le Bovier de Fontenelle, the eminent seventeenth- and eighteenth-century French writer on astronomy and letters, HM is Herman Melville, and the other contributors are the scientists Neils Bohr, Fred Hoyle, and J. B. S. Haldane):

MP: minds, but eventually die.... Scientists never change their minds, but eventually die.... Scientists ne

BLF: ver died.... As long as roses could remember, no gar-dener e

HM: ver contracting towards the buttonlike black bubble at the axis of that slowly wheeling circle, like another Ixion I did revolve.... Round and round, then, and e

NB: veryday language, we can only hope to grasp the real facts by means of these images.... Quantum theory thus provides us with a striking illustration of the fact that we can fully understand a connection though we can only speak of it in images and parable.... since we can only describe natural phenomena with our e

> FH: verse. . . . Grant me the hydrogen atom, and I will deduce the uni
>
> JBSH: verse is queerer than we think. The universe is queerer than we can

This passage, with its swirls and spirals, its complex symmetries and unexpected disjunctions—and, in short, its chaotic order, means to justify a kind of language that might come closer than "everyday language" to describing our apprehension of the state of things. I am reminded of David Bohm, the hidden variable physicist become philosopher, who has called (in *Wholeness and the Implicate Order*) for "a *new mode* of language," specifically a "rheomode ('rheo' is from a Greek verb, meaning 'to flow')," that could better reflect the world as physicists have come to know it. Intensely labored yet not laborious, Kenney's own invention—one of several in this volume—comports with the idea of energy shaping itself.

Toward the other end of the volume, the penultimate part, the "Epilog," consists of a scrambling, perhaps (ideally) in some degree aleatory, of bits of the quotations in the "Colloquy." I quote another self-exemplifying passage, chaotic without being disorderly:

> ter and then it was extremely solemn. We knew the world would
>
> not be the same I re
>
> member no gardener ever died. As long as roses could remember
>
> the line from the Hin
>
> disputable authority that the end of the world was to be finally accomplished by a catastroph
>
> es. The unleashed power of the atom has changed every
>
> day language, we can only hope to grasp the real fact
>
> er of the fundamentals of scientific theory.

Finally, every section of the volume—there are thirteen in all—is designated either by an astrological sign (each of which is also an *alchemical* sign in the cases of the seven unnamed interludic sections) or another symbol (the second and twelfth sections, the "Colloquy" and the "Epilog"). The identifiable sectional signs in the order of their appearance are as follows: (1) the moon (silver); (3) Mars (iron); (4) fixed star (or is this a stylized wheel—or gear?); (5) Mercury (quicksilver); (6) Earth; (7) Jupiter (tin); (8) Neptune; (9) Venus (copper); (10) comet; (11) Saturn (lead); and (13) the sun (gold). The two planets not represented are the two unknown to the early alchemists, Uranus and Pluto. The correspondent second and twelfth sections are both accompanied by a circle diagonally cut by a line, or a "pierced cipher," the computer's symbol for zero.

I hasten to assure the "Dear Reader" who is determined to continue in the role that this book is much more user friendly, sensuous, passionate, and playful than the preceding adumbration can begin to indicate. The thing is that Kenney is something of a polymath, with centrifugal aspirations, ranging from a pure lyricist's love of the pun—the splitting of the etym, as Joyce had it—outward to the storyteller's love of the narrative, just as his sponsors range from Erato through Clio to Calliope. An unequivocal bid for major attention, this book cannot be "dealt with" in a short essay. What one can do is to quote and contextualize a passage or two from one of the four narrative chapters. The following lines come from "Lucifer," the last of the four narratives, which centers on the experience of a man named Lew, the navy SEAL who, on his first parachute jump, had both his parachutes fail. In these lines—characteristically expansive, maximalist, sewn with off-rhyme—the second chute fails, even as Lew's feet are tangled up in the shrouds of the first:

>   Plucked
> untimely from your buttonhole! And now the unmade
> paroxysm of the Future, Reader: ripped
> *pop* (hear?—imagine this sound audible
> in midair, too, the littlest apocalyptic
> tickle where your palm tree shirt's reserve chute
> should have opened, whiffling out across the epoch)—

Up, down: Here's Lew's figure once again, all doubled
over, flapping, fumbling with a winged shoelace
shroud that binds his ankles now, all spacetime shirred
like silk scarves in the wind, open now, now poked
back through the black magician's fist—

                                    A first
approximation of the metaphor (preferred);
the word permits a second solution: spacetime shirred like
    shell-
less zeroes hatched inside this queer ceramic pickle-
jar of pure imaginary numbers.

Lew falls for many pages, as such moments dilate and give way to other meditations and so on. In fact, rather like Milton's fallen angel—and Lucifer's name could be shortened to Lew—he falls through time as well as space. Like Milton's angel's fall, too, Lew's parallels *the* Fall, which in Kenney's version probably occurred in the Renaissance, when for all practical purposes the zero was invented for Western culture, or appropriated from the originally Hindu numbering system, and the possibility of atomic physics and digital computers was born. Of course *born* has ironic overtones in this context, as this passage's opening allusion to *Macbeth* itself suggests. (The same play gives Brian Rotman the title of his book, *Signifying Nothing: The Semiotics of Zero,* which has perhaps had some effect on Kenney, along with Roger Penrose's *The Emperor's New Mind* and N. Katherine Hayles's *Chaos Bound.* But the list of influencing works would be a very long one.) Eventually, Lew's shroud lines, as knotted about his feet as the metaphors in Kenney's narrative are about *his* feet, magically come clear and the narrative ends with the SEAL floating limpidly to Earth as the poet reflects on universal order and meaning:

        But this is my story. Whether or not the grand
orrery is gone for good, when once upon
a time at last a parachute plucks open
in a dream's cloud chamber, time stops, scales
start on my skin, and one green man in a glass mask hangs

> pendant, by his heartstrings, as it were, it looks
> from where I stand like nothing so much as the frail calyx
> of a flower, an invisible flower, or a very blue
> flower from the heart, the day sky, blooming.

Well, it's everybody's story, although no one else could have closed with lines beautiful in this special way, and although (as he points out) Kenney arbitrarily chooses a happy ending, as the "nothing" that came of nothing is a zero, an opening parachute, a flower, the sky, and thus the whole blooming universe.

I think that some readers will feel, as R. P. Blackmur felt about Hart Crane's *The Bridge,* that Kenney has called upon an essentially lyric gift to do epic work. So that, for instance, the dense clustering of detail and the heavily enjambed lines rather work against the premise of different speakers and incidents and gum up the plot of the whole. Some people will probably also feel that he has an advanced case of Spenser's syndrome, the compulsion to use arcane and archaic terms, and that now and again the poems sound rather like encyclopedia entries versified. For my part, these aspects of Kenney's book are not defects so much as distinguishing characteristics of one of the most splendidly aspiring long poems in America in this now nearly waned century.

A Boundless Field

It makes little difference where we take up our story, to paraphrase Parmenides, since we must return there in the fullness of time. Any attempt to summarize Frank Bidart's new book of poems *Desire* will somehow acknowledge the relevance of that venerable witticism—or insight. For one thing, *Desire* is less the kind of book—and it is assuredly, even aggressively a *book* rather than a collection of poems (its components aren't even all in lines)—that has an Aristotelian beginning, middle, and end than it is the kind of book that has a dizzying Augustinian density, such that its unity implies centers everywhere and a circumference nowhere. If in this respect *Desire* also conjures Plotinus' universe, according to which "God is not external . . . but is present with[in] all things," that's no wonder, because from the outset Bidart's scrupulous, ambitious, and affecting volume explicitly evokes it, too.

In his single, modest, responsible concluding "Note" (and what a relief it *is* not to find pages of authorial annotations reinstructing us in Greek mythology or Gnostic principles or whatever, as though the poet were both the inspired Milton and the tireless Merritt Hughes), Bidart recognizes that his long poem, "The Second Hour of the Night," which makes up the second half of his book, "throughout is indebted to Stephen MacKenna's translation of Plotinus." Helpful as it is in regard to the book's last poem, that tribute also reminds us that the book's first poem opens with this allusion to the Neoplatonist:

Review of *Desire* by Frank Bidart and *The Vigil* by C. K. Williams. From *The Yale Review*, Spring, 1998.

> AS THE EYE TO THE SUN
> To Plotinus what we seek is VISION, what
> wakes when we wake to desire
>
> *as the eye to the sun*
>
> It is just as if you should fall in love with
> one of the sparrows which fly by
>
> *when we wake to desire*

Plotinus' vision, then, is there in both beginning and end. So, too, is the fundamental procedure of weaving: first poem and last, for instance, and roman and italic type in the preceding excerpt. Where does this book "begin"? Perhaps we can suspend the question, however knowingly.

This opening poem, "As the Eye to the Sun," derives most of its material from Marcus Aurelius' *Meditations* as translated by George Long (see Bidart's "Note"), so that, for example, the simile involving the sparrows springs from *Meditations* 6.15, with its Heraclitean and ecclesiastical recognition of the transience of all things:

> Motions and changes are continually renewing the world, just as the uninterrupted course of time is always renewing the infinite duration of ages. In this flowing stream, then, on which there is no abiding, what is there of the things which hurry by on which a man would set a high price? It would be just as if a man should fall in love with one of the sparrows which fly by, but it has already passed out of sight. Something of this kind is the very life of every man, like the exhalation of the blood and the respiration of the air.

But whereas his excerpt from Marcus Aurelius, at least when contextualized, points us in the direction of flux, Bidart's opening allusion suggests a motif in Marcus Aurelius' successor Plotinus, who was ultimately interested less in the ephemeral nature of things than in their ineffable unity. (Though we might note that Marcus Aurelius himself writes on several occasions about the possibility of "one intelligent source" of all things and "the connections of all things" to one another.) In one of the *Enneads* that invokes terms Bidart also uses, Plotinus tells us that the One (also known as "It") can be known, "if at all, by vision.... We must not run after It, but must fit ourselves for the vision and then wait tranquilly for it as the eye waits on the rising of the sun."

To sum up the opening lines of Bidart's opening poem we might say that the poet is drawn on one hand to a radiant vision of the unified whole (Plotinus also refers to the One as the Good, and the Beautiful, as well as It) and on the other to a recognition of the vanity of such aspirations in view of mutability. It is then perhaps not too much to see these alternatives that I have indicated reflected in the lines that follow those already quoted:

> But once you have seen a hand cut off, or
> a foot, or a head, you have embarked, have begun
>
> *as the eye to the sun*
>
> The voyage, such is everything, you have not come to
> shore, but little children and their sports and
>
> *when we wake to desire*

What is certain is that the image of the severed body part has been excised from Marcus Aurelius, *Meditations* 8.34 (a passage that Djuna Barnes must have recollected several times in the course of composing *Nightwood*):

> If thou didst ever see a hand cut off, or a foot, or a head, lying anywhere apart from the rest of the body, such does a man make himself, as far as he can, who is not content with what happens, and separates himself from others, or does anything unsocial. Suppose that thou hast detached thyself from the natural unity—for thou wast made by nature a part, but now thou hast cut thyself off—yet here there is this beautiful provision, that it is in thy power again to unite thyself. God has allowed this to no other part, after it has been separated and cut asunder, to come together again.

It is in this context that one must read the concluding line of Bidart's opening poem, which requotes Marcus Aurelius: "But once you have seen a hand cut off you have begun." That last period, I must note, is mine. It is not in Bidart's text because Bidart does not want to stop the beginning he has begun the book with, so to speak. To put it another way, by cutting out this precise section of Marcus Aurelius, Bidart invites us to complete the fragment ("you have begun 'again to unite thyself,'" for example) and thus to engage in the process that he means reading this book to be. To put that yet another way, to recognize or to recreate the relationship between Marcus Aurelius (c. 121–80) and Plotinus (c. 205–70) is to begin to apprehend the complex thing that *Desire* is, and that apprehension is in turn a synecdoche for a quest for the immanent One, to use Plotinus' term. Indeed, "the One" is everywhere both sought and unspoken in "As the Eye to the Sun," from its first rhyme to its last, both of which join *sun* with *begun*, especially since in Plotinus vision and light are indistinguishable: "the quester is lifted and sees, never knowing how; the vision floods the eyes with light, but it is not a light showing some other thing, the light is itself the vision. No longer is there object seen and light to show it, no longer Intellect and the object of Intellection; this is the very Radiance that brought both into being" (6.7.36).

It will make sense, then, that *Desire* concludes with a pointed couplet. Here are the last five lines of "The Second Hour of the Night," in which declaration, supplication, and summation merge:

> *infinite the sounds the poems*
> *seeking to be allowed to* SUBMIT,—*that this*
> *dust becomes seed*
> *like those extinguished stars whose fires still give us light*
>
> •
>
> This is the end of the second hour of the night.

At the end, the "*light*" that dies out in the "night" lives on in the rhyme. And among "*those extinguished stars,*" we must number Plato and Plotinus and Marcus Aurelius and others, "*dust become seed*" themselves in the fertile ground of "*poems*" like this one, which seek also to propagate the "VISION" the book began with.

If it seems that I can't tell whether I'm talking about Frank Bidart's poetics or his metaphysics, well, I think that's the point. His *buon maestro* here is the T. S. Eliot of *Four Quartets,* whose "uncertain hour before the morning / Near the ending of interminable night" anticipates Bidart's "second hour of the night" and whose cadences in different parts of the *Quartets* are occasionally apparent in *Desire.* Eliot concludes his own visionary quest with these lines in "Little Gidding":

> A condition of complete simplicity
> (Costing not less than everything)
> And all shall be well and
> All manner of thing shall be well
> When the tongues of flame are in-folded
> Into the crowned knot of fire
> And the fire and the rose are one.

Even as Eliot's *complete simplicity* specifies both the spiritual state he aspires to and his language (virtually unpunctuated and monosyllabic by the end), this *fifth* section of his *fourth* quartet narrows to *tri*meter in this, its *second* part, which ends with *one*—a "one" that is also, because it is a "knot," a "naught," all of them represented by or infolded into the final "point" (the term is central in *Four Quartets*) or period that he (exactly unlike Bidart in the poem quoted earlier) provides. That's the kind of dovetailing of metaphysics and poetics that I think Bidart has in mind as a model.

At the beginning of "Borges and I," which takes its title from one of Jorge Luis Borges's pieces in *Labyrinths,* and rings a further change on it since in *Desire* "I" is also "Frank," we are told that "We fill pre-existing forms and when we fill them we change them and are changed." That resonant statement makes marvelously short work of Ezra Pound's peremptory claim that there are two kinds of form, one that water takes when poured into a pitcher and the other that a tree takes when growing. Bidart's book and even Bidart himself—his statement is radically reflexive—fill forms used by Marcus Aurelius, Plotinus, Eliot, Borges, Dante ("Love Incarnate"), Catullus (whose "Odi et amo" couplet is echoed in at least two of these poems), Lady Bird Johnson, an anonymous person quoted in what I take to be a published account of coerced fellatio ("Adolescence"), and others, some identified and some not, change them, and are changed in the process. The main form filled in "The Return," as Bidart suggests in his "Note," comes from Tacitus' *Annals*. The specific source turns out to be book 1, chapter 2, which recounts the engagement of the Romans, under Germanicus, with the Bructeri, under Arminius, and includes a brilliant flashback to the annihilation by the Bructeri, on the same site some six years earlier, of the Roman legions commanded by Varus. To watch Bidart iterate and change and reiterate Tacitus, in this context of the Roman return to the Teutoburgian Wood, is to take an intensive course in storytelling. Tacitus is gripping, and Bidart adds the dimension of the work itself in progress, so that now when we read of Germanicus' general Caecina and his troops following orders "to reconnoitre the dismal / treacherous passes, to attempt to build bridges and / causeways across the uneven sodden marshland," we find their actions refracted in Bidart's renderings of Tacitus' prose. Each line break and stanza break is a deep pass to be negotiated, each rhetorical stratagem a contribution to the route with its "bridges and causeways" (that unexpected rhyme *en passant* of *and* with *marshland* makes one little bridge) that returns us to the time and place of the earlier catastrophe.

That "catastrophe": Varus' defeat? Germanicus' sortie itself? In Tacitus, though Arminius escapes for a time, the Germans are massacred. Bidart, however, ends ominously: "Arminius, relentlessly pursued by / Germanicus, retreated into pathless country." The effect in Bidart's conclusion—strikingly like that in the conclusion to Elizabeth Bishop's "Brazil, January 1, 1502," surely another one of his "pre-existing forms"—is that of an endlessly frustrating mission. And indeed Arminius remained a thorn in the Roman side for some time. Or is that earlier catastrophe a preceding attempt to versify Tacitus? The reader coming backwards into this poem from "The Second Hour of the Night" at the book's end might well call up Eliot in "East Coker," who learns that "what there is to conquer / By strength and submission, has already been discovered / Once or twice or several times" and that "each venture / Is a new beginning, a raid on the inarticulate, / With shabby equipment always deteriorating."(In this context, one earlier venture will have been by Pound, whose own poem "The Return," which an impressed Yeats compared to a sight translation of an unknown Greek masterpiece, seems to lament the passage of classical heroes, much abused in the process, into the modern era. The poem most *like* Pound's "The Return" in Bidart's book is, however, "A Coin for Joe, with the Image of a Horse; c. 550–525 B.C.") Bidart's first-person speaker, for his part, has just two lines, the poem's penultimate sentence, perfectly consonant with this last gloss: "I have returned here a thousand times, / though history cannot tell its location." The point might well be Eliot's in "The Dry Salvages," "We are only undefeated / Because we have gone on trying," and in "Little Gidding":

> We shall not cease from exploration
> And the end of all our exploring
> Will be to arrive where we started
> And know the place for the first time.

The motif of the voyage, important in *Four Quartets*, figures also in the longest poem in *Desire*, "The Second Hour of the Night" (with its "infinitely varied / voyagings in storm and in calm"), which recurs to another motif in Eliot, desire itself. In *Four Quartets*, of course, desire is a two-edged sword. At one and the same time desire turns us toward God (Love, stillness) and yet, precisely because it entails movement, remains of this world. So

> Desire itself is movement
> Not in itself desirable;
> Love is itself unmoving,
> Only the cause and end of movement.
> ("Little Gidding," 5)

"The Second Hour of the Night," in contrast, stresses desire and movement—or "appetency," in Eliot's term. Another of Bidart's inspired collages, this poem's materials include parts of Hector Berlioz's poignant recollection in his *Memoirs* of the death of his wife, Henriette, with its numerous glances back at the tortuous history of their relationship, which in turn began with his fierce desire for an actress whom he didn't even know, and sections of Ovid's version of the tale of Myrrha and Cinyras, her father (a tale put by Ovid in the mouth of Orpheus), whose incestuous coupling, made inevitable by her unquenchable desire for him, led to the conception of Adonis. These two plots, each more agonizing than the other, are framed and fleshed out by a tender third (which might be more or less original or might have its origin in Er's vision in book 10 of Plato's *Republic* or in Plotinus' discussions of reincarnation), according to which the soul after death seeks the body of a congenial former being in which to return to the physical world—though *soul* and *body* are ambiguous terms, to be sure, since throughout this poem the understanding is once more that "We fill pre-existing forms and when we fill them change them and are changed."

Beginning at last to suspect that such glossing as the preceding will be useful if at all only to readers with at least a cursory knowledge of "The Second Hour of the Night," I find myself wanting to stand back from the poem and to remind us of some general observations that might have ramifications as well for the whole of *Desire*. For one thing, Bidart's handling of the narrative here is an exemplary intercalation of desire and deferral. Like the book as a whole, the poem keeps intimating completion and staving it off, so that the reader is continually shuttling back and forth and shuffling its parts. For another, the poem animates (gives *anima* to) vessels that we might in our self-assurance have thought beyond resuscitation (here Berlioz and Ovid, elsewhere Plotinus and Marcus Aurelius). For yet another thing, the poem reminds us, both by way of refrain ("*Four steps forward then / one back, then three / back, then four forward*") and by way of theme ("*thy son whose sister is his mother / in secrecy conceived within / the mother whose brother is her son*": somewhere William Faulkner positively wriggles with satisfaction), that to go forward is to go back. If pastiche is the defining characteristic of the postmodern, Bidart is its poetic master.

183

Whose heart doesn't sink when the reviewer, at such a juncture, takes a shallow breath and continues, "X could not be more different from Y, and yet . . ."? And yet there's no straighter way from Bidart's *Desire* to C. K. Williams's *The Vigil* than the dividing line of difference—unless it's the connecting line of high achievement. Or perhaps the "line" of Eliot, now that I ponder the matter further. In any event, I am confident that Walt Whitman—himself a progenitor of that last line, who promised near the end of the last century, in regard to "the needs and possibilities of American imaginative literature," that there was in the future "a boundless field to fill," just as there had been in the universe's origins an infinite space to occupy, before the advent of "the definitely-form'd worlds themselves, duly compacted, clustering in systems, hung up there, chandeliers of the universe, beholding and mutually lit by each other's lights"—that Whitman himself would embrace alike the far-flung constellations of Bidart and Williams. Where Bidart meticulously selects and arranges a multitude of extant materials and makes them cohere to new effects, Williams pursues a confessional mode that mostly eschews allusion, never mind extensive quotation, and that offers a reader virtually nothing to think about (nothing!) except contemporary American English itself. When Williams entitles a poem "My Fly," he might well invite us to consider not only irrelevant sartorial details but also such predecessors as James Merrill's "The House Fly," Yeats's "The Long-Legged Fly," and Emily Dickinson's "I heard a fly buzz—when I died," but he doesn't demand that we do any homework, even though his poem is dedicated to the memory of the well-known sociologist (evidently his friend or mentor) Erving Goffman. On the contrary, he asks us to follow, through its faultlessly thoughtless path of evasion, "One of those great, garishly emerald flies that always looks generated from fresh excrement" to its escape, through a window opened by the poet, in "one final moment of felicity," its "brilliant ardent atom swerving through" in a kind of minimalist rebirth (perhaps reminiscent, though not certainly so, of the conclusion of John Barth's *Chimera*).

As "My Fly" suggests, *desire*—or "ardor," to introduce his recurrent term—is a major theme in Williams's new volume, too, though of course that circumstance won't distinguish *The Vigil* from many other volumes. What will begin to distinguish *The Vigil* from most contemporary work is its combination of transparency, seemingly unfiltered emotion, insistently lucid reflection, including carefully calculated transitions, and tight syntactic and prosodic control. Like Bidart's verse—or rather, *un*like Bidart's, which features fractures rather than parallelisms—Williams's verse is "free," so my use of *prosodic* pertains to line and stanza rather than foot. More like Whitman than, say, Sharon Olds, to pick a contemporary who also aspires to a certain transparency, Williams almost never enjambs and instead breaks his lines and his stanzas at syntactical and "logical" units, so that the effect is of a Jamesian discourse, with its discriminations and differentiations heightened and hence more immediate. Williams's verse has what Robert Pinsky identified years ago as "prose virtues."

The Vigil is framed by poems about women, whom I take to offer versions of the lyric Muse. In the book's first poem, the principal is a neighbor, a resident in a "firetrap in the Village." Here is the volume's gutsy opening stanza, characteristic in the expansiveness of its lines, the directness of its language, the length of its period, and the amplitude of its detail, which involves the use at the outset of more modifiers than most workshop teachers would sanction:

> Her five, horrid, deformed little dogs, who incessantly yap
>   on the roof under my window,
> her cats, god knows how many, who must piss on her rugs—
>   her landing's a sickening reek;
> her shadow, once, fumbling the chain on the door, then the
>   door slamming fearfully shut:
> only the barking, and the music, jazz, filtering as it does day
>   and night into the hall.

Characteristic, too, is the scrupulous construction: the syntactical parallelism of the first three lines—complemented by the ever tighter focus (roof, landing, door with a glimpse on an interior)—and the rounding out of the whole by the repetition of the barking, only to have it all sprung open by that one mitigating factor, the music. The music that the poet proceeds to specify is a song by Chris Connor—a jazz singer in the dark, husky-voiced mode of Anita O'Day—whose "Lush Life," popular in the 1960s, was a favorite of the poet's "college sweetheart," whom he not only left high and dry but then humiliated, one night thirty-odd years ago, when she was drunk and trying to make up with him at a party. In the poet's imagination, though he declines to make the connection explicit, the image of the old girlfriend must transfer to the neighbor, whose own voice is "hoarse, harsh, hollow," when she calls out to her dogs (or seems to), "Come back, darlings, come back, dear ones, my sweet angels, come back." (Bidart might have made something of the link with MacDuff's famous lament; Williams, though he goes on to refer us to Medea, does not.)

While his neighbor in effect repeats his girlfriend's pathetic plea, she also articulates Williams's own feelings when he remembers his unconscionably cold rejection of his "old love," and behind both the neighbor and the poet is the haunting voice of Chris Connor singing of "regrets and depletions." Williams epitomizes the network of longing and sorrow that the poem sketches in clearly Whitmanian fashion (the parallel triplings, the rhetorical question, the attraction to intersections) near its end: "What pathways through pain, what junctures of vulnerability, what crossings and counterings?"

If "the god of frenzied, inexhaustible love" presides over the volume's first poem, a related force pervades its last poem, "Old Man": "always the erotic murmur—I'm hardly myself if I'm not in a state of incipient desire." The unlikely triad of women in "The Neighbor" repeats itself here in the figure of the poet's wife, a recollected pre–World War II studio portrait of "an absolute angel" of a Polish girl who later "died in the camps," and a photo on a newsstand's magazine—featuring a "*Special: Big Tits*"—of a "lush, fresh-lipped blonde . . . with her sham heat and her bosom probably plumped with gel." Although she is as much a "counterfeit Venus" as "The Neighbor" is a caricature of the girlfriend, or a déclassé muse, this blonde, tripartite in her last invocation (in the final three-line stanza), is also more than that, in spite of herself:

> Vamp, siren, seductress, how much more she reveals in her
>   glare of ink than she knows;
> how she incarnates our desperate human need for regard,
>   our passion to live in beauty,
> to be beauty, to be cherished, by glances if by no more, of
>   something like love, or love.

In "Spider Psyche," Williams's "ardor" manifests itself as "want." An extraordinary meditation, this poem is seamlessly unpunctuated, so that it can distill its whole being into one utterance. Its "mummified spider," at the brink of death "in its own web," is explicitly not "human" but, magically, somehow human at the same time, perhaps partly because mummification is a human process, partly because the poem's syntax mimics the web that holds the spider, and perhaps partly because the spider turns out to have had its own "psyche." Indeed, precisely by virtue of that psyche, the spider, this "tiny nub," becomes a concentrated particle of all life in the dense network of the universe. Remarkably like the fly, that "brilliant ardent atom," driven by an unfathomable desire, the dying spider *wants*—"you want / no matter what this last moment of holding . . . / even if brain swoons nearly trying to hold its last thought last fusion of will and cognition"—with the result that "there is no end in this ending no contingent condition of being this glare of perception / hurl of sensation all one sense and intention act and love my psyche my spider love and hope." So the poem takes us as close as it can get us to the impossible, infinite point or endless instant in which "the wave of not-here take[s] the shore-edge of here," when the self acknowledges "its portion / of being the blare of light in the corner the grain in the wood and the old odors and the space" of the entire hylozoic universe—which is again not unlike Augustine's notion of deity, with a fulcrum everywhere (spider-nub, wood-knot, psyche) and a perimeter nowhere. Using the first person plural for the only time, the poem ends with a little prayer of proleptic gratitude for becoming one with "all we ever wanted" and of course without a full stop:

> take us dear spider of self into your otherness into having
> > once been and the knowledge of having
> in all this been once in wonder so every instant was thanks
> > and all else was beneath and adrift
> my spider psyche all awe now all we ever wanted to be now
> > in this great gratitude gone[.]

Other poems here that effloresce from quotidian origins to spectacular conclusions include "The Hovel" and "Cave." "The Hovel" begins to build itself from "Slate scraps, split stone, third hand splintering lumber" and continues through a bitter, millennia-long accumulation of abjection and wrenching particulars—"rags, flies, stench . . . crops charred, wife ravished, children starved, stolen, enslaved"—to an image of Everyman in his natural habitat:

> Back bent, knees shattered, teeth rotting; fever and lesion,
> > the physical knowledge of evil;
> illiterate, numb, insensible, superstitious, lurching from lust
> > to hunger to unnameable dread:
> the true history I inhabit, its sea of suffering, its wave to
> > which I am froth, scum.

In contrast, a kind of companion poem to "The Hovel," there is "Cave," which discovers its proto-human speaker, a veritable Caliban, lurking in a "lobe of a cave" surrounded by "cracked-open, gnawed-open bones" in a "Cold, cold ending; rain rising and ending, ever menacing night circling." In this instance, however, the despair—now that of Lear rather than Caliban—gives way through "dream" and "ardor" to a kind of "singing; toneless, nearly . . . but singing":

> Not yet in a garden, of morality or of mind, not yet in the
> > shimmering prisms of reflection,
> there must still be past the prattle and haggle of breath
> > some aspiration to propel me.
>
> A gust of upgroaning ardor, flurries of sad meditation,
> > nostalgia for so much already lost:
> in a stumble of uncountable syllables spun from pulse and
> > passion something sings, and I sing.

In its insinuation of a creation ex nihilo, of a precipitation of "aspiration" out of nothing but "breath" and the attendant etymological pun, this poem recalls other remarkable recent poems of desire, including Robert Pinsky's "The Want Bone," in which the "mouthbones of a shark" washed up on a shore make a "welded-open shape," a rictus, an "O," which naught nevertheless frames a song of desire, and the last section of Galway Kinnell's *The Book of Nightmares,* in which, when at the end

> there is nothing, nothing
> left,
> in the rust of old cars,
> . . . .
> in river-mist smelling of the weariness of stones,
> the dead lie,
> empty, filled, at the beginning,
> and the first
> voice comes craving again out of their mouths.

To these poems we might add the concluding stanzas of John Berryman's "Homage to Mistress Bradstreet" ("I renounce not even . . . nothing" and "In the rain of pain & departure, still / Love has no body and presides the sun, / and elfs from silence melody") and Eliot's "East Coker," in which the dull round of mortality—its ecclesiastical subjects inexorably keeping

> The time of the seasons and the constellations
> The time of milking and the time of harvest
> The time of the coupling of man and woman
> And that of beasts

in their dance of "Dung and death"—somehow yields the seedphrase *Dawn points.*

In Williams's confessional mode, then, as well as in Bidart's postmodern collages, we find traces of Eliot's *Quartets* (which sequence is incidentally the first major modern poem that I know of to be called "confessional"—by Robert Lowell, then a very young poet, in an appreciative review). In fact, Williams's sequence entitled "Symbols," which makes up part 2 of his book, concludes with a poem called "Garden" that has overtones of Eliot's rose garden. As in "Burnt Norton," for instance, a bird shows the poet the way, and in the final lines stillness, rose, and world intersect:

> Then, on my hand beside me on the bench, something, I
>   thought somebody else's hand, alighted;
> I flinched it off, and saw—sorrow!—a warbler, grey, black,
>   yellow, in flight already away.
> It stopped near me in a shrub, though, and waited, as
>   though unstartled, as though unafraid,
>
> as though to tell me my reflex of fear was no failure, that if
>   I had believed I had lost something,
> I was wrong, because nothing can be lost, of the self, of a
>   lifetime of bringing forth selves.
> Then it was gone, its branch springing back empty: still oak,
>   though, still rose, still world.

"The Bed" ends with a similar vision of a unified world, this time associated explicitly with a new beginning. Many beds that are the sites of seemingly endless suffering and tribulation through this utterly original poem come together in the end, even as the poem's alternating voices—one confessional, in italics, and one impersonal, in roman print—also couple. Its last lines conjure Whitman (who in the wake of his experience as a nurse testified that "I was the man, I suffered, I was there" and who could thus conceive of himself as a "kosmos") and Wallace Stevens ("The palm at the end of the mind" in "Of Mere Being") as well as Eliot (who also knew that *patience* comes from a root meaning "to suffer"):

> *I echoed, I knelled, I sobbed and repented, I bandaged the*
>   *wrists, sighed for embryos lost.*
>
> A nation of beds, a cosmos, then, how could it still happen,
>   the bed at the end of the world,
> as welcoming as the world, ark, fortress, light and delight,
>   the other beds all forgiven, forgiving.
>
> *A bed that sang through the darkness and woke in song as*
>   *though world itself had just wakened;*
> *two beds fitted together as one; bed of peace, patience, arrival,*
>   *bed of unwaning ardor.*

If these lines are also sanguine, in the very teeth of the poem's admission of the evils of the world, they seem to me representative of *The Vigil* as a whole. The word *vigil*, in all its contemporary uses, suggests a night watch (*watch* itself seems to come from the same Proto-Indo-European root) that precedes a morning revival (*wake, vigor,* and *reveille* derive from the same source). In this various light, then, to borrow from Andrew Marvell, Williams's "Storm" strikes me as a nearly plausible epitome of a volume that is, however, too variegated to be summed up. "Storm" begins with an "interminable, intermittently torrential dark afternoon downpour" and works up by degrees to an apocalypse: "twelve vast suns of purification . . . then twelve cosmic cycles of rain: no tree / left, no birdsong, / only the [*nota bene*] vigilant, acid waves." And then it surprises us and at last falls into place with this epiphanic tercet:

> Imagine then the emergence: Oh, this way, the sky streaked,
>   Oh, that way, with miraculous brightness;
> imagine us, beginning again, timid and tender, with a
>   million years more this time to evolve,
> an epoch more on all fours, stricken with shame and
>   repentance, before we fire our forges.

At just this point, as Fortune would have it, I've come across a review of Bidart's *Deisre,* by one Adam Kirsch, in the *New Republic.* A long if thoroughly bemused castigation of the book that I began this review by praising, it condemns (along with several epiphenomena) an element I'd meant to conclude by extolling in these two quite different volumes: the "attempt to see beyond the everyday into a dimly apprehended perfection." Bidart, it seems to Kirsch, is "always looking past the actual" toward "the ideal," and thus he is subject to the same disabling criticisms as "Wordsworth and Eliot"—as well as, by implication, Plato, Plotinus, Augustine, Milton, John Donne, George Herbert, William Blake, "the Romantics," any mystic one cares to mention, Gerard Manley Hopkins, Whitman, Hart Crane, H.D. . . . As antidotes to such pernicious idealistic influences, Kirsch offers "the Tennyson of *In Memoriam* [as though the poet were of a single materialist mind during the seventeen years he wrote his tortuous elegy], Matthew Arnold [whom until now I had thought was the author of "Thyrsis" and "The Scholar Gipsy"], the underappreciated George Meredith, Thomas Hardy, Philip Larkin, and late-period Robert Lowell [as though this figure, too, even if the "late period" were definable, were somehow monolithic]."

The argument in its nutshell, naturalistic and moralistic at once if I may say so, is that "we live most deeply when we live *in* the world, not when we are straining to see beyond the horizon or beneath 'the unexceptionable surface.'" Hmm. But wait one Paterian moment: what if living "in the world" somehow *involved* "straining to see beyond" the empirical, as, for instance, Bidart's stoical model Marcus Aurelius himself notably strained—not to mention Søren Kierkegaard (pastmaster of irony, the one scheme and trope that Kirsch explicitly approves), and Rainer Maria Rilke, Yeats, and Stevens, to pick at random a few more thinkers on the subject. And what if living truly most intensely "in" the world even *entailed* a vision of something beyond it? These are questions—ineradicable and perhaps unresolvable and unrecognized by the *New Republic*'s reviewer—that are raised by both Bidart and Williams. Indeed, one thing that sets them apart from most of the poets and reviewers of the late twentieth century is their willingness to think in eschatological terms. That, and the attention (each in his own way) to the poetic line, which is of course itself a matter of nothing if not ending and beginning.

The Poetics of Plash and Speed

It is now finally clear enough that postmodernism, still alive and thriving even at the century's end, right along with its classical mate and nemesis modernism, began in Eden. If Adam, our protomodernist, earnestly dubbing his animals and plants, acted in the name of definition and fixity, of things as they were and thus should be, playful Eve, uneasy with hierarchy and alert to new possibilities, spoke up on behalf of change—or the cultivation of mystery rather than mastery. One of Eve's eloquent successors was Walt Whitman, who in *Democratic Vistas* foresaw (as other romantics, including Wordsworth and Coleridge, had periodically foreseen before him) a "new order":

> new law-forces of spoken and written language—not merely the pedagogue forms, correct, regular, familiar with precedents, made for matters of outside propriety, fine words, thoughts definitely told out—but a language fann'd by the breath of Nature, which leaps overhead, cares mostly for impetus and effects, and for what it plants and invigorates to grow—tallies life and character, and seldomer tells a thing than suggests or necessitates it [a riveting alternative]. In fact, a new theory of literary composition for imaginative works of the very first class, and especially for highest poems, is the sole course open to these States. Books are to be call'd for, and supplied, on the assumption that the process of reading is not a half-sleep, but, in [the] highest sense, an exercise, a gymnast's struggle; that the reader is to do something for himself, must be on the alert, must himself or

---

Review of *Smokes* by Susan Wheeler and *Going Fast* by Frederick Seidel. From *The Yale Review,* Winter, 1999.

herself [this circumspection in 1868, mind you] construct indeed the poem . . . —the text furnishing the hints, the clue, the start or frame-work.

Whitman advocates a heuristic, imprudent process, a kind of improvised pas de deux between composed page and deciphering mind, implicitly preceded by an equally athletic relationship between blank page and composing mind, that will turn out to be better or worse but in no case perfect or final. Promulgating new forms and correspondingly fresh responses, he makes the case for a poetry that is original and resistant, a poetry that unabashedly contains multitudes of meanings and points of view and yet expects to be read within the provisional parameters it makes bold to chalk out.

It's hard to imagine Susan Wheeler reacting to Whitman's desiderata with anything but applause and huzzahs. Her own poetry—*Bag 'o' Diamonds* and most recently *Smokes*, chosen for publication by Robert Hass, who has written an engaging afterword—characteristically gets along like a wildfire: "fann'd by the breath of Nature," if I may, it "leaps overhead," values above all momentum and discovery, and propagates itself by means of the barest contiguities. To put the point another way, if all poems have specific enemies, and if all good poems resist those enemies, it is clear that two of Wheeler's poems' enemies are regularity and predictability. A basic principle of her poetics is "That each second escorts a fresh plash. . . . Its drive is for the offbeat, the cack-handed, the apocopated. It sings with regret for its thrum" ("Clock Radio"). Her personae are slippery as soap in the shower, her narratives are discontinuous, her juxtapositions are sometimes inexplicable even in retrospect, and her range of reference is catholic, so that hymns, cartoons, fairy tales, slogans, and literary classics collide as in a pile-up on a foggy freeway. It is perhaps less apparent that her poems' other enemies include arbitrariness and randomness. I am thinking in part of her frequent use of conventional infrastructures—couplets, rhymed quatrains, sonnets, a pantoum, a ballad—and in part of her steely grammatical and syntactical control. In this last respect she is unlike John Ashbery—to whom one of her poems is dedicated and with whom she certainly has affinities—who is known for his liberal and inspired use of anacoluthon, fuzzy antecedent, dangling modifier, and other staples of undergraduate essays. She likes oddball puns and neologisms, but she perpetrates fewer of the latter than a cursory reader might surmise. (As far as I know, for example, while *garp* does not exist, John Irving notwithstanding, nor does *masticulate,* though Lewis Carroll is somewhere green with envy, *cackhanded* means more or less "with shitty fingers," and *fribbling* means "faltering, feeble, or frivolous"—as the *Oxford English Dictionary* will attest.)

Because Wheeler's poems live so insistently from moment to moment, they are difficult to excerpt or to summarize, so perhaps I'll be forgiven for walking us (according to my lights) through a poem or two. (*Caveat lector:* you might find yourself following as it were in the steps of the proverbial bloodhound, who would run out on to the lawn after his owner, in clear view and only yards away, and yet zig and zag for a couple of minutes because he didn't want to know where the man was but how he had gotten there.) "Run on a Warehouse" is a poem in two parts, with seven quatrains in part 1 and three quatrains in part 2. In the first part—which was originally published by itself in a journal—the quatrains rhyme *axax,* and the meter alternates between iambic and trochaic lines (or, to preempt dispute, between rising and falling rhythms). That seems ordinary enough, but here are the opening stanzas:

> What he had said came back to him.
> Sectioned seat, sectioned seat.
> The lift caught wind and swayed him in.
> Big armoire, big armoire.
>
> For some time he had felt it stir.
> Sideboard door, sideboard door.
> He sashayed through the conifers.
> Dad's chair, dad's chair.
>
> He had not known how far he'd come.
> The blanket chest, the blanket chest.
> A sourceless light suffused the run.
> Love seat, love seat.

Far from conventional, then, these stanzas might seem at first perversely enigmatic. But by the time we have digested the poem, we have begun to see that Wheeler is interposing narratives. In the odd-numbered lines she is sketching out a story, which I like to think of as Hitchcockian, about a man with a mission on a snowy mountain. (The *Run* of the title is a ski run.) In each of the even-numbered lines she doubles up an item in a furniture sale at a warehouse. By virtue of the influence of the first narrative, we can imagine someone strolling among these items just as the other figure moves through "the conifers." (*Run* also signifies an overwhelming response to an ad for the sale.) At the middle of this section—the fourth of its seven stanzas—the two quests dovetail:

> He had not come for his own sake.
> All fixtures new, fixtures new.
> Before the end he'd need to break.
> Wall to wall, wall to wall.

Of course "he" did not come for his own sake. In this field of force he came for the sake of his alter ego in the other narrative, who, for someone else's sake, is searching through the warehouse inventory. At the same time that this "someone else" has to be the "he" of the first plot, their relationship is a convenient metaphor for the relationship of writer and reader, both searching something out, who must convene à la Whitman for the poem's sake.

In the following stanzas the way seems to be lost in a kind of whiteout that is ironically paralleled by the plethora of "wall to wall" offerings:

> So buckily he bore his load.
> Filigreed frame, filigreed frame.
> He could not see the lodge for snow.
> Canopied bed, canopied bed.

But there is hope. The whimsical and the careful might cooperate, like two searchers, or indeed like the random and the orderly:

> He'll not forget the moment soon.
> Cuckoo clock, cuckoo clock.
> Now over snow a glimpse of moon.
> Savvy desk, savvy desk.

Precisely savvy and charmingly cuckoo at once, this first part concludes with a muted epiphany that immediately undermines itself:

> There were but two things he required.
> Glass breakfront, glass breakfront.
> The slope was steep and he was tired.
> Just a hutch, just a hutch.

As the form has led us to suspect all along, with its meshing plots and its mirrorings in every other line, the "two things . . . required" really amount to one, which point Wheeler makes ingeniously in several ways, first by reiterating (as her nonce form requires) the single item "glass breakfront"—a move adumbrated by the earlier line, "Before the end he'd need to break." Again, in the last line, the "hutch" that is a *chest* in the warehouse plot is a temporary *shelter* in the mountain-climbing plot. But Wheeler shies from closure even here and confesses that she has at best—as the reader has—"just a hunch." (The approximateness of that pun is an earmark of the postmodern; you wouldn't find it in Eliot or Pound or Williams.)

Part 2 of the poem picks up the stubborn impulse to regularity or continuity, as a "heathen man" comes down out of the hills to argue that "there has to be / A way to bargain that will instead / Be harbingers or history"—which proposition, however, his little postmodern congregation rudely dismisses:

> How come, one said, and then one of each
> Joined in finding an earnest fool
> The gentleman with the counterpoint
> Who could not get the present rule.

Having served in part as "The gentleman with the counterpoint," as "heathen man" is now called, or as a methodist who cannot quite acknowledge the "rule" of randomness, this reader is prepared to retire—only to be stopped on the way out by the final stanza's unexpected and vehement admission that this whole poem has been the product after all of some regrettable factitiousness: "What frippery. This narrative could not / Have less to do with whim. I'm bored." Yet in this evidently interminable tergiversation or flirtatiousness "whim" seems to get the last word: "It's now that the bodice and the dots / Become the hedge for wonders scored." If *hedge* means a counterbalancing investment, as in this very image of "bodice and dots" where the reassertion of whim defends against what to the poet has come to seem an excess of composition, or "scoring," the poem rather wonderfully completes itself precisely by opposing itself. Such a structure might even be said to close by virtue of its insistence on openness.

Wheeler's fondness for disjunction has ramifications for the "voice" in her poems and for her implicit definition of "self." Like the work of many of the Language poets and other postmodernists, her poems are permeable by all manner of speech and sponsor heterogeneous points of view. In lieu of the more or less dramatic monologist characteristic of many confessional and neoformalist lyrics alike, Wheeler can rustle up at a moment's notice a little crowd of voices—as in "Run on a Warehouse," where the speaker's voice gives way to that of heathen man, which is in turn overwhelmed by different responses from his audience. Michael Palmer has explained in an interview how for him and others of a similar sensibility "language inhabits" the poet, whose work consequently sponsors "a whole variety of selves and nonselves which propose themselves as language on the page." In *The Changing Light at Sandover,* James Merrill, to invoke a quite different kind of postmodernist, describes a related feeling of being the host for innumerable selves in the way that the body's cytoplasm is the host for mitochondria. On this view of things, the poet is not so much a speaker or a maker as a listener or a transmitter; in Palmer's phrase, the poet "learns to listen to the poem as it unfolds."

This position has an analogue if not a source in Mallarmé's thought ("the pure poem entails the elocutionary disappearance of the poet, who grants the initiative to the words") and bears a close relationship to the speculations of Mikhail Bakhtin about dialogism—though Bakhtin would be surprised to hear it. Bakhtin, who didn't care about poetry and seems not to have read Mallarmé, proposed that "the poetic symbol presupposes the unity of a voice with which it is identical, and it presupposes that such a voice is completely alone in its discourse. As soon as another's voice, another's accent, the possibility of another's point of view breaks through this play of the symbol, the poetic plane is destroyed." Enter the writer of fiction, who "takes a completely different path" and "welcomes the heteroglossia and diversity of the literary and extraliterary language into his work.... It is in fact out of this stratification of language ... that he constructs his style." While Bakhtin's notions about poetry are patronizing, convenient, and circular, one might use his thoughts on heteroglossia to approach much postmodern poetry—poetry almost written to contravene his view of the genre, one might say—including Palmer's own little echo chambers, Ashbery's eerie orchestras, and Berryman's cacophonous *Dream Songs*.

Wheeler's "Notes" point out two allusions to Berryman, one of which is in her volume's last line, "Bone collating—now *that's* a job," which implicitly acknowledges her reconstruction of earlier writers, but his spirit hovers over other poems too, perhaps most notably "Ethic":

> Manman got a special s'rup 't cures the lonelies.
> All the night, up the tree'f the pickling shed
> Ise drinking from it elixir.
>
> Afters the sunup the hacked meat it come.
> The truck it seethes on its brakes and the driver he look
> Ise singing from t'friendly tree.
>
> Then it smote. What business was mine
> in the cardboard rune, in the native rap?
> I on the tree stump, I missing all.

If Berryman's interlocutor's lingo parodies the speech of the vaudeville end-man, which speech itself is a parody of vernacular African American, this poem reads at first like a parody at third remove—whatever that might mean. How else to explain the awkward elisions (I take "syrup that cures" and "tree off the pickling shed" to be the expanded phrases) and the implausible solecisms, especially in the presence of words like *elixir, smote,* and *rune*? If we extend that hypothesis, we can perhaps understand the poem not as a blatant imitation or send-up of Berryman but as a sympathetic criticism of him—and in the first place of the mode of this very poem, at once a "rune" and a "ru'n" or "ruin." (Harking back to those other odd elisions, I cannot but notice that *Ethic* is potentially a shortened form of *Ethnic*.)

The poem's last lines, quoted earlier, aptly suggest that the white poet might well have no right to "the native rap" or to this intermittent pseudo-dialect, since she or he would be "missing all" the experience that it arises from and bodies forth. The further achievement of this scrappy little poem, however, is that, even as it confesses its experiential inadequacy, it tries to represent a part of that missing experience affectingly. To put that another way, "Ethic" is a riddle poem, and the question is, "What business was mine?" Beyond the answer to the rhetorical question noted earlier, one answer is "none," because African Americans could have no "business" at all in this country for long after they were brought here. (Bringing them here was a business that they were not part of, so to speak.) Beyond that answer and even as a consequence there is another: "suicide." It will be an indication of the fineness of Wheeler's textures that this inference is indirectly borne out by a reference in her author's notes, in regard to *another* poem, to Flannery O'Connor's story "The Lame Shall Enter First," in which a child "hanged herself." In Wheeler's other poem, "Exemplification Avenue," the child, "swinging back and forth beneath the / attic's peak, misses the telescope." ("Misses," precisely.) It's no accident that the speaker in "Ethic" is "swinging" from a tree and that he is "missing all." In this lurid "sunup" light, the astonishment of the packing company's truck driver makes logical sense—and his merchandise, "hacked meat," makes metaphoric sense.

Wheeler's lovely, difficult, poignant, eccentric "Beavis' Day Off" is a tour de force of different perspectives:

> He'd been doing a lot of cull-twanging,
> he thought, walking back and forth on the deck
> of his battleship *whoa! correction:* loft.
>
> Small fires burned on the outskirts of Soho;
> Fanelli's lit up under a stickered sky:
> cirrus pitched to the top of its firmament.
>
> How long could he crimp the diesel in the dark?
> the bedlam was breathing its own air now;
> the parrot shivering in the freezer glared at the hen.
>
> *Please it's time* said Meg. And each infernal
> truism struck a package deal for tin.
>
> What hast thou, O nut job, with paradise?
> The sparks O they crested the floor then they floated
> and she lay down on fine braids and she cried.

At the poem's outset the speaker nominally distinguishes herself from Beavis, but it is soon apparent that much of the poem is as though from his point of view—whoever "he" may be beyond the dismayingly popular TV character. We hear his voice at its purest in "*whoa! correction,*" when he catches himself up as it were in the middle of a loony fantasy—by virtue of which he has transformed his SoHo loft, evidently not far from the venerable Fanelli's Cafe on Prince Street, into a "battleship"—but the one voice fades into the other. If there are also overtones of Ahab, they would comport with the rest of the poem, since one of its most important voices is that of another famous paranoid. Though Ezra Pound is never named, Wheeler alludes to him (as her notes confirm) in the first line of the final stanza; and meanwhile (or so I suspect) he begins to emerge by way of Elizabeth Bishop's poem about him, "Visits to St. Elizabeths." St. Elizabeths, the hospital to which Pound was committed following his trial for treason and the court's finding of insanity, is known in Bishop's inspired adaptation of the form of "The House That Jack Built" as "The house of Bedlam." Moreover, one of her central figures is a "sailor" who seems to believe he is (as of course he *is*) at sea, since his progress is associated with "a roadstead all of board," "a creaking sea of board," and so on. In Bishop's poem the sailor and the other specified figures—a widowed "Jew in a newspaper hat," "a boy that pats the floor / to see if the world is there, is flat," a "soldier home from the war," and "the poet," who cast himself as Odysseus in the *Cantos*—all bleed into one another, until "bedlam" seems a kind of magnification of the poet himself. In Wheeler's poem the "compound ghost," to borrow Eliot's phrase, in addition to Ol' Possum himself, master of ventriloquism and polyphony (*"Please it's time* said Meg"), the Beavis of the animated cartoon (and probably not Bevis of Hampton, though Wheeler might welcome in this context the themes of exile and imprisonment in the Anglo-Norman ballad), Ezra Pound, and of course the original speaker—or listener—herself.

"What hast thou, O nut job, with paradise?"—the last stanza's first line—exemplifies the delicacy of these relationships. The nominal speaker, Wheeler qua poet, reminds us that even as he was in the psychiatric ward Pound was writing the later *Cantos*, which are explicitly in search of "paradise." (His actual situation, in contrast, is implied in the allusion to *The Waste Land* and the reference to the "infernal," as well as those astonishing stand-ins for the mad patients, the parrot and the hen.) At the same time, the framing terms in Wheeler's line derive from the opening of Pound's lyric of some forty years before his confinement, "Blandula, Tenella, Vagula":

> What hast thou, O my soul, with paradise?
> Will we not rather, when our freedom's won,
> Get us to some clear place wherein the sun
> Lets drift in on us through the olive leaves
> A liquid glory.

So to all the other voices we must add that of the young Pound, who as Christine Froula has informed us was himself echoing Hadrian and Marcus Aurelius, and who is here ironically maneuvered into admonishing his aging, tragic self. As Wheeler surely wants us to realize, when his freedom *was* won from St. Elizabeths, Pound took himself off to the "clear place" of Italy, where he could meditate under the olives. Her concluding lines heighten the complexity of the emotional chord struck at the same time that they end the poem with an arabesque embellishment: "The sparks O they crested the floor when they floated / and she lay down on fine braids and she cried." The female figure cannot but conjure the poet, whose sympathy, admiration, and repugnance the poem has so magically braided together. As Wheeler well knows, a "cull" is a dupe, as was the Pound infatuated by Mussolini, and *to twang* used to mean "to thrust through." But there is another, broader sense in which this poem is indeed some kind of "cull-twanging," which is to say a combination of diverse motifs and voices (a "cull" is also a selection) played as though on a musical instrument. Even in its flourish of a conclusion, then, the poem frays out in other directions, and all in all it strikes me as a good example of what N. Katherine Hayles identifies in *Chaos Bound,* her book on postmodern literature and science, as "orderly disorder" or "nonlinear dynamics."

Most of Wheeler's other poems similarly invite the reader to discover coherence in—or at least to negotiate—the apparently chaotic. In "Carnivorous Fowl, and Otherwise," for instance, the implied task is to ascertain the relationship among a good ol' boy moved to Los Angeles (near "Miracle Mile . . . the clam dogs weren't / anything to ~~right~~ write home about"), "a vixen she" whose parts call up "Mo's Ravine," and the speaker, hardly more literate than his friend, who has nonetheless read his William Carlos Williams. Here is a part of his letter home:

> Weren't long before we'd sent that one
> back up to Lonnie's Gulch, since there's no room
> for bullies here. Anyway, she ate the plums,
> the plums I was saving, plums for you.

Even when the poems' principles of selection and arrangement are not altogether clear, their parts are often irresistible. Who would not succumb to the opening of "The Blanching Heart," where the illusion of high specificity somehow emerges from a mercurial voice, which in six lines changes from the judicious through a kind of knowing Stevensian lyricism and deadpan surreal comedy to the mock literary?

> The hero, such as he was, in the classroom,
> in the evening, found the crosstalk overtaxing.
> He'd come, driving, from fields lit like rivers,
> glittering under autumnal sun.
> The machete mobile clanged;
> the instructor tipped (ho, bland) his spectacles.

The last two stanzas of "Fractured Fairy Tale" cover tremendous ground as they move from an inventive ironic commentary on intellectualism through the simplest evocation of ordinary, everyday sadness to a wild summary of this century just now breathing its postmodern last:

> Several men rest their rakes at their crotches and begin to talk.
> They are having an ur-argument. They are arguing over
> pure and impure analyticity, or error theory or a nonfactualist
> theory about ethics. It might be the Chinese Room Argument.
> The light through the elms reminds them of dinner.
> The hunger reminds them of loss.
>
> Doze Doll Does Wiz Biz—a century that, her sleeping,
> a stenotic century self-circling, noodling its tunes, drug
> by the scuff of its kitchen to stand, squinting, at *thing*
> coherent, drooping from clouds, bungeeing to boot.

Any quatrain that can invent a perfect *Daily Variety* headline for a story about the box office success of *Sleeping Beauty,* use the term *stenotic* with the word *noodling,* ring "the scruff of its neck" into a new shape altogether, and pun with a hoot on the phrase *to boot* goes more than its part of the bail for the century of which this poem, itself "self-circling," is an admitted part.

Is the postmodern especially conducive to personal inaccessibility? We have Carlos Castaneda, Thomas Pynchon, and the somewhat less invisible Don DeLillo to muse on—successors all to J. D. Salinger—but almost no poets, at least in the so-called Western world. Mallarmé's early invisibility was only aesthetic or theoretical, since he appeared and held forth at his well-known "evenings" and elsewhere, and many Language poets, regardless of hypothetical underpinnings, regularly entertain audiences. Forty years ago, when the practice seemed almost vulgar, poets who did not read in public were easily in the majority; today, most poets, published or not, thrive on readings. Frederick Seidel does not—and while I do not know that he has never read in public, I have never talked to anyone who has heard him do so. His publicist recently told me that Seidel might consider an invitation to a motorcycle race but would probably not be amenable to any other performance. I had inquired about sponsoring a reading because for years I have been an intrigued follower of the work. The first time I came across his name was when I was thinking about Robert Lowell's poems and encountered an interview with Lowell conducted by Seidel. It was a perspicacious interview, and in subsequent years I would read volumes of Seidel's own poems—*Final Solutions* was the witty title of the first book, then *Sunrise, These Days, My Tokyo,* and now *Going Fast*—with admiration. Lowell blurbed the first book by saying that "when I read [Seidel], I have envious, delighted, jolted feelings, and suspect the possibilities of modern poetry have been changed." Three decades later Seidel still writes poems so differently striking that one can hardly write about them. Like all works of highest caliber they seem to beggar description, challenge assessment, and demand to represent themselves— to be quoted.

Identifiable as they are, Seidel's poems resemble Wheeler's in certain regards, one of which is that they grip you line by line. They are so cleanly written that, in the first place, each line comes bearing its gift and that, in the second, the gift can take the form of a single, exquisite touch. "Hotel Carlyle, New York" turns out to be about an evening in 1991 when the

Prufrockian speaker "didn't dare" to make an advance to a woman. Look at how Seidel approaches the subject:

> Inside the dining room it was snowing.
> Men and linen stayed warmly candlelit.
> The gay waiters returned from the heat of the kitchen
> Unsmilingly cold as Lenin.

No sooner do we understand that it is the tablecloths that suggest snow than we are given the weirdly ineluctable substitution of *linen* for *women* and then the devastatingly antithetical off-rhyme of *linen* with *Lenin*. In spite of the poem's title and subject we are suddenly an inch away from the Russian Revolution, and the following lines, where "women" finally appear in their own right, immediately obliterate that distinction:

> Women were vast white estates
> Measured in versts.
> The chandeliers were Fabergé sleighs
> Flying behind powerful invisible horses,
> Powerful invisible forces,
> On runners of serfs over
> The foam of snowdrifts of fine linen.
> Take us
> Home from the ball
> Through the dark, in the deepening snow!

At once suavely and startlingly, conventionally and radically, the Carlyle's dining room unfolds into a vision of Russia in 1917. But art isn't life, and the conceit breaks down—or maybe art *is* life (Seidel has this effect) and *as* the conceit breaks down, the poet remembers that when the critical point came, he couldn't "overthrow" himself and "take over" at the dinner table. "Life achingly said, *Do* something. / And I didn't dare." Surely this is one proper use of the beautifully wrought: to serve as a setting for such translucently simple lines as those this poem ends on.

Seidel also recalls Wheeler in his ability to generate new "forms"—forms necessarily as bound to their occasions, that is, as they are exigent. "The Resumption of Nuclear Testing in the South Pacific," which never explicitly refers to that lamentable event, is a poem in fourteen distichs that has a stop after every three- to four-beat line and a full stop after all lines but two. In these self-imposed narrow limits it gets along by means of the smallest adjustments of the relationship between *two* and *one*. A kind of minimalist jazz, with each improvisation becoming structurally indispensable, it begins modestly enough, even unpromisingly:

> People in their love affairs.
> People in their loneliness.
>
> People in their beds alone.
> People in each other's arms.
>
> I woke up this morning.
> I went to sleep last night.
>
> I woke up this morning.
> I went to sleep last night.

Nothing's going on? The poet's treading water? But the allusion to the medieval lyric "Western Wind" and the incorporation in the last four quoted lines of a blues stanza's repetons will correct that thought. And before long, "the horrific complications," to lift a phrase from Sylvia Plath's "Little Fugue," a poem about nothing but black and white. Single people set off against couples in stanza 1 are followed in stanza 2 by an inversion of that opposition, and then we have the two "identical" stanzas. Each of these stanzas seems at first to revert to the theme of loneliness, but each of them also pairs morning with night, and it figures that in the last analysis each stanza has to do with both situations. That is, coupling hardly excludes loneliness. It is probably a prerequisite for it. The following stanzas deal out diverse other pairs, the last of which seems uncannily to have been inspired by last week's news:

> The beauty of Tahiti.
> That lagoon in Huahiné.
>
> Manta rays were mating.
> One on top the other.

> Venus with Chinese eyes,
> On the motu at Maupiti.
>
> I wish I was a head of state.
> I'd wave away my bodyguards.
>
> I'd never been unhappy.
> Now, I'd never be.

Having followed his theme into the international arena, Seidel proceeds ominously to pair two presidents and ironically to set the realm of politics and power off against the realm of love and longing:

> A *force de frappe* is Gaston Flosse.
> Tahitians always call him Gaston.
>
> Gaston did this. Gaston said that.
> Nobody better mess with Gaston!
>
> The president of French Polynesia,
> Gaston Flosse, has flown in to Paris.
>
> Their Kingfish, their Huey Long,
> Is very close to Jacques Chirac.
>
> They're strolling down the rue de Seine.
> Chirac is France's president.

The simplest means have brought the poem a long way indeed. In fact, what does it leave out? "People in each other's arms" have evolved into people in each other's *arms,* and the mating of the latter portends the annihilation of the former. Arms off arms. *Mundus idem et alter.*

Seidel is a cyclophile, as I have indicated, and the title sequence, the pièce de resistance that ends *Going Fast,* refers not only to *vita brevis* but also to brute velocity:

> Red
> As a Ducati 916, I'm crazed, I speed,
> I blaze, I bleed,
> I sight-read
> A Bach Invention.

Ducati pizzicati. How carefully plucked these rapid syllables are by the admirer of this "Invention," designed by Massimo Tamburini (whose name itself is a little musical passage), "Which ought to be in the Museum of Modern Art," this "Stradivarius / Of motorcycles," this "Donatello by way of Brancusi, smoothed simplicity," this "nightingale" that "sings . . . more sweetly than Cole Porter," that is "Slender as a girl" and "Sudden as a shark" ("Milan"). It will be apparent that the Ducati 916 is one model for the poems that Seidel is making. They often want to be sleek, wind-tunnel shaped, spare as a good mathematical equation. Ideally, not a line is wasted, and the poem speeds on. Another poem in this sequence, "Poem Does" (cf. "Simon Says"), is more explicit: "Life is going ahead as fast as it can, / Which is what a poem does." Earlier in this poem we get another version of the poetics of speed, this one based on the coronary effect of nitroglycerin and ending with a wacky rephrasing of Mallarmé's dictum that it is the poet's duty "*Donner un sens plus pur aux mots de la tribu*":

> The god in the nitroglycerin
> Is speedily absorbed under the tongue
> Till it turns a green man red,
> Which is what a poem does.
> It explosively reanimates
> By oxygenating the tribe.

This is the beginning of "Stars," which is about how everything in our world goes all too fast:

> None of the Above
> Stays down here below.
> My going very fast
> Describes the atmosphere.
> Heady.
>
> And when I die,
> We orbit way
> Above the sky of
> And return
> From stars.

> We fall from stars
> In all the colors of Brazil,
> Of Africa, Iran.
> We stir a black hole swirl, star
> Figure skaters twirling on the black, galaxies
>
> Unspooling on the surface tension
> Of the morning coffee
> In the cup.

Every line here has to have been worked and reworked—and then revised and retouched. The meter is a firm and adroitly varied iambic. The rhymes are dexterously scumbled over: *die* and *sky*, *Above* and *of*, *fall* and *all*, *stir* and *star*, and *swirl* and *twirling*. The colors of the map and the colors of the cultures and the corresponding national flags contribute inseparably to the little composition at the beginning of the third stanza. The syntax, the enjambment, and the figures interact to sweep microcosm into macrocosm and back in the last five lines (an involvement forecast in the switch from *I* to *We* in the second stanza). But it is all done with an eye to the accidental, so to speak, and in this respect it differs remarkably from the art of Brancusi and Ducati.

Rarely linear, Seidel's poems can be described in terms of fragments as readily as in terms of unity. They are usually shot through with *trouvailles,* and they often take "complex irregular forms," to borrow a term from Hayles again—forms analogous to "coastlines, for example, or mountain landscapes, or the complex branchings of the human vascular system." Fractal geometry—Benoit Mandelbrot's invention, which has inspired other postmodern poets, notably Alice Fulton, who has proposed that we "call the poetry of irregular form *fractal verse*"—involves such configurations. Fractals put in a brief appearance in one of Wheeler's poems ("The Lip of the Snow in Lapland") and are likely familiar to Seidel, as other contemporary versions of nonlinear dynamics will be. The handsome, multicolored dust jacket of his new book is a computer-generated combination of ocular ovals perhaps representing a black hole (as someone has suggested to me) produced by Chris Perez and Robert Wagoner of Stanford's Department of Physics. Seidel must have selected it in part to anticipate certain images in his opening poem, "Midnight," a kind of postmodern Genesis that implies that the creation is ongoing:

> God begins. The universe will soon.
> The intensity of the baseball bat
> Meets the ball. Is the fireball
> When he speaks and then in the silence
> The cobra head rises regally and turns to look at you.
> The angel burns through the air.
> The flower turns to look.

As even that passage might intimate, one thing that characterizes Seidel's approach to structure is an alertness to local effects that can generate their own miniature systems within the arrangement of the whole poem. Such minisystems are sometimes sonically based, as in the third stanza of "A Pretty Girl," a poem largely without rhyme, in which for a moment comic echo takes over. Like many of these poems, it is set in Italy.

> Bare, thick, spare, pure,
> Umber, somber, brick Bologna.
> This year's fashion color is manure,
> According to the windows
> Of fogged-in manikins
> In Piazza Cavour.
> Reeking of allure
> Arcades of demure
> Young women dressed in odorless brown pneumonia
> Give off clouds of smoke,
> Dry ice in the fog.

While this riff contributes something to the poem's plot, it is here because it has its own pixillated order, which bridges antithetical rhymes (*pure, manure, demure*) with other phrases (*Piazza Cavour* and *Reeking of allure*) and virtually dissolves *Bologna* into *pneumonia* by way of smoke, dry ice, and fog. This is writing that is itself paradoxically "Bare, thick, spare, pure."

Another instance, at the center of which is a bawdy pun, occurs in the middle of "Yankee Doodle":

> When an earring in one ear makes a pioneer,
> Gender Studies finds *Tender Buttons*
> Is all about the sacred body
> Of the rhino and author, Miss Stein,
> And parts of her companion, Miss Toklas.

"Miss" and "Miss" indeed. Mr. Seidel will score no points with feminists. But it is hard not to appreciate the eerie ringing across the first line, the tacit interpretation of the single earring in clitorial terms in the following lines, the implicit discovery that *Gender Studies* has the same initials as *Gertrude Stein,* and the triple valence of *rhino,* which not only refers indelicately to Ms. Stein's appearance but also suggests the dildo that keeps coming up in her prose poems and the source of a famous aphrodisiac powder. (The same medication occurs in another poem here.)

In the conclusion of "Milan," a paean to the motorcycle, the binding element is not the rhyme or the lubricious semantics but the part of speech. In the penultimate stanza, in a kind of foreplay, we have heard about the Ducati 916, that "Stradivarius / Of motorcycles" on Via Borgospesso as well as Donatello, Brancusi, and Cole Porter, and the final stanza (in which the full stop is used to wonderful effect) is an orgy of proper nouns:

> The president of Cagiva Motorcycles,
> Mr. Claudio Castiglioni, lifts off in his helicopter
> From his ecologically sound factory by a lake.
> Caviga in Varese owns Ducati in Bologna,
> Where he lands.
> His instructions are Confucian:
> Don't stint.
> Combine a far-seeing industrialist.
> With an Islamic fundamentalist.
> With an Italian premier who doesn't take bribes.
> With a pharmaceuticals CEO who loves to spread disease.
> Put them on a 916.
>
> And you get Fred Seidel.

Which is to say that we cannot "get" him at all; the 916 is going too fast.

Earlier in "Milan" there is a passage that we might think of as analogous to a feedback loop (a mechanism by which "output feeds back into the system as input," as Hayles puts it with exemplary concision) that has its own little labyrinthine structure. Seidel's subject, a quasi-Proustian recollection, has been presaged by a reference to "Cupid's bow," not to mention George Herbert's "Love 3":

> Oh Milan, I feel myself being pulled back
> To the past and released.
> I hiss like an arrow
> Through the air,
> On my way from here to there.
> I am a man I used to know.
> I am the arrow and the bow.
> I am a reincarnation, but
> I give birth to the man
> I grew out of.
> I follow him down a street
> Into a restaurant I don't remember
> And sit and eat.

This passage, like others in *Going Fast,* suggests that Seidel is one of the few poets so far to be influenced—as distinct from overpowered—by Sylvia Plath. (I'm thinking in this instance especially of "Ariel.") Be that as it may, this stanza's fulcrum is its central line, "I am the arrow and the bow," and the surrounding twelve lines—from the breathtaking puns on *pulled back* and *released* through the rhymes and the Möbius strip-like twist of the Wordsworthian paradox that "The child is father of the man," to the implicit resurrection of the etymological source of *restaurant*—are of a piece with it, so that again we have a kind of minipoem within a complex poem.

A more extended instance of a complexly ordered digression occurs in "Victory," a meditation set in the first-class section of an airplane on an international flight to Southeast Asia (Seidel's real enjoyment of luxury is everywhere unfashionably apparent). We gather that the poet has a hankering for a woman traveling in his section—or perhaps a flight attendant. In the background an in-flight film is running, and somehow the circumstances of the making of the film are surmised. Like Wheeler, Seidel often drops quotation marks and other signs of discreteness and shifts from one level of diction to another without warning—and with rather outrageous results:

> My penis is full of blood for you
> Probably won't win her hand.
> But you bet
> Susanna the movie has to pull in the Elders.
> She has designs.
> She was designed to. She is audience response
>   questionnaire-designed to
> Get them to feast their eyes.

The "questionnaire" might have been distributed to the airline's passengers or to the movie's likely audience at any theater—it is all the same. The following several stanzas' phantasmagoria of scenes in the airplane, in the jungle beneath, and in course of the film's production coheres chiefly by changes rung on the phallic image: "sixteen kinds of snakes," "the head / Of the British fleet, here for the joint / Naval exercises" (the line breaks are crucial), "The Steadicam . . . Holding its head in the air like a King Cobra," "about to Big Bang," "The poisonous viper," "a ten-foot lizard," "Bananas."

Thanks to the serpentine motif, which recalls the book's first poem, with its *god* and *cobra head,* and which withdraws after this section, the different scenes are woven together. In the poet's punning proposition (which is close to a definition of a fractal) "the set itself is a subset of itself, / A jungle set in the jungle." Seidel puts the idea the other way in a recursion to the desired woman and a sly revision of St. Augustine's principle ("God is a circle whose center is everywhere and whose circumference is nowhere"):

> God is everywhere you're not,
> And you are everywhere. I wish I knew your name.
> Congestion in the brain is cleared
> By the tropical haze which mists the coconut palms
> And by the horrible heat of heaven.

Which is to say, as Seidel does at poem's end, with glancing references to *Four Quartets,* another poem about God in the world, that

> The jungle is within. The jungle also comes down
> To the heavenly warm water lapping the sand.
> The jungle is the start and the jungle is the end.
> The jungle is behind. The jungle is ahead.
> Ahead of me is heaven.

And hell, no doubt, in view of "the horrible heat." It is perhaps pertinent that *jungle* is one of those words with histories of opposite meanings. As far back as we can trace it, it meant "wasteland" or "desert." If we find the Godhead and other "heads" latent in the repeated *Ahead* in the last lines, the inference is pretty much the same: the universe is one complex irregular form whose most distant parts are unpredictably but significantly interrelated, and this poem in its process and connections—like so many others in this collection, itself scrupulously arranged—means to suggest that complex form.

If you're looking for something else, or rather something in addition, try "Dune Road, Southampton," as impeccably tight and chilling a brief poetic narrative as any I have read for years; or the translation of Ovid's story of Myrrha, which (especially when considered along with Frank Bidart's version in *Desire*) makes it almost incredible that this tale has been so infrequently read in our time; or the raunchy, razor-sharp anecdote of an encounter between Noel Coward and Tallulah Bankhead in the salaciously entitled "The Great Depression"; or the unimprovable oedipal lyric "The Pierre Hotel, New York, 1946"; or . . .

If Wheeler and Seidel are indicative, and I think they are, we'll take the sharp curve into the next century in good poetic hands.

Breaking and Making

To begin with endings then: as much as anyone in her generation, Heather McHugh has been concerned to remind us that the sole difference between poetry and prose is that poetry is committed in lines. Economy, eloquence, and even—in the right conditions—rhyme and meter are available also to the prose writer (one of the sequences in McHugh's new volume, *The Father of the Predicaments,* includes several sections in fine iambic prose), and poetry begins just where prose ends. Only the poet, that is, controls her own right margin (and, if she chooses, her left), while the hapless prose writer is at the mercy of the tyrannical typesetter, whose obsessive project, ordinarily interfered with only by the occasional paragraph, becomes the erection of that perfectly justified wall of whiteness around the teeming words. Writing a poem is more like blazing a trail across the tundra. In other words, if there is a sense in which prose is endless—the representative work here would be *Finnegans Wake,* whose famous opening phrase begins in the middle of and proleptically finishes the book's concluding sentence fragment, so that it is a great, snaky river, rather like the ancient Greeks' encompassing ocean, with its tail in its mouth—there is a sense in which poems get along by stopping. In McHugh's succinct and elegantly reversible formulation, "The making of the line is the breaking of the line." But because the poetic line breaks less in the way that a branch breaks than in the way that a wave breaks, or dawn, it breaks or can break out of itself and into new places—or (words

---

Review of *The Father of the Predicaments* by Heather McHugh, *The House of Entertaining Science* by Lynne McMahon, and *Swarm* by Jorie Graham. From *The Yale Review,* Winter, 2000.

going back and down as far as they do) into dark, old places, as jampacked with strange treasures as tombs in the Valley of the Golden Mummies.

So it is that McHugh can call her book of essays (just reissued with revisions) *Broken English: Poetry and Partiality*. On its cover, the two words of the main title are set or broken at a right angle, so that we see how the last two letters of the first word are repeated in the first letters of the second. McHugh worries syllables, phonemes, graphemes, everything linguistic, and her attention to the breaking of the line comports with what uncanny Joyce, to call on him just once more, referred to as the "splitting of the etym." Her work recalls the anecdote about Edgar Degas, the superb painter, who went to his friend Stéphane Mallarmé and pleaded with him to teach him how to write poems, because he had some "marvelous ideas to express." "But, mon ami," said Mallarmé, more or less, "poems aren't made of ideas; they're made of words." Then of course there is Remy de Gourmont's more imperious pronouncement on the subject: "Ideas are well enough until you are twenty; after that only words will do." If only words will do, perhaps that's because of all that they can do. They can make us aware, as McHugh insists, of the contradiction "inside all diction." Michel Foucault, focusing on the amazing disparity between the number of words in the world and the number of events, extols language's "wealth of poverty," and McHugh, revising a workshop-worn credo, declares as follows: "No infinity but in finity." Because its fractures eventuate in such paradoxes, poetry "verges on the unsayable, the unspeakable." "A poem," McHugh continues, "is untoward"—by which she means in part that it is inevitably improper, perverse, and awkward and in the main that it is ideally what she calls Emily Dickinson's work, "a winging out of bounds."

Here is the opening of "Not Unterrified"—the first poem in part 2 of *The Father of Predicaments*—whose original title, "Carriage Return," explicitly indicated both a woman wheeling a baby stroller and the poet playing her typewriter:

Edge-rich, the beach
is a batcher of changes:

> five long bands of upwash
> stretch a cove into an afternoon,
> and deepen it to evening there, where ten
> sandpipers race along the liquefaction's froth.
> It beats, at their needling, a quick retreat; wherefrom they turn
>
> three feet uphill to find
> the last tide's hemline, run its whole cove-length of
>   lacework back—then tack
> and race and tack and
> race again—the long and the short of it is life for them,
>   who poke
> through frillwork at
> such breakneck speed, make tracks like some unholy
>   Underwood—till each
> new tide-line's trove of trash
>
> has been sandpipered, dashed along.

The lines not only wash in and out like waves but also trace the movements of the birds. If "the long and short of it is life" for the sandpipers, it is as well for the poet, whose lines are "Edge-rich" also in that many of them break on words having to do with margins (*beach, changes, upwash, froth, turn, tack*), while others, by means of enjambment, sharpen the point of the sandpipers' "needling" ("and / race," "poke / through," "at / such," and "each / new," which last rhymes neatly with "poke / through")—and of course the poet's, who knows that to describe the water's action "we need the binding / stitcheries of / syntax." Probably not since Elizabeth Bishop's "Sandpiper" has that bird been put to such good metaphoric use. Running on and not, making and—braking, then not, these lines conjure verse as differently wizard as A. R. Ammons's "Corson's Inlet" and Ezra Pound's "Canto II." The poem's concluding questions—"What's bolted? What is fast?"—reflect on the paradox of form in movement that poetry like music embodies as they balance terms each of which contains its antithesis, since *bolted* means both "fastened down" and "run away" and *fast* means both "rapid" and "firm."

Such self-interfering puns come naturally to a sensibility as aporetical as McHugh's. In "Out of Mind" she compares her two homes, one in the Pacific Northwest and the other in Maine. The one landscape is lush and verdant, "an embarrassment of riches," while the other is "austerer," and her lineation corresponds to the geography. The opening stanza about the Northwest comprises expansive lines, while that about the Northeast coast narrows to two or three beats:

> I miss
> the knuckling down
> on landscapes known
> as necks and heads;
> what's sharpened into
> etcheries of age—arthritic
> bush, twig dignity.

The third stanza mediates in length and content alike, as McHugh asks how one can ever

> choose one's kind? Part-time I'm missing
> all of somewhere else. My Maine is bone;
> my west is flesh. The latter has no place
> without the former, but the former
> has a future out of mind.

Her dilemma presents itself in syntax and punctuation as well as in argument, because each line has a strong medial caesura—except the last, in which the poet does finally imply a choice after all by locating Maine in both the indefinite future and the immemorial past. In light of the last line, the multivalence of *Maine* discloses itself, and in addition to the name of the state we hear the meanings "strength" or "power" and "essential part" (as well as perhaps "household," for which meaning the usual spelling was *meinie*).

McHugh's two homes correspond to her two inclinations, centripetal and centrifugal, minimalist and maximalist. On one hand, she wants to put it all in a word or two ("What's bolted? What is fast?"). "My Maine is bone" epitomizes (and rhymes with) the already dense preceding anatomical phrasing, "the knuckling down / on landscapes known / as necks

219

and heads." Here is the whole of "Fast," a poem that translates love into the relations among the four elements as Heraclitus viewed them:

> If he's the rock, then I'm the water.
> If he's the water, I'm the wind.
> If he's the wind, I must be moonlight
> driven in wavelengths to rock.

Fast is again both "solid" and "quick," partly because the "wavelengths" have to do with light waves and ocean waves and partly because *rock* is a noun and a verb. The same epitomizing impulse fuels "One Woe," a ten-line scholium on the little conundrum in Revelation 9:12: "One woe is past; and behold, there come two woes more hereafter." Having provisionally identified one woe as "past" and one as "future," McHugh, here the consummate Occamite, concludes even more grimly:

> (How was any
> woe begun?) No need to wonder.
>
> One woe's present.
> So it can't be done.

The tendency to wrap everything up by way of buried rhyme near the poem's end—in this instance, the four-times-repeated *un* sound—also attests to McHugh's minimalism.

Her minimalist vein recalls Emily Dickinson, as in the following passage, which could come right out of the fascicles, concluding ellipsis and all, if TV screens had existed earlier (the ellipsis is the poet's): "their monitors abuzz with *is*'s / Etymologies. . . . " As a maximalist, by contrast, she sounds like Wallace Stevens:

> What do we take
> arriving for? Only the best
> asbestos, most expensive
> avocado?

(She is punning zanily on the Spanish for "advocate" or "lawyer," *abogado*.) More often, she conjures Gerard Manley

Hopkins. In "Spill of Howl" we come upon the following parenthesis:

> (the there of that
>
> befallen happenstance,
> given a moon full-blown, a current
> near to flood, a wind-struck view
> of shivers sur-subliminal, near pure
> precision).

In "Qua Qua Qua," which is one of many poems here to suggest that McHugh might be the funniest American poet alive, the duck's speech merges with the philosopher's:

> Oh duck, it doesn't
> bother you. You live in a dive, you daub the lawn,
>
> you dabble bodily aloft: more wakes
> awake, where sheerness shares
> its force.

"In a dive" indeed! "Moon and TV," in which the poet is a kind of woman-in-the-moon, gives us this hilarious imitation of the Jesuit poet:

> Unthinkably far-off, I am
> the moon-monkey's semblable, caught in the same
> sublunes of cycle—brought-up, let-down,
> mob-summed, mum-sobbed, inmate of
> a bleeding narrative, forever being
> seized, released, shaken, mistaken,
> molded to the mercies of
> a mimic muscle—
> spell-bent,
>   heart-rent,
>   spawn of a spondee. . . .

Her maximalist propensity insists that she acknowledge what she calls in a charming cavalierism the "Linking mechanisms in the universe." These mechanisms are responsible not just for the two carriages in "Not Unterrified" but also for the juxtaposition of that poem, from which the preceding quotation comes, and "Past All Understanding," which links with it by virtue of the woman-with-baby motif. (Beginning with its title—which comes by way of a felicitous linguistic warp from Aristotle's genealogy of the *kategoria,* or "predicaments," as it was translated into Latin and then English: "The father of the predicaments is being"—much of this book has to do with family.) "Past All Understanding" itself proceeds by unpredictable linkage: a woman at the park and her baby, "balancing back to back," makes a "casual covalency into / a human idiogram, / spontaneous Pilobolus" that so disturbs the poet's dog, Kooch, that he barks at what he can only see as a monstrosity, a beast with two fronts, so that his owner must explain to the woman his rude intervention, which explanation involves poor Kooch's misunderstanding also of crippled people, and "Meanwhile a wind / rose at the kiosk," that synecdoche for universal linking mechanisms, "stapled with yard jobs, sub-clubs, bands somebody named for animals." Such a digressive structure is "extravagant" in Henry Thoreau's radical sense—a sense that McHugh, inveterate etymologist that she is, would approve and that indeed corresponds nicely with her definition of a poem as "a winging out of bounds."

It is perhaps because she is logophilic through and through that McHugh must be maximalist and minimalist both. It takes two to make her one. She ends "Verdict" (the title's roots combine "truth" with "saying"), which is I think addressed to an alter ego, thus:

> One of us
> is wrong, that's evident, but who? By all
> that's just, adjudicate: the only un-
>
> committed one is you.

As the doubling in the juxtaposition "just, adjudicate" intimates, the *One* is the *who* that rhymes with *you,* while the *un-* is the *you* who is the *one*. Semantically, to put that another way, the last four end-words rhyme: *us, all, un-, you*. Together, we—"all" of "us"—are one or *un* (and one and *un* add up to two). Is that the history of the world in a French syllable? (To elaborate excruciatingly on the same bifurcation Sylvia Plath turned to a German syllable in "Daddy": "You do not do, you do not do." The single "old shoe" he is presently identified with is of course one of a pair.)

The self's duplicity prompts "Neitherer Brings Charges." The reader cannot but think at the outset that the speaker opposes her addressee, but doubts set in about the time that the cry of someone in the audience, "Author! author!" doubles itself. As for the audience, they always divide up into

> the fighters and the fuckers,
> those who take, and those who give. There's room
>
> for one kind or the other, half of all
> Binarydom should live. It's man
>
> or beast—you take your pick. It's
> logos or it's low. We cannot be
>
> at one unless you choose.

At poem's end, however, the poet's personae, like the indecisive Casey Stengel squared, make their minds up both ways at once, as each declines the either-or alternative:

> It's them or us, it's
> yes or no, it's time the father
>
> or it's pussy-whipped. I tell you outright,
> I'm a neitherer. But what are you? You are a bother.

Which is to say, an "un- / committed one."

Like poets of the earlier seventeenth century—with whom she has affinities, as her essay in Jonathan Post's collection *Green Thoughts, Green Shades* will confirm—McHugh's love of wordgames lives cheek by skull with her preoccupation with mortality. The first poem in *The Father of the Predicaments*—its longest and most impressive work, the sequence that includes the iambic prose—is entitled "Not a Prayer." The title works in several ways. The sequence is an elegy for a friend's mother, and its title suggests that in the end none of us has a prayer of surviving. It also indicates negatively the nature of this poem. As McHugh puts it near the conclusion,

> All I can call upon
> is words—unsatisfactory to say
> the least—a nomen always aiming
> for amen, a pupil meaning
> well, pre-emptively.

The universal linking mechanisms see to it that at the other end of the book, in "Qua Qua Qua," the penultimate poem, which is a wry self-portrait, the duck is addressed in these terms:

> from a log
> to a logos and back, you go flinging
> the thing that you are—and you sing
>
> as you dare—on a current of
> nerve. On a wing
> and a wing.

Not "a prayer." The latter's absence rhymes, so to speak, with the absence of *air* in the preceding line, where *nerve* substitutes for it. It takes two wings to fly, two wings to sing. "No infinity but in finity." In McHugh's world, the poetry of praise and remembrance is a kind of logos rolling. When logodaedaly becomes an Olympic event, she will take the gold medal. Like no one else's, her rock rocks.

Although we are lucky enough to live in a time in which American poetry is surely more various and indeed vigorous than ever, so that McHugh has ample company, we nonetheless—and inevitably: when was it ever *not* thus?—have a dull, quiescent mainstream. Along with others, many of whom are also, alas, teachers of workshops, I often think of this mainstream as "workshop poetry." Donald Hall has dubbed the typical product, unforgettably, "a McPoem." My own aversions, which are not necessarily those of Hall (or Joseph Epstein or Dana Gioia or Mary Kinzie or Mary Karr, all of whom have individually inveighed against aspects of contemporary poetry) include the following: the contemporary plain style, an emphasis in content on the outré, an attainment of the latter through minimalism, an absorption by certain poets born no earlier than Stanley Kunitz, a light regard for prosodic matters, and an anti-intellectual bias or pose.

Though unlike some of her contemporaries she does not provide endnotes, Lynne McMahon is an example of the poet who unabashedly rereads Homer—as well as Virgil, the Romantics, Walt Whitman, Emily Dickinson, and, especially in her new book, *The House of Entertaining Science,* Hopkins. In spite of the radical nature of the work of several of her mentors, hers is a distinctively level-headed, circumspect, ambitious, yet self-effacing verse that testifies at once to an eager curiosity, a broad education, a sure prosodic hand, a discriminating ear, and an appreciation of what I want to call—though perhaps the term *is* still a redundancy—grammatical syntax. I don't mean that McMahon's work is conservative, especially as compared with McHugh's (not to mention Jorie Graham's). Or do I? To be sure, "Wuthering Heights," the last poem in her preceding book, *Devolution of the Nude,* is characteristic in its clear-eyed assessment of the deracinating potential of the Romantic sensibility and in its tribute to "that other / nineteenth century virtue ill-defined by . . . charity, serenity, / love." There as usual McMahon is thoughtful, probative, self-possessed. She refuses to laugh—or refuses *merely* to "laugh at Marianne Moore's remark—'I like the nude . . . but *in moderation,*'" and indeed in that poem she craftily echoes Moore's modus operandi. But I certainly don't want to suggest that her work is distant or undramatic. In her salutary combination of cool meditation and vivid observation, she reminds me of Elizabeth Bishop more than of Moore—though it is still Hopkins who provides the subtext for much of *The House of Entertaining Science.*

The poem entitled "All quail to the wallowing," after a passage in "Harry Ploughman," can suggest his importance to McMahon. It begins like this:

> *All quail to the wallowing,*
> Hopkins wrote, punning bird and verb,
> mud and clumsy baseness, and his favorite

> entirety "all," near-rhyme with "ah" and
> that *ah* his abruptly intaken breath, that awe,
> whose *bright wings, my dear, touched*
> *in your bower of bone, are you!* led me
> from poem to poem: *ah, there was a heart right* . . .
> *this air I gather and release* . . . *the heir*
> *to his own selfbent so bound* . . . *Ah, well where!*
> to his final troubling pun, *ah, let life*
> *wind off* . . .
> Was there ever a man so tormented, my Victorian
> professor asked, twinning *ah* with the frequent *alas,*
> ever so circumscribed by the fact of the body?
> Hopkins was circumcised six days
> after his ordination. Is that something
> we need to know? he asked the class.

In its italicized phrases the delicate little pastiche links up quotations from no fewer than seven sources—"God's Grandeur," "The Wreck of the Deutschland" (sections 18 and then 29), "Duns Scotus's Oxford," "Ribblesdale," "The Golden Echo," and "Spelt from Sybil's Leaves"—before ending with the professor's allusion to the sonnet beginning, "My own heart let me more have pity on," where Hopkins pleads "[let] not live this tormented mind / With this tormented mind tormenting yet." That plea might well be the professor's also, and even McMahon's, caught up as she is in the poet's various toils. We note, for instance, the echo of *tormented* in *Victorian* and of *circumscribed* in *circumcised*. Even as that last iteration has its humorous side and mocks a certain body-based exegesis now in vogue ("do we need / the speculation about masturbation / as well?"), McMahon perhaps looks askance at her own critical practice, which has included an essay, entitled "The Sexual Swamp: Female Erotics and the Masculine Art," which might seem to comport with what this poem wickedly refers to as "the mudhole of posterity and its fashionable / interpretations." In any event, she tells us,

> I think I may cut back my critical forays
> for a while. Let go of the new talk.
> Was there ever a man so intoxicated by fields,

so worddrunk and dazzled?
He fathers forth whose beauty is past change.
Praise him.

By quoting the conclusion to "Pied Beauty," that paean to all God's "dappled" things, the final two lines invite us to read her own collage as a tribute in kind to "Whatever is fickle, freckled," "plotted and pieced." In this case, however, the work extolled is not God's but Hopkins's, as McMahon assures us by printing the last words in Roman and thus claiming them also for herself. The exaltation is itself Hopkinsesque. "I am all at once what Christ is, since he was what I am," Hopkins dares to write in one poem, and Harry Ploughman is a figure somewhere between the salt of the earth and the light of the world.

Another poem titled after a phrase from Hopkins, "Are you beam-blind?" is a model of subtle counterpointing in the service of a meditation on the sensual and the sacred. In its original context, the sonnet entitled, "The Candle Indoors," Hopkins's self-directed question perhaps means, "Are you blind to God's light?" Or perhaps, since *beam* can signify *rood* or *cross*, "Are you blind to the consequences of the crucifixion?" Hopkins must also have in mind Matthew 7:5, where Jesus enjoins the hypocrite "first [to] cast out the beam out of thine own eye; and then shalt thou see clearly to cast out the mote out of thy brother's eye." Ever the scholar, McMahon allows for these glosses but stresses two others. The first definition of *beam* in the *Oxford English Dictionary* is "tree," after all (hence "rood" and "cross"), and she could not help but imagine "the painful rough-barked / sap and needle of a *tree*." "For years I tried to make it beam of light, / light ray, dazzling and blinding possibly," she tells us, but the possibility that nonetheless haunted her was that the phrase meant blinded in the manner of Polyphemus. Having recalled Jesus' adjuration to the hypocrite, and having touched on evergreen needles, she frames the act as a kind of "ocular counterpart" to the image later in Matthew (19:24) in which Jesus cautions us that "it is easier for a camel to go through the eye of a needle than for a rich man to enter into the kingdom of God." As soon as she notes in passing that the parable at least has "the virtue of sticking it / to the rich," her poem takes a strange turn, and on the basis of "beam-blind" man she conjures a cartoon by R. Crumb, the creator of the scurrilous "comix" that feature Angelfood McSpade and friends, including "Mr. Natural with a beam in his pants and another in his eye, a walking bracket / of venery." Because she regards Hopkins's question, "Are you beam-blind?" as "self-distressing," we have to see *this* Mr. Natural as her own version of the priest—Hopkins with a stalwart hard-on.

Now Hopkins, if beset by temptation, would surely recall, as McMahon does, yet another verse in Matthew (5:29): "And if thy right eye offend thee, pluck it out, and cast it from thee: for it is profitable for thee that one of thy members should perish, and not that thy whole body should be cast into hell." When McMahon goes on to consider Hopkins's "self-chastisement," she remembers his obsession with "the parish newspaper account of a young man, / of medical training, who tore his eyes out / with a heated wire" and "whose eyeballs were found soon after / in a nettle patch" and splices that account with a dry query from one of the poet's letters to Robert Bridges: "Can there be gout / or rheumatism of the eye? . . . If so, I think I have it." She leaves it to the readers to combine the inflammation and the stiffness associated with rheumatism with the offense of the "eyeballs"—about which tender organs Freud has instructed us—but she abets us by borrowing (again without indicating her source) from another lyric, "Binsey Poplars," where with stunning compression Hopkins laments their vulnerability to expeditious loggers of a lovely woods, which, "like this sleek and seeing ball, / But a prick will make no eye at all." In McMahon's poem the pun on *prick* that Hopkins assuredly did not make suddenly exposes itself—the prick blinds one spiritually—as she implicitly confirms by referring us to *Lear*'s Gloucester, who apprehends the truth when deprived of the sense of sight and realizes conversely that "I stumbled when I saw." McMahon's conclusion, however, which incorporates a phrase from Hopkins's "Morning Midday and Evening Sacrifice," counters that proposition:

> Insight instead of sight, the better gift,
> a holy man decrees. But ah,
> poor swap for Hopkins' silk-ash mastery
> of sight. Poor swap for Hopkins' trees.

The buried rhyme, *trees* with *decrees*, beats down the "holy man" even as it resurrects the felled poplars and reaffirms the physical experience. Under the pressure of such language as Hopkins's, the poem asks, who can pretend to disentangle the sacred from the sensuous?

McMahon's own sensuous language has a distinctive postmodern glow. "No Damascus," the first poem in "In the American Grain," is a scornful indictment of vulgar masculinism inspired by an infamous bumper sticker:

> I caught this evening evening's genie,
> epoxied to the chrome in light-
> sensitive fluorescent script
> repeating in each headlight's sweep
> *No Fat Chicks. No Fat Chicks,*
> unegged, unknifed, not yet set aflame
> or painted out, a crud anomalous
> even in the sixties when I saw it first.

The echoes of Hopkins, not just in the first line's clanging parody but also in the subtler allusions (the "headlight's sweep" recalls the "skate's heel [that] sweeps," "not yet set aflame" recalls "the fire that breaks from thee," and so on), keep "The Windhover" consistently between the lines and insist on the heavy irony of the term *sensitive*—and of the dramatic difference between this image and that in Hopkins's "chevalier" with his "Brute beauty and valour and act." Perhaps the most satisfying such collaboration occurs when McMahon remembers thinking "what seventeen was going to mean": "This is what the boys say: gash, quim, / twat, and snatch. Almost a nursery rhyme, / though it wasn't then." Or almost a series in Hopkins, who adored special four-letter words (her *crud*, too, he would have been fond of)—and who of course called on *gash* on several memorable occasions. In a brilliant little touch, McMahon snidely rhymes *quim* with *the driver's whim*. But such a "beam-blind" driver, as the title "No Damascus" intimates, is no Saul of Tarsus on the brink of a revelation, nor is he any John Bunyan about to extricate himself from the "dung-hill" of his previous existence. If the poet has her way, he will have no entry to exit whatever:

> Driver, for whom all flesh is dross
> and all entry blocked, who will stay
> to redeem you now? No hitchhiker
> will wave you down. There's no grace
> abounding. No future town.

The light and internal rhymes are characteristic of McMahon's deftness. Her "Elegy" is shot through with rhymes like *drawn/song, words/urn,* and *fruit/conduit.* In "Love Poem" she watches her husband sleep fitfully under the influence of illness and homeopathic remedies. She half-jealously notices "a dream of sex, perhaps, keeping / [him] erect but torn":

> The herbs,
> the Carrickfergus flint and poisoned sea pinch
> together a near-sayable word—
>
> but the hasp of meaning unfastens
> into breath. The insignificant sibilance
> I strain to fashion
> into sense, whose chance
>
> syllable might be a name,
> dissolves for good and I give up,
> mindful once again that the nameless
> soul wanders ceaselessly. Your body is gift enough.

This is Hopkins rarefied, this little tour de force of assonance, consonance, and hitherto unspecified varieties of rhyme. What shall we call the connection between *unfastens* and *fashion,* whose antonymic relationship (reflected in the coupling of *name* and *nameless*) is mimicked in the lisping near rhyme? McMahon's book's title, *The House of Entertaining Science,* which derives from the name of the apartment complex where

Anna Akhmatova lived in misery in 1939, is strangely right for a collection of poems that are at once so accommodating and so technically exact. (As though to emphasize technique and study, her cover reproduces Leonardo's drawing known as "The Proportions of the Head.")

"Anniversary" is so nicely turned that we cannot but see the root of *verse* in its title. Starting with the coincidence of Halloween and the date of John Keats's birth, the poem ends with these verses, which bring together, as though in a memorial "twist of flowers," lines from Keats's beloved *King Lear,* allusions to the death (also by tuberculosis) of Keats's brother Tom, and images from "To Autumn":

> The future
> passed the sentry at his mother's door,
> and then poor Tom's a-cold.
> The cold warmth on the granary floor
>
> still seems a meager recompense,
> that twist of flowers spared by the scythe.
> So little of the loss restored.
> We were thinking about it tonight
>
> on our meandering course down the road
> celebrating this autumn's close.
> A holiness of wraiths and creeps,
> death-eating Deaths. Our breath
>
> visible in the pumpkin-lighted streets.
> The cold traveled centuries to show us that.
> We looked, but the dead had all gone back.
> No one dressed as Keats.

Tom Keats's death presaged that of the poet, who could see his future in the past. If both men were genetically liable to consumption, "The future / passed . . . his mother's door" at their very births. Keats had Autumn's "hook / [Spare] the next swath and all its twined flowers," so McMahon can touch on them here, but of course Keats himself could not be spared. The last stanza's slab-flat rhymes, clipped syntax, and objective tone are of a piece. "The dead had all gone back"—back home in the form of creeps and trick-or-treaters, and back to the grave in the shape of the wraiths. McMahon herself has gone back to her sources and, her own claim notwithstanding, is for a moment "dressed as Keats." Somewhere he approves.

Jorie Graham's *Swarm* is abuzz with beginnings and rife with endings. To complicate matters, more than most volumes it asks to be read all at once. In this regard it is akin to other determinedly experimental, metaphysically ambitious, spiritually aware, eclectically informed, obsessively revised, and self-consciously subversive projects. If T. S. Eliot's *Four Quartets* were to collide with *The Waste Land*, the debris pattern might look like this. Among recent books, Frank Bidart's *Desire* and Michael Palmer's *Sun* share qualities with *Swarm*—qualities that appear earlier in David Jones's *Anathemata*, which Graham credits in her mercifully selective endnotes, and the work that made these others possible, Ezra Pound's *Cantos*. An aggregate of perceptions, reflections, monologues in the voices of mythical characters, and glosses on other works in a variety of free verse forms, *Swarm* seems to want to have no edges, no boundaries, no unchanging shape. When we read in the book's penultimate utterance (like most others here, it is not a complete sentence) of "the atom / saturated with situation," we have to remember "the atom still at the bottom of nature" in the first poem and all of the references to atoms between. "More atoms, more days, the noise of the sparrows, of the universals" is one of Graham's vividly disconcerting attempts to summarize at once the world—from its simplest component (at root *atom* means "not cut" or in Graham's formulation "already as little as it can be") to its comprehensive and axiomatic principles—and this collection.

This book's universe (everything "turned into one") is a congregation of mixogamous bits each "saturated with situation" or thoroughly imbued with its context—though the concept of "context" might have to be altered: "Bless, blame, transvaluate— / Change context— / Unexpect context," she counsels us in "Eve"—so that as in a swarm of bees the distinction between unicity and multiplicity seems irrelevant. "To swarm," the jacket copy reminds us, "is to leave an originating organism—a hive, a home country, a stable sense of one's body, a stable hierarchy of values—in an attempt, by coming apart, to found a new form that will hold." If that rather overbearing definition leaves the species *Hymenoptera* in its rapidly broadening wake—the wake of the *Arbella* and its flotilla might come to mind instead—it nonetheless suggests the behavior of these poems. As in her earlier *Region of Unlikeness*, St. Augustine supplies the epigraph to this volume ("To say I love you is to say I want you to be"), and it might be that in conceptualizing its "swarm" we should think also of his description of God as a circle whose center is everywhere and whose circumference nowhere. Graham's "Prayer," an unusually straightforward poem indebted to Friedrich Hölderlin, ends with these lines: "I called you once and thought you once. / You travel to me on your allotted paths, // a light embrace, miraculously omnipresent."

In any case God is relevant. The first poem in *Swarm* presents itself as a fragment "from The Reformation Journal," and its title's religious overtones are soon reinforced. The poem begins with a bold statement as to how to read this book. As in *The End of Beauty*, where she numbered them, Graham separates her lines, in this case with extra leading and sometimes an asterisk:

> The wisdom I have heretofore trusted was cowardice, the leaper.
> *
> I am not lying. There *is no* lying in me,
> *
> I surrender myself like the sinking ship,
> *
> a burning wreck from which the depths will get theirs when the heights
> have gotten theirs
> *
> My throat is an open grave. I hide my face.
> *
> I have reduced all to lower case.
> *
> I have crossed out passages.
> *

I have severely trimmed and cleared.
*
Locations are omitted.
*
Uncertain readings are inserted silently.
*
Abbreviations are silently expanded.
*
A "he" referring to God may be capitalized or not.

A rejection of her mode hitherto—which had been increasingly disjunctive but which she now wryly views as retrograde and cowardly and identifies with "the leaper," a figure that would be appropriate in George Puttenham's nomenclatorial inventions in *The Art of English Poesie* (where we find other terms we could adapt to our advantage here, including *the trespasser, the straggler,* and *the disabler*)—this passage outlines the new aesthetics, the reformation of the poet.

The new aesthetics springs from the Augustinian motivation to confront candidly whatever the case may be. Although we might find it hard to trust a statement such as "There is no lying in me," Graham certainly intends no irony—nor is she, I think, disingenuous. Regardless of whether she can possibly vouch for her own honesty, her claim implies an ambition and sets a standard. The aim is that of the aggressive spiritual exercise. Graham has not yet quite eliminated all humor from her poems, but the grim irony of the fourth line quoted earlier is about as funny as she gets (she asks near the book's end, "what do I do with my laughter"), and for the most part she is engaged in a struggle so strenuous that it makes one think of Jacob, teeth gritted, as it were, muscles bunched, bearing down as though in childbirth. And let the reader beware: to approach this book in good faith you must commit yourself to some version of the same agon. There are no extended luscious passages here, no spacious pastoral interludes in which you can loaf and invite your soul, no discursive retreats, no plots grassy or otherwise to fall back on. Indeed, there are precious few uninterrupted sentences. Some time ago Graham seems to have taken literally Pound's advice to "Leave blanks for what you do not know," and here her implicit ignorance joins with a certain *askesis* to produce as *hard* a text as I have encountered recently. One has to get at it in a new way— a way roughly analogous to that in which one first got at John Berryman's *Homage to Mistress Bradstreet* or Emily Dickinson's more elliptical poems in their manuscript forms. Some poets need to devise a language within the language.

The Dickinson poem Graham alludes to and says in an endnote "animates the book throughout" is number 640 in Thomas Johnson's edition of *The Complete Poems*. As Graham informs us, the title of her "For One Must Want / To Shut the Other's Gaze" misquotes the fourth stanza of Dickinson's poem, one of her fiercest proclamations of love in separation. In the original, "One must wait / To shut the Other's Gaze down," but that verb is evidently not avid enough for Graham. The situation of the Dickinson poem, however, is to Graham's purpose. Beginning "I could not live with You— / it would be Life— / And Life is over there," it addresses a lover who eclipses the deity: "Your Face / Would put out Jesus'," Dickinson blasphemes, and

> You saturated Sight—
> And I had no more eyes
> For sordid excellence
> As Paradise.

Because of the ruinous potential of the love,

> We must meet apart—
> You there—I—here—
> With just the Door ajar
> That Oceans are—and Prayer—
> And that White Sustenance—
> Despair.

Graham's poem, whose imagery harks back to that of the shipwreck in the opening lines of the book, is a dark night of the soul in which she reflects on her predecessor's plight and her own:

> What are you thinking?
> Here on the bottom?
> What do you squint clear for yourself
> up there through the surface?
>
> Explain   door ajar.
> . . . .
> Here: tangle and seaweed
> . . . .
>
> Explain   saturated.
> Explain   and I had no more eyes.

Whether Dickinson's problematic poem is ultimately religious or not, Graham's must be, in the sense that it reiterates the search for the God mentioned at the outset. God also appears, I take it, in another guise with Dickinsonian connotations: "A wise man wants? // A master," Graham admits in "Underneath (9)," and then later in "Underneath (Always)":

> But, master, I've gone a far way down your path,
> emptying sounds from my throat like stones from my
>   pockets,
> emptying them onto your lips, into your
> ear warm from sunlight.
> Not in time. My suit denied.

Not in time: Graham uses the phrase three more times in the ten lines following. The echo of Eliot's phrase in "Burnt Norton" has here two senses: the quester is too late, as it were, yet it is precisely only "not in time" (outside time, that is) that she can be successful. Near the end of her book, speaking as Eurydice, the poet still asks, "Where is my master? with whom share death?"

Graham casts her search in psalmic terms in "Probity," in one of the simplest passages in the volume:

> I have shown up sweet lord
>
> have put my hand out
>
> have looked for a long while

> have run a hand along
>
> looked for a symbol at the door
>
> a long while
>
> devices   prejudices
>
> have felt for the wounds
>
> have tired eyes

But they also might not be served who stand and wait. In Graham's relationship, too, there is still that "Door ajar / That Oceans are—and Prayer" between the two principals. Like Thomas the doubter she has "felt for the wounds," but unlike him she has been neither satisfied nor shamed. To be sure, the "sweet lord" she seeks does not always resemble Jesus. She also identifies deity with "atoms" (the "saturated" motif is just one link between the meditation on Dickinson and the book's opening and closing poems) and "universals." But whatever deity is, it has to do with telos, which has to do with death. In "Underneath (8)" the devastating possibility is put like this:

> As in they shall seek death
> *
> and shall not find   it
> *
> What if there is   no end?
> *
> What if there is no
> *
>   punishment?
>   *
> As in   *it is written.*

God has to do, as that last phrase hints, with narrative. The speaker's search is a journeying across a "Desert / Dune," as one poem is called, a pursuit as by ghost riders over a wasteland ("invisible crowd, dust-risen faces . . . then cooling sand, then crack of voices riding by, // some laughter ticked-out over sand, // deeper and deeper into the open") of "the seriously wounded narrator" (not the poet, nota bene), who would be the author of "the true story" ("Underneath [9]"). The Fisher-King also puts in appearances as Odysseus, Agamemnon, Oedipus, Lear, and others, while Graham's "invisible crowd" recalls the "crowd [that] flowed over London Bridge," and perhaps also, in a book called *Swarm,* "those hooded hordes swarming / Over endless plains." But Graham's story is more fragmented than Eliot's.

It is at the point precisely of story, of narrative, that writing and teleology intersect. To write consistently in full sentences and in lines without lacunae or to provide a "true story" would be for the poet to collude in the creation of the fable of purpose and unity. To break the sentence is to admit that the *sentence* is: to be broken. ("What if there is no // * // punishment?" What if Thomas cannot be shamed?) The pun on *sentence* is featured, along with related others, in "Fuse," in which the speaker is the Watchman in the beginning of Aeschylus' *Agamemnon* who waits, alone and seemingly interminably, for the lighting of the last in a chain of beacons that relay the news that Troy has fallen. "It is a sentence   the long watch I keep," because until the watch is ended, it is a kind of punishment. The fragmented sentence is the sentence levied upon the Watchman. Later he tells us that, waiting for the "syntax" of signal fires to complete itself, he is "Always drowsy. Never spelled." ("Thy name is all, if I could spell," George Herbert exclaimed. What if the beacon is never lit?) "Dear   sentence   so filled with deferral": the apostrophe is the Watchman's and the poet's. The grammatical sentence beginning thus is itself never completed but after forty lines frays out in several directions and in this respect seems to refigure the book. Of course to the extent that the sentence is a life sentence, its conclusion can only be in death. Maybe death bestows meaning, in short—but it might also be that there is no end, no purpose. Perhaps "Chance replaces punishment," as the last poem hypothesizes. In other words, "Explain   accident," as Graham has it elsewhere.

One of the crucial accidents in *Swarm* repeats an event recorded in *Region of Unlikeness* in a poem called "The Phase after History." The first indication of it in this volume is in the second poem, "Try On":

> Wings thickly lifting off the hidden
> nest.
>
> The sound of a hand-sized stone hitting dry ground
> from a certain height.

Other inchoate references appear now and again, and then more than fifty pages later, in "Underneath (1)," they all come into focus:

> Painful to look up.
> No. Painful to look out.
>
> Heard the bird hit the pane hard.
> Didn't see it. Heard nothing
> drop.
>
> To look out and past the shimmering screen to the miles of grasses.

Now when we look back through such small foreshadowings as "Wrecks left at the bottom, yes. // Space   birdless" to that first mention, and to its anticipation in "I surrender myself like the sinking ship, // * // a burning wreck," the poem coheres around the image of the bird—probably a sparrow, because sparrows appear elsewhere in *Swarm*, so that Hamlet's meditation on accident and providence is drawn into the orbit of the image, which image also helps to account for another rich phrase, repeated three times, in the opening poem: glassy ripeness. Whatever else these words signify, they could refer to the instant of the bird's death in the collision with the windowpane. *Glassy* might glance at Paul's promise in 1 Corinthians 13 to the effect that we shall one day, instead of apprehending God as through a glass darkly, see him face to face, and *ripeness* might well call up Lear's pronouncement ("Men must endure / Their going hence, even as their coming hither: / Ripeness is all"), and in any event we will reflect on Graham's insistent if always undermined conjunction of death and revelation. As she has it in her concluding poem, in almost her last words,

> The woman of clay;
>
> I wanted to be broken, make no mistake.
>
> I wanted to enter light—and everywhere its mad colors.
>
> To be told best not to touch.
>
> To touch.
>
> For the farewell of it.

The speaker is in part Mary Magdalene wanting to touch the risen Christ ("Noli me tangere," he warns her), but she has read the later *Cantos*. In "Canto XCII," for instance, Pound beseeches "Lux in diafana, / Creatrix," that his daughter be able to "walk in peace in her basilica, / The light there almost solid"—and we find an "Invisible basilica your willingness its floor" in Graham's "Daphne," where she also writes "Let light come into taste light," as well as "light touching everything / grace and slenderness of its touching" in juxtaposition with "to make the basilica of divine hazard" in her "Underneath (Uplands)." If, earlier in this same poem, which is "Underneath (Calypso)," we might suspect another more eccentric allusion to EP, especially since, according to his *donnée* he is the Odysseus to whom Calypso speaks—

> Why should the exile   return home?
> Era?   Period?

—we might be forgiven on the basis of the dense intertextuality of the book, which is in the end not a collection of poems or a sequence, really, but indeed a swarm.

Images comparable in structural importance to that of the bird abound in the book. In a longer essay one could follow among others the changes rung on the "door ajar," veils, empire, mirrors, and conjunctions of ear and mouth. That is the nature of *Swarm* as one warms to it: it's busy as bees, coherent but uncontainable, on the move, unpredictable, part of a process, and always reforming itself. The wineglass shattered underfoot in the Jewish wedding ceremony portends wholeness. For her part, Graham is deeply antinomian, perhaps philosophically anarchist, but never chaotic. She is grammatically and punctuationally promiscuous in the service of fidelity to a kaleidoscopic vision of things as she thinks they are, things that again remind us of Hopkins, things

> variegated   dappled   spangled   intricately wrought
> complicated   abstruse   subtle   devious
> scintillating with change and ambiguity

Graham's final lines (which might allude to Michelangelo's painting of Adam's initial human movement as well as to Eve's transgression and Mary Magdalene's impulse) are as follows:

> To be told best not to touch.
> To touch.
> For the farewell of it.
> And the further replication.
> And the atom
> saturated with situation.
> And the statue put there to persuade me.

Statue derives, of course, from a root meaning "to stand, to be placed, to be erected," while *persuade* comes from words having to do with sweetness, pleasure, enticement. Graham's book concludes—pauses, rather, on a threshold—with an emblem sonorously, sensuously saturated with inception.

UNDER DISCUSSION
David Lehman, General Editor
Donald Hall, Founding Editor

Volumes in the Under Discussion series collect reviews and essays about individual poets. The series is concerned with contemporary American and English poets about whom the consensus has not yet been formed and the final vote has not been taken. Titles in the series include:

Robert Hayden
edited by Laurence Goldstein and Robert Chrisman
Charles Simic
edited by Bruce Weigl
On Gwendolyn Brooks
edited by Stephen Caldwell Wright
On William Stafford
edited by Tom Andrews
Denise Levertov
edited with an introduction by Albert Gelpi
The Poetry of W. D. Snodgrass
edited by Stephen Haven
On the Poetry of Philip Levine
edited by Christopher Buckley
Frank O'Hara
edited by Jim Elledge
James Wright
edited by Peter Stitt and Frank Graziano
Anne Sexton
edited by Steven E. Colburn
On Louis Simpson
edited by Hank Lazer
On the Poetry of Galway Kinnell
edited by Howard Nelson
Robert Creeley's Life and Work
edited by John Wilson
On the Poetry of Allen Ginsberg
edited by Lewis Hyde
Reading Adrienne Rich
edited by Jane Roberta Cooper
Richard Wilbur's Creation
edited and with an introduction by Wendy Salinger
Elizabeth Bishop and Her Art
edited by Lloyd Schwartz and Sybil P. Estess